EVERY BITE
A DELIGHT
AND OTHER SLOGANS

EVERY BITE
A DELIGHT
AND OTHER SLOGANS

LAURENCE URDANG
& JANET BRAUNSTEIN

WITH TINA K. SPEAGLE & CEILA DAME ROBBINS

ILLUSTRATIONS BY TERRY COLON

VISIBLE
INK
PRESS

DETROIT   WASHINGTON, D.C.   LONDON

EVERY BITE
A DELIGHT
AND OTHER SLOGANS

Art Director: Arthur Chartow
Cover Design: Cynthia Baldwin
Interior Design: Mary Krzewinski
Illustrations: Terry Colon

Printed in the United States of America
All rights reserved

10 9 8 7 6 5 4 3 2 1

Contents

Introduction

Good to the last drop. Reach out and touch someone. Does she or doesn't she? We try harder. Breakfast of champions. It takes a licking and keeps on ticking. Quality is Job 1. Let your fingers do the walking. Where's the beef? When it rains, it pours. 1/4 cleansing cream. All the news that's fit to print. His master's voice. Get a piece of the rock. A diamond is forever. Just do it. Think.

These and thousands of phrases like them are instantly recognizable elements of modern American speech. They form part of our shared mass-culture lexicon along with fragments like "I don't think we're in Kansas any more," "beam me up, Scotty," and "hee-e-e-re's Johnny." Typically promoting a purpose or product, these slogans are stashed in our language bank, although we made no effort to deposit them there. We might not even immediately identify them as advertising slogans, but as messages from some higher force. After all, it *is* "good to the last drop." Some slogans, time capsules from decades ago ("melts in your mouth, not in your hands"), sit cheek-by-jowl with the latest soundbite from the cola wars ("Gotta have it"). Our awareness of these simple but ingenious advertising lines means that their creators were successful. And that, soon, if they don't stop (they won't), the confluence of past and present great lines in advertising will lead to the dreaded condition of slogan gridlock.

The truth behind the jingle you find yourself humming all day—even when you hate the product, the ad, or both—is simple. A good slogan gets under your skin. And five thousand of them found their way into this book.

Sometimes a phrase comes to symbolize an era. Americans instantly recognize "Hell, no! We won't go!" as a Vietnam-era rallying cry, and "Read my lips: No new taxes" as the despoiled promise that helped George Bush win the presidency for the Republican Party in 1988. Other slogans don't achieve symbol status but, like snapshots, still tell us a great deal about the time in which they were written. Most visible, and most revealing, are the commercial catch-phrases companies use to persuade us we need or want their products and services.

Who's Buying

The world in which a stove was advertised: "A choice of over a million women" was obviously not the one we know today, peopled as it is with working women and executive vice presidents who are called "Mommy" when they get home from work. And here are a couple of slogans likely to make contemporary women grimace, especially those who can actually remember what it's like to wear a corset or a girdle: "It's smart to conform with Reo-Form" and "Puts your best figure forward." No company today would risk ignoring female buyers—who make or influence eighty percent of all car purchases—with a line such as Packard's "Ask the man who owns one." And note how the pantyhose slogan "Gentlemen prefer Hanes" evolved to "The lady prefers Hanes" as women began to realize there's more to self-esteem and dressing well than pleasing men. Meanwhile, advertisers openly acknowledge that women are no longer the only consumers dying their hair, using skin-care products, and dousing themselves with designer fragrance (other than aftershave). This book collects recent slogans encouraging men to alter their facade too.

With the realization that women don't appreciate ads that treat them as simple-minded, and with the onset of the AIDS epidemic, previously taboo subjects are openly advertised. The slogan "For the anemia of RETRO-VIR-treated HIV-infected patients" may be cumbersome, but it shows how AIDS has become part of our lives. We still rarely see condom ads on television. But print slogans such as "For natural feeling and sensitivity" and "Prolong sexual pleasure for both partners" aim to convince consumers that protection against disease needn't prevent sexual enjoyment. Intermixed with slogans for various birth control products are slogans such as "Easy to read, unmistakable result" describing a home pregnancy test, and " ... for the period before your period," offering a PMS remedy.

Imagine getting away with touting cigarettes using slogans like "Not a cough in a carload," "For digestion's sake, smoke Camels," or "Ask Dad, he knows"—all from the decades before the public understood the dangers of smoking. Now tobacco-related slogans compete with lines such as "If you've got the will, now you've got the power" for Habitrol, a prescription skin-patch that delivers tiny doses of nicotine for smokers working to become non-smokers.

Standards for selecting healthy food have also changed. "Wholesome sweets for children" and "Meals without meat are meals incomplete" wouldn't cut it with today's health-conscious consumers, who want natural ingredients with little fat, cholesterol, or calories. Today we're more susceptible to a pitch like "Medically proven to help you lose weight." Nor would we grab for "the gum with the fascinating artificial flavor." The wisdom of statements such as "Have a glass of Guinness when you're tired" or "Guinness and oysters are good for you" would be considered questionable at best. More a sign of the times is the slogan "What beer drinkers drink when they're not drinking beer" for O'Doul's, reflecting the growing popularity of alcohol-free beverages.

We live in the era of the microwave oven and disposable contact lenses, so pardon us if we find it morbidly fascinating to pore over a stack of slogans for baking goods. Baking has become a hobby for those with the luxury of time, and those old slogans have a glow of nostalgia about them. But looking back cuts both ways; the most basic sensitivity against racism would prevent the old Aunt Jemima pancake flour slogan "I'se in town, honey" from appearing in any medium today.

Slogans trace the changes in entire industries. Look at all the grandiose phrases promoting airlines that no longer fly, banks that failed, car companies long extinct. The broadcast industry is no longer dominated by three commercial networks. Hence such lines as: "The total sports network" and "Weather you can always turn to."

Who's Selling

Computer-makers started out struggling to convince consumers—mostly businesses—of the usefulness of their machines. "A tool for modern times," was an early IBM slogan. Newer slogans show that neither businesses nor Joe and Jane Consumer need to be persuaded of the need for computers. Instead, slogans like "It's the next thing," for an Apple laptop computer work to reassure customers they'll be keeping up with the rapid escalation in computing power we've grown accustomed to. Slogans such as "The information service you won't outgrow" for CompuServe and "You've got to get this thing," for Prodigy, both information services that any PC user can easily tap into, give a sense of how the computer is becoming more a routine part of our daily lives.

On the other hand, some advertising is remarkable for how little it changes. Without a few important clues, it would be hard to tell auto slogans present from auto slogans past. For example, how much difference is there between "The front-wheel-drive youngmobile from Oldsmobile " and "The new generation of Oldsmobile"? (About 20 years.) The first slogan is for the 1970s Toronado. The second was used to help distinguish Oldsmobile of the late 1980s from the early 1980s, when cars by General Motors' Cadillac, Buick, and Oldsmobile divisions all looked alike. And today's wave of nostalgia advertising, bringing back favorite campaigns from the 1950s, 1960s, and 1970s, further proves that the slogans don't have to change to be effective; in fact, if they resonate with phrases you've already learned, they'll probably gain in power.

This book is a collection of snapshots from the past and present. And really, like other mass culture fragments, they're part of what goes into the huge family album of commonality that ties Americans together. But this book is just the beginning. Slogans are all around us, on TV and radio commercials, on billboards, in magazines and newspapers, on the bottles, cans, boxes, and bags that fill our cupboards and closets. Whether we like it or not, some of them will head toward our language bank, and the "quicker picker-upper" in our brain will select some more snapshots for the album.

Janet Braunstein
Ann Arbor, 1992

We'll Always Have Room for More?

A User's Guide to the Book

Table of Thematic Categories. Alphabetically arranged, with **See** and **See also** cross references, for finding slogans on particular topics. The corresponding text offers an organization of the slogans by these categories, similar to that of a thesaurus, bringing together material of a related nature. This allows for comparison and contrast that is difficult or impossible with a straight dictionary format.

The Slogans. Under each of the 126 category sections used in the text can be found the appropriate slogans, arranged in alphabetical order, along with source information as complete as could be verified by our research. For further convenience, the category cross references found in the Table of Thematic Categories have been included in the text at the appropriate places.

Index. All slogans are listed in one alphabetic order, furnishing the opportunity for alphabetic access to the slogans in dictionary order. Slogans beginning with **A**, **An**, or **The** are listed twice, once alphabetized by the article and words following, and once alphabetized beginning with the words following the initial article. References are to page numbers in the text.

Table of Thematic Categories

In the following table, categories used throughout the text and synonyms that are cross-references to categories are combined in one alphabetic order.

ADHESIVES

ADVERTISING

AEROSPACE
See also AIR TRAVEL AND CARGO, ELECTRONICS INDUSTRY

Agriculture
See FARMING SUPPLIES AND EQUIPMENT

Air Conditioning
See HEATING AND AIR CONDITIONING

AIR TRAVEL AND CARGO
See also AEROSPACE, TRAVEL

Airplanes
See AEROSPACE

Alcoholic Beverages
See BEER AND ALE, LIQUORS, WINES

Ale
See BEER AND ALE

Appliances
See HOME APPLIANCES AND EQUIPMENT

AUDIO EQUIPMENT
See also ELECTRONICS INDUSTRY, MOVIES AND ENTERTAINMENT, RECORDINGS

AUTOMOBILE RENTAL SERVICES
See also AUTOMOBILES

AUTOMOBILES
See also AUTOMOBILE RENTAL SERVICES, AUTOMOTIVE PARTS AND PRODUCTS, AUTOMOTIVE SERVICE

AUTOMOTIVE PARTS AND PRODUCTS
See also AUTOMOBILES, AUTOMOTIVE SERVICE, TIRES

AUTOMOTIVE SERVICE
See also AUTOMOBILES, AUTOMOTIVE PARTS AND PRODUCTS, PETROLEUM PRODUCTS

BABY PRODUCTS
See also FOOD, MISCELLANEOUS; SOAP; TOYS AND GAMES

BAKED GOODS AND BAKING SUPPLIES
See also FOOD, MISCELLANEOUS; KITCHEN PRODUCTS AND UTENSILS

Banks
See FINANCIAL SERVICES AND INSTITUTIONS

BATH ACCESSORIES
See also SHAVING SUPPLIES, SOAP, TOILETRIES

Bathing Suits
See SWIMWEAR

Batteries
See ELECTRICAL PRODUCTS AND SERVICES

Beauty Aids
See TOILETRIES

BEDS AND BEDDING
See also FURNITURE

BEER AND ALE
See also BEVERAGES, MISCELLANEOUS; LIQUORS; WINES

BEVERAGES, MISCELLANEOUS
See also BEER AND ALE; COFFEE; DAIRY PRODUCTS; FOOD, MISCELLANEOUS; LIQUORS; SOFT DRINKS; TEA; WINES

BOATS AND BOATING EQUIPMENT
See also SEA TRAVEL AND CARGO

Books
See PUBLISHING

BROADCASTING
See also RADIO EQUIPMENT, TELECOMMUNICATIONS, TELEVISIONS

BUILDING SUPPLIES
See also HARDWARE, INTERIOR DECORATION, METALS INDUSTRY, PAINT AND PAINTING SUPPLIES

BUS LINES
See also TRAVEL

Business Machines
See COMPUTER EQUIPMENT, OFFICE EQUIPMENT AND SUPPLIES

Campaign Slogans
See PRESIDENTIAL CAMPAIGNS

Camping Equipment
See RECREATIONAL EQUIPMENT

CANDY AND GUM
See also FOOD, MISCELLANEOUS

Cargo
See AIR TRAVEL AND CARGO, RAIL TRAVEL AND CARGO, SEA TRAVEL AND CARGO

Carpets
See FLOOR COVERINGS

Cars
See AUTOMOBILES

Cassettes
See RECORDINGS

Ceramics
See GLASS AND CERAMICS

CEREALS
See also FOOD, MISCELLANEOUS

Charitable Organizations
See PUBLIC SERVICE

CHEMICAL INDUSTRY
See also CLEANING AND LAUNDRY PRODUCTS, PEST CONTROL

CHINA AND CRYSTAL
See also GLASS AND CERAMICS, KITCHEN PRODUCTS AND UTENSILS

Cigarettes
See TOBACCO PRODUCTS

Cigars
See TOBACCO PRODUCTS

CLEANING AND LAUNDRY PRODUCTS
See also CHEMICAL INDUSTRY, SOAP

CLEANING SERVICES

Clocks
See WATCHES AND CLOCKS

CLOTHING, MISCELLANEOUS
See also FOOTWEAR, HOSIERY, SWIMWEAR, UNDERWEAR, WARDROBE ACCESSORIES

COFFEE
See also BEVERAGES; MISCELLANEOUS; TEA

Communications
See TELECOMMUNICATIONS

Companies
See CORPORATIONS, MISCELLANEOUS

COMPUTER EQUIPMENT AND SOFTWARE
See also ELECTRICAL PRODUCTS AND SERVICES, ELECTRONICS INDUSTRY, OFFICE EQUIPMENT AND SUPPLIES

CONDIMENTS AND SPICES
See also FOOD, MISCELLANEOUS

Confections
See CANDY AND GUM

Construction
See BUILDING SUPPLIES, MACHINERY

Contact Lenses
See EYEGLASSES

Contraceptives
See DRUGS AND REMEDIES

Cooking Fuels
See HEATING AND COOKING FUELS

Cookware
See BAKED GOODS AND BAKING SUPPLIES, KITCHEN PRODUCTS AND UTENSILS

COPYING EQUIPMENT
See also OFFICE EQUIPMENT AND SUPPLIES

CORPORATIONS, MISCELLANEOUS

COSMETICS
See also HAIR CARE, TOILETRIES

Cruise Ships
See SEA TRAVEL AND CARGO

Cutlery
See HARDWARE

DAIRY PRODUCTS
See also BEVERAGES, MISCELLAENOUS; FOOD, MISCELLANEOUS

DENTAL CARE
See also TOILETRIES

Deoderants
See TOILETRIES

Detergents
See CLEANING AND LAUNDRY PRODUCTS

Dishes
See CHINA

DRUGS AND REMEDIES
See also HEALTH AND FITNESS

Dry Goods
See SEWING AND KNITTING SUPPLIES

Earthmovers
See MACHINERY

ECONOMIC DEVELOPMENT
See also TRAVEL

**ELECTRICAL PRODUCTS
AND SERVICE**
See also ELECTRONICS
INDUSTRY, HEATING AND
AIR CONDITIONING,
HOME APPLIANCES AND
EQUIPMENT, LIGHTING
PRODUCTS, PUBLIC
UTILITIES

Electricity
See PUBLIC UTILITIES

ELECTRONICS INDUSTRY
See also AEROSPACE,
AUDIO EQUIPMENT,
BROADCASTING,
COMPUTER EQUIPMENT
AND SOFTWARE,
CORPORATIONS,
ELECTRICAL PRODUCTS
AND SERVICE, RADIO
EQUIPMENT,
TELECOMMUNICATIONS,
TELEVISIONS, VIDEO
EQUIPMENT

ELEVATORS

EMPLOYMENT AGENCIES

Energy
See HEATING AND
COOKING FUELS

Entertainment
See MOVIES AND
ENTERTAINMENT

EYEGLASSES
See also WARDROBE
ACCESSORIES

Fabrics Industry
See SEWING AND
KNITTING SUPPLIES

**FARMING SUPPLIES AND
EQUIPMENT**
See also MACHINERY,
TRUCKS AND TRUCKING
INDUSTRY

Fashion Accessories
See CLOTHING,
COSMETICS, WARDROBE
ACCESSORIES

Feed
See FARMING SUPPLIES
AND EQUIPMENT

Fertilizer
See FARMING SUPPLIES
AND EQUIPMENT

Film
See PHOTOGRAPHIC
EQUIPMENT

**FINANCIAL INSTITUTIONS
AND SERVICES**
See also INSURANCE,
INVESTMENT

Finishes
See PAINT AND PAINTING
SUPPLIES

FIREARMS

FISHING SUPPLIES
See also RECREATIONAL
EQUIPMENT, SPORTING
GOODS

Fitness
See HEALTH AND FITNESS

Flatware
See CHINA, JEWELRY AND
SILVER

Flavorings
See CONDIMENTS AND
SPICES

FLOOR COVERINGS
See also BUILDING
SUPPLIES, INTERIOR
DECORATION

FOOD, MISCELLANEOUS
See also BABY PRODUCTS;
BAKED GOODS AND
BAKING SUPPLIES;
BEVERAGES,
MISCELLANEOUS; CANDY
AND GUM; CEREALS;
CONDIMENTS AND
SPICES; DAIRY PRODUCTS;
FRUITS AND NUTS;
MEATS; PET FOOD AND
PRODUCTS; RESTAURANTS

FOOTWEAR
See also CLOTHING,
MISCELLANEOUS;
WARDROBE ACCESSORIES

Fragrances
See PERFUMES AND
FRAGRANCES

Fruit Drinks
See SOFT DRINKS

FRUITS AND NUTS
See also FOOD,
MISCELLANEOUS

Fuel
See AUTOMOTIVE
SERVICE, HEATING AND
COOKING FUELS,
PETROLEUM PRODUCTS,
PUBLIC UTILITIES

FURNITURE
See also BEDS AND
BEDDING, INTERIOR
DECORATION

Games
See TOYS AND GAMES

Garden Products
See LAWN AND GARDEN
PRODUCTS

Garters
See HOSIERY

Gasoline
See PETROLEUM
PRODUCTS

Gauges
See INTSRUMENTS AND
GAUGES

Gems
See JEWELRY AND SILVER

GIFTS AND GREETINGS

GLASS AND CERAMICS
See also CHINA AND
CRYSTAL

Glasses
See EYEGLASSES

Gloves
See WARDROBE
ACCESSORIES

Glue
See ADHESIVES

GOVERNMENT SERVICE
See also PUBLIC SERVICE

Greetings
See GIFTS AND
GREETINGS

Gum
See CANDY AND GUM

Guns
See FIREARMS

HAIR CARE
See also COSMETICS,
TOILETRIES

Handbags
See WARDROBE
ACCESSORIES

Handkerchiefs
See WARDROBE
ACCESSORIES

HARDWARE
See also BUILDING
SUPPLIES, TOOLS

Health and Beauty Aids
See COSMETICS,
TOILETRIES

HEALTH AND FITNESS
See also DRUGS AND
REMEDIES, RECREATIONAL
EQUIPMENT, SPORTING
GOODS

5

HEARING AIDS

HEATING AND AIR CONDITIONING
See also ELECTRICAL PRODUCTS AND SERVICES, HOME APPLIANCES AND EQUIPMENT

HEATING AND COOKING FUELS
See also PETROLEUM PRODUCTS

Herbs
See CONDIMENTS AND SPICES

HOME APPLIANCES AND EQUIPMENT
See also HEATING AND AIR CONDITIONING, KITCHEN PRODUCTS AND UTENSILS

Home Maintenance
See CLEANING AND LAUNDRY PRODUCTS, PEST CONTROL

HOSIERY
See also CLOTHING, MISCELLANEOUS; FOOTWEAR; UNDERWEAR; WARDROBE ACCESSORIES

HOTELS AND MOTELS
See also TRAVEL

Insecticides
See PEST CONTROL

INSTRUMENTS AND GAUGES

INSURANCE
See also FINANCIAL INSTITUTIONS AND SERVICES, INVESTMENT

INTERIOR DECORATION
See also BUILDING SUPPLIES, FLOOR COVERINGS, FURNITURE, PAINT AND PAINTING SUPPLIES

INVESTMENT
See also FINANCIAL INSTITUTIONS AND SERVICES, INSURANCE

Jets
See AEROSPACE, AIR TRAVEL AND CARGO

JEWELRY AND SILVER
See also WARDROBE ACCESSORIES

Job Placement
See EMPLOYMENT

Juices
See BEVERAGES, MISCELLANEOUS

KITCHEN PRODUCTS AND UTENSILS
See also BAKED GOODS AND BAKING SUPPLIES, CHINA, HOME APPLIANCES AND EQUIPMENT

Knitting Supplies
See SEWING AND KNITTING SUPPLIES

Lamps
See LIGHTING PRODUCTS

Laundry Products
See CLEANING AND LAUNDRY PRODUCTS

LAWN AND GARDEN PRODUCTS
See also PEST CONTROL

LIGHTING PRODUCTS
See also ELECTRICAL PRODUCTS AND SERVICE, HOME APPLIANCES AND EQUIPMENT, INTERIOR DECORATION

Linens
See BEDS AND BEDDING

Lingerie
See UNDERWEAR

LIQUORS
See also BEER AND ALE; BEVERAGES, MISCELLANEOUS; WINES

Locks
See HARDWARE

LUGGAGE
See also TRAVEL

Lumber
See BUILDING SUPPLIES

MACHINERY
See also ELECTRICAL PRODUCTS AND SERVICE, FARMING SUPPLIES AND EQUIPMENT, TRUCKS AND TRUCKING INDUSTRY

Magazines
See PERIODICALS AND NEWSPAPERS

Maintenance
See CLEANING AND LAUNDRY PRODUCTS

Make-up
See COSMETICS

Marketing
See ADVERTISING

Measuring Devices
See INSTRUMENTS AND GAUGES

MEATS
See also FOOD, MISCELLANEOUS

Medications
See DRUGS AND REMEDIES

METALS INDUSTRY
See also BUILDING SUPPLIES

Motels
See HOTELS AND MOTELS

Motor Oil
See PETROLEUM PRODUCTS

MOTORCYCLES
See also AUTOMOBILES, RECREATIONAL EQUIPMENT

MOVIES AND ENTERTAINMENT
See also AUDIO EQUIPMENT, BROADCASTING, PHOTOGRAPHIC EQUIPMENT, TELEVISIONS, VIDEO EQUIPMENT

MOVING AND STORAGE
See also TRUCKS AND TRUCKING INDUSTRY

MUSICAL INSTRUMENTS

Nautical Supplies
See BOATS AND BOATING EQUIPMENT

Newspapers
See PERIODICALS AND NEWSPAPERS

Notions
See SEWING AND KNITTING SUPPLIES

Nuts
See FRUITS AND NUTS

OFFICE EQUIPMENT AND SUPPLIES
See also COMPUTER EQUIPMENT, COPYING EQUIPMENT, PAPER PRODUCTS, WRITING INSTRUMENTS

Outboard Motors
See BOATS AND BOATING EQUIPMENT

Outdoor Supplies
See RECREATIONAL EQUIPMENT, SPORTING GOODS

Ovens
See HOME APPLIANCES AND EQUIPMENT

7

PAINT AND PAINTING SUPPLIES
See also INTERIOR DECORATION

PAPER PRODUCTS
See also KITCHEN PRODUCTS AND UTENSILS, OFFICE EQUIPMENT AND SUPPLIES

Pencils
See WRITING INSTRUMENTS

Pens
See WRITING INSTRUMENTS

PERFUMES AND FRAGRANCES
See also BATH ACCESSORIES, COSMETICS, SHAVING SUPPLIES, TOILETRIES

PERIODICALS AND NEWSPAPERS
See also PUBLISHING

PEST CONTROL
See also CHEMICAL INDUSTRY, LAWN AND GARDEN PRODUCTS

PET FOOD AND PRODUCTS
See also FOOD, MISCELLANEOUS; PEST CONTROL

PETROLEUM PRODUCTS
See also AUTOMOTIVE SERVICE, HEATING AND COOKING FUELS

Pharmaceutical Products
See DRUGS AND REMEDIES

Phonographic Equipment
See AUDIO EQUIPMENT

Phonographs
See AUDIO EQUIPMENT

PHOTOGRAPHIC EQUIPMENT
See also MOVIES AND ENTERTAINMENT

Physical Fitness
See HEALTH AND FITNESS

Pipes
See SMOKING ACCESSORIES

Plumbing Supplies
See HARDWARE

POLITICAL ISSUES
See also PRESIDENTIAL CAMPAIGNS

Pottery
See GLASS AND CERAMICS

PRESIDENTIAL CAMPAIGNS
See also POLITICAL ISSUES

PUBLIC SERVICE
See also GOVERNMENT SERVICE

PUBLIC UTILITIES

PUBLISHING
See also PERIODICALS AND NEWSPAPERS

RADIO EQUIPMENT
See also AUDIO EQUIPMENT, TELECOMMUNICATIONS

RAIL TRAVEL AND CARGO
See also TRAVEL

Ranges
See HOME APPLIANCES AND EQUIPMENT

RECORDINGS
See also AUDIO EQUIPMENT

Record Players
See AUDIO EQUIPMENT

Records
See RECORDINGS

RECREATIONAL EQUIPMENT
See also BOATS AND
BOATING EQUIPMENT,
FIREARMS, FISHING
SUPPLIES, HEALTH AND
FITNESS, MOTORCYCLES,
SPORTING GOODS,
SWIMWEAR, TOYS AND
GAMES

Refrigerators
See HOME APPLIANCES
AND EQUIPMENT

Relishes
See CONDIMENTS AND
SPICES

Remedies
See DRUGS AND
REMEDIES

RESTAURANTS
See also FOOD,
MISCELLANEOUS

RETAIL STORES

Scales
See INSTRUMENTS AND
GAUGES

SCHOOLS

SEA TRAVEL AND CARGO
See also BOATS AND
BOATING EQUIPMENT,
TRAVEL

Seeds
See FARMING SUPPLIES
AND EQUIPMENT

**SEWING AND KNITTING
SUPPLIES**
See also TEXTILES

Shampoo
See HAIR CARE

SHAVING SUPPLIES
See also BATH
ACCESSORIES, PERFUMES
AND FRAGRANCES, SOAP,
TOILETRIES

Shipping
See AEROSPACE, RAIL
TRAVEL AND CARGO, SEA
TRAVEL AND CARGO,
TRUCKS AND TRUCKING
INDUSTRY

Shoes
See FOOTWEAR

Silver
See JEWELRY AND SILVER

Skin Care
See COSMETICS,
TOILETRIES

SMOKING ACCESSORIES
See also TOBACCO
PRODUCTS

SOAP
See also BABY PRODUCTS,
BATH ACCESSORIES,
CLEANING AND LAUNDRY
PRODUCTS, SHAVING
SUPPLIES, TOILETRIES

Social Issues
See POLITICAL ISSUES

Socks
See HOSIERY

Soda
See SOFT DRINKS

SOFT DRINKS
See also BEVERAGES,
MISCELLANEOUS; COFFEE,
TEA

Software
See COMPUTER
EQUIPMENT

Spices
See CONDIMENTS AND
SPICES

SPORTING GOODS
See also BOATS AND
BOATING EQUIPMENT,
FIREARMS, FISHING
SUPPLIES, FOOTWEAR,
HEALTH AND FITNESS,
RECREATIONAL
EQUIPMENT, SWIMWEAR,
TOYS AND GAMES

Stationery Supplies
See OFFICE EQUIPMENT
AND SUPPLIES, PAPER
PRODUCTS, WRITING
INSTRUMENTS

Stereos
See AUDIO EQUIPMENT

Stockings
See HOSIERY

Storage
See MOVING AND
STORAGE

Stoves
See HOME APPLIANCES
AND EQUIPMENT

Sunglasses
See EYEGLASSES

Sweets
See CANDY AND GUM

SWIMWEAR
See also CLOTHING,
MISCELLANEOUS;
RECREATIONAL
EQUIPMENT; SPORTING
GOODS

Tableware
See CHINA, JEWELRY AND
SILVER

Tape Decks
See AUDIO EQUIPMENT

Tapes
See RECORDINGS

TEA
See also BEVERAGES,
MISCELLANEOUS; COFFEE;
SOFT DRINKS

TELECOMMUNICATIONS
See also BROADCASTING,
RADIO EQUIPMENT

TELEVISIONS
See also ELECTRONICS
INDUSTRY, HOME
APPLIANCES AND
EQUIPMENT, MOVIES AND
ENTERTAINMENT, VIDEO
EQUIPMENT

TEXTILES
See also INTERIOR
DECORATION, SEWING
AND KNITTING SUPPLIES

Timepieces
See WATCHES AND
CLOCKS

TIRES
See also AUTOMOTIVE
PARTS AND PRODUCTS

TOBACCO PRODUCTS
See also SMOKING
ACCESSORIES

TOILETRIES
See also BATH
ACCESSORIES, COSMETICS,
DENTAL CARE, HAIR
CARE, PERFUMES AND
FRAGRANCES, SHAVING
SUPPLIES, SOAP

TOOLS
See also HARDWARE

Toothpaste
See DENTAL CARE

Tourism
See TRAVEL

TOYS AND GAMES
See also BABY PRODUCTS,
RECREATIONAL
EQUIPMENT, SPORTING
GOODS

Tractors
See FARMING SUPPLIES
AND EQUIPMENT

Transportation
See AIR TRAVEL AND
CARGO, BUS LINES, RAIL
TRAVEL AND CARGO, SEA
TRAVEL AND CARGO,
TRUCKS AND TRUCKING
INDUSTRY

TRAVEL
See also AIR TRAVEL AND
CARGO, AUTOMOBILE
RENTAL SERVICES, BUS
LINES, ECONOMIC
DEVELOPMENT, HOTELS
AND MOTELS, LUGGAGE,
MOVING AND STORAGE,
RAIL TRAVEL AND
CARGO, SEA TRAVEL AND
CARGO

Travelers Checks
See FINANCIAL
INSTITUTIONS AND
SERVICES, TRAVEL

**TRUCKS AND TRUCKING
INDUSTRY**
See also FARMING AND
SUPPLIES AND
EQUIPMENT, MACHINERY,
MOVING AND STORAGE

Typewriters
See OFFICE EQUIPMENT
AND SUPPLIES

Umbrellas
See WARDROBE
ACCESSORIES

UNDERWEAR
See also CLOTHING,
MISCELLANEOUS; HOSIERY

Utensils
See KITCHEN PRODUCTS
AND UTENSILS

Varnish
See PAINT AND PAINTING
SUPPLIES

VIDEO EQUIPMENT
See also MOVIES AND
ENTERTAINMENT,
TELEVISIONS

Wallets
See WARDROBE
ACCESSORIES

WARDROBE ACCESSORIES
See also EYEGLASSES,
FOOTWEAR, HOSIERY,
JEWELRY AND SILVER

WATCHES AND CLOCKS

Whiskey
See LIQUORS

WINES
See also BEER AND ALE;
BEVERAGES,
MISCELLANEOUS;
LIQUORS

WRITING INSTRUMENTS
See also OFFICE
EQUIPMENT AND
SUPPLIES

IT'S BUG TESTED

The Slogans

ADHESIVES

A million and one uses
      Fix-All Liquid Cement Co.

Best glue in the joint
      (*Elmer's Glue All*) Borden Chemical Division, Borden Inc.

Holds the world together
      H. B. Fuller Co.

Join with Bostik for better bonding
      B. B. Chemical Division, United Shoe Machinery Corp.

Mends everything but a broken heart
      Fix-All Liquid Cement Co.

ADVERTISING

Advertise for action
      (*Yellow Pages*) AT&T

Advertising is the power of an idea multiplied
      D'Arcy Advertising Co.

Advertising with a basic idea
      J. Walter Thompson Co.

Advertising. Without it, you wouldn't know.
      American Advertising Federation

Advertising

An agency is known by the clients it keeps
Gottschalk–Humphrey

A true expression of heart-felt sympathy
Florists Association

Better business is our aim
Business Advertising Agency

Bright by day, light by night
Pyrograph Advertising Sign Corp.

Built on bedrock
Johnson, Read & Co.

Find it faster in the Yellow Pages
AT&T

Idea Creators, not just illustrators
Martin Ullman Studios

Let your fingers do the walking
(*Yellow Pages*) AT&T

Merchandise well displayed is half sold
Russell H. Spoor Co.

Meredith moves merchandise
Meredith Publishing Co.

Put it up to men who know your market
Federal Advertising Agency

Repetition makes reputation
Emil Brisacher & Staff

Signs of long life
Artkraft Sign Co.

Teaching the millions to buy
Millis Advertising Co.

The interrupting idea
Federal Advertising Agency

Thematic advertising
Grey Advertising Agency

The shortest distance between two points
J. L. Arnold Co.

Think of it first
Ideas Inc.

To sell millions, tell millions
National Transitads Inc.

True salesmanship in print
Lord & Thomas

We stick up for everybody
(*bill posters*) McClintock Co.

AEROSPACE
See also AIR TRAVEL AND CARGO, ELECTRONICS INDUSTRY

Built for permanence, calibrated for performance
Bendix Aviation Corp.

Capability has many faces at Boeing
Boeing Co.

Dutch. Dedicated. Dependable.
Fokker Aircraft USA

Easy to buy, easy to fly
(*Stinson*) Consolidated Vultee

Family car of the air
Cessna Aircraft Co.

Garrett *is* experience
Garrett AiResearch, The Garrett Corp.

In the air or outer space Douglas gets things done
Douglas Aircraft Co. Inc.

Look to Lockheed for leadership
Lockheed Corp.

Look to the leader for good safe planes you can afford to
buy and fly
Piper Aircraft Corp.

More people buy Cessna twins than any other make
Cessna Aircraft Co.

More people have bought Pipers than any other plane in the world
Piper Aircraft Corp.

Aerospace

Pacemakers of aviation progress
   Bell Aircraft Corp.

The business jet that's backed by an airline
   (*Fan Jet Falcon*) Business Jets Division, Pan American World Airways Inc.

The jet that justifies itself
   (*Sabreliner*) North American Rockwell Corp.

The modern magic carpet
   (*helicopters*) Bell Aircraft Corp.

The world is smaller when you fly a Beechcraft
   Beech Aircraft Corp.

This one means business
   (*The DH 125*) Hawker Siddeley Group Ltd.

Uncommonly versatile, uncommonly productive
   (*Gulfstream IV business jet*) Gulfstream Aerospace

When science gets down to business
   Rockwell International

World's first family of jets
   Boeing Co.

World standard
   Bell Helicopter Co.

Years ahead in the science of flight
   Lockheed Corp.

Your personal plane IS HERE
   Aeronca

AGRICULTURE
See FARMING SUPPLIES AND EQUIPMENT

AIR CONDITIONING
See HEATING AND AIR CONDITIONING

AIR TRAVEL AND CARGO
See also AEROSPACE, TRAVEL

A friend of the family
  Air Canada

A great name in aviation
  Pacific Northern Airlines

A great way to fly
  Singapore Airlines

Air-freight specialists
  Flying Tiger Line Inc.

Airlines of Spain
  Iberia

All over the world BOAC takes good care of you
  British Overseas Airways Corp.

America's airline to the world
  Pan American World Airways

America's favorite way to fly
  Eastern Airlines Inc.

À votre service
  Air France

A most remarkable airline
  Continental Airlines Inc.

Australia's round-the-world jet airline
  Qantas Airways

Coast to coast overnight
  American Airlines Inc.

Coast to coast to coast
  National Airlines Inc.

Delta is ready when you are
  Delta Air Lines Inc.

Determined to serve you best
  Eastern Airlines Inc.

Europe's foremost airline
  British European Airways

Europe's most helpful airline
>Sabena Belgian World Airlines

Fast, frequent and friendly
>SAA—South African Airways

Find out how good we really are
>Trans World Airlines Inc.

First across the Pacific; first across the Atlantic; first throughout Latin America
>Pan American World Airways Inc.

First airline in the Americas
>Avianca

First in airfreight with airfreight first
>Flying Tiger Line Inc.

Fly anywhere in Europe via Air France
>Air France

Fly the friendly skies of United
>United Air Lines Inc.

Fly the planes that fly the U. S. Flag
>Airlines of the U. S.

Gets there first
>Air Express

Golden nugget jet service
>Alaska Airlines Inc.

Great people to fly with
>Pakistan International Airlines

It takes a big airline
>Allegheny Airlines

Just plane smart
>Southwest Airlines

Nationwide, worldwide depend on ...
>Trans World Airlines Inc.

Packages prefer United AirExpress
>United AirExpress

Pan Am Makes the going great
        Pan American World Airways Inc.

Sailing the South Pacific skies
        UTA French Airlines

Serving America's billionaires
        Northwest Airlines Inc.

Ski lift to the Italian Alps
        Alitalia Airlines

Something special in the air
        American Airlines

Specialists in international jet service to Texas or South America
        Braniff Airways Inc.

Swisscare. Worldwide.
        Swiss Air Transport Co. Ltd.

Take us for all we've got
        Virgin Atlantic Airways

The airline run by fliers
        Transcontinental & Western

The airline that knows the South Pacific best
        Air New Zealand

The airline that treats you like a maharajah
        Air–India

The best connections in West Africa
        Nigeria Airways

The calm beauty of Japan at almost the speed of sound
        Japan Air Lines

The country's top on-time airline. With more U.S. gateways to Asia
    than any other airline in the world.
        Northwest Airlines

The fan-jet airline
        Northwest Airlines Inc.

The friendly way, C. P. A.
        Canadian Pacific Air Lines

The jet with the extra engine
    Western Air Lines Inc.

The new way to fly daily non-stop to Brazil
    TransBrasil Airlines

The Pacific's number one
    Air New Zealand

The pioneer of low fares to Europe
    Icelandic Airlines

The things we do to make you happy
    Trans World Airlines Inc.

The way to get there
    Iberia Air Lines of Spain

The world is going our way
    Northwest Orient Airlines

The world's favourite airline
    British Airways

Up up and away
    Trans World Airlines Inc.

USAir begins with you
    USAir

We earn our wings every day
    Eastern Airlines Inc.

We'll go to the ends of the earth for you
    Continental Airlines

We know where you're going
    Air France

Welcome aboard
    United Air Lines Inc.

We love to fly and it shows
    Delta Air Lines Inc.

We started small. And made it big.
    Saudi Arabian Airlines

We treat you as an honored guest
    Korean Air Lines

We've earned the trust of American Business
    Emery Worldwide

When it absolutely, positively has to be there overnight
    Federal Express

When you need it overnight, we deliver
    Federal Express

Where only the plane gets more attention than you
    Iberia Air Lines of Spain

Why fool around with anyone else?
    Federal Express

World's largest charter airline
    World Airways Inc.

World's most dependable air freight service
    Airborne Freight Corp.

You're better off with Pan Am
    Pan American World Airways Inc.

You're not just flying. You're flying the friendly skies.
    United Air Lines

You want it. You got it.
    Purolator Courier

AIRPLANES
See AEROSPACE

ALCOHOLIC BEVERAGES
See BEER AND ALE, LIQUORS, WINES

ALE
See BEER AND ALE

APPLIANCES
See HOME APPLIANCES AND EQUIPMENT

AUDIO EQUIPMENT
See also ELECTRONICS INDUSTRY, MOVIES AND
ENTERTAINMENT, RECORDINGS

After years of giving people smaller electronics, Sony now makes
electronics for smaller people
(*My First Sony*) Sony Corp. of America

Anything else is a compromise
(*car stereos*) Concord

Because the music matters
(*Pioneer Audio Systems*) Pioneer Electronics (USA) Inc.

Be finicky
(*Shure cartridges*) Tandy Corp.

Don't just tape it. TDK it.
(*cassettes*) TDK Electronics Corp.

Feature rich
(*Aiwa*) Selectron International Co.

For those who can hear the difference
Pickering and Co. Inc.

Full color sound
(*audio tape*) Sony Corp. of America

Getting closer to the source
(*speakers*) EPI

Great sound starts with the source
(*speakers*) Pyle Driver

Hearing is believing
Koss

His master's voice
RCA Corp.

Imagination has just become reality
(*audio tape*) Fuji

In a class by itself
(*car stereo*) Kenwood Electronics Inc.

Innovation. Precision. Integrity.
(*cartridges*) Audio Technica

Is it live? Or is it Memorex?
   (*Memorex recording cassettes*) Memorex Corp.

It speaks for itself
   (*Audiotape*) Audio Devices Inc.

Kenwood: the sound of leadership
   (*receivers*) Kenwood Electronics Inc.

Made in Japan by fanatics
   (*tape decks*) Teac

Miles ahead in sound experience
   (*Delco car stereo*) General Motors Corp.

Move at the speed of sound
   (*car stereos*) Clarion

Music you'll love to stay home with
   JVC

Our state-of-the-mind is tomorrow's state-of-the-art
   Harman–Kardon Inc.

Our woofers bark, but don't bite
   (*car speakers*) Maxima

Plays all records, natural as life
   Vitanola Talking Machine Co.

Portable phonographs of distinction
   Caswell Mfg. Co.

Power & Grace
   (*speakers*) Electro-Voice Inc.

Putting more pleasure in sound
   (*receivers*) Sansui

Quality. Technology. Value.
   (*car stereos*) Maxima

Setting new standards in sound
   Electro-Voice Inc.

Simply, the best
   O'Sullivan Industries Inc.

Sound shapers have no equal
   (*equalizers*) ADC

Studio sound for the home
(*equalizers*) Numark

That's life
(*cassette decks*) Sanyo

The leader in digital audio
Sony Corp. of America

The longer you play it, the sweeter it grows
Cheney Talking Machine Co.

The name that means MUSIC to millions
(*Wurlitzer phonograph*)

The phonograph of marvelous tone
Vitanola Talking Machine Co.

The phonograph with a soul
Edison

The Science of Sound
(*Technics*) Matsushita Electric Corp. of America

The sound approach to quality
Kenwood Electronics Inc.

The sound of excellence!
(*amplifiers*) SAE Two

The tape of the stars
Ampex

True in every sound
Victor Talking Machine Co.

We take you there
JVC America Inc.

What you want is a Wollensack
(*tape recorders*) Revere–Wollensack Division, Minnesota
Mining and Mfg. Co.

When it's the sound that moves you
(*car stereos*) Jensen Sound Laboratories

World's most wonderful phonograph
Aeolian Vocalion

You never heard it so good
   (*receivers*) Akai

AUTOMOBILE RENTAL SERVICES
See also AUTOMOBILES

America's wheels
   Hertz Corp.

Anywhere in the wide world
   Hertz Corp.

Going all out
   General Rent-a-car

Let Hertz put *you* in the driver's seat
   Hertz Corp.

Maybe we're better
   National Car Rental System Inc.

Right on the airport. Right on the money.
   Dollar Rent a Car

The biggest *should* do more. It's only right.
   Hertz Corp.

The customer is always No. 1
   National Car Rental System Inc.

The smart money is on Budget
   Budget Rent a Car

We're trying harder than ever
   Avis Inc.

We try harder
   Avis Inc.

Where all the miles are free
   Alamo Rent a Car

Your vacation car company
   Value Rent-a-Car

AUTOMOBILES
See also AUTOMOBILE RENTAL SERVICES, AUTOMOTIVE PARTS
AND PRODUCTS, AUTOMOTIVE SERVICE

A blending of art and machine
> Jaguar

A car for every purse and purpose
> General Motors Corp.

A car you can believe in
> Volvo of America Corp.

A different kind of company. A different kind of car.
> (*Saturn Corp.*) General Motors Corp.

Advancing the art of driving
> (*Merkur*) Ford Motor Co.

All our best ideas in one car
> (*Jetta*) Volkswagen of America Inc.

All this and the quality of a Mercury
> (*Lincoln-Mercury*) Ford Motor Co.

America's favorite fun car
> (*Mustang*) Ford Motor Co.

America's finest motor car for America's finest families
> Pierce–Arrow Motor Car Co.

America's first car
> Haynes Automobile Co.

America's first truly fine small car
> Marmon Motor Car Co.

America's friendliest factory
> Studebaker Corp.

America's most distinguished motorcar
> (*Lincoln Continental*) Ford Motor Co.

America's most luxurious motor car
> (*Stearns-Knight*) Willys–Overland Inc.

America's smartest car
> (*Ranier*)

A more enlightened approach
    (*Mercury*) Ford Motor Co.

An air bag is only as good as the car it's attached to
    Volvo North America

A new kind of excitement
    (*Pontiac*) General Motors Corp.

A new time. A new GM.
    General Motors Corp.

As fine as money can build
    (*Chrysler*) Chrysler Corp.

Ask the man who owns one
    (*Packard*) Studebaker–Packard Corp.

A twentieth century expression of the French civilization
    (*Renault*) Renault Inc.

Audi: the art of engineer
    Volkswagen of America Inc.

Baseball, hot dogs, apple pie ... and Chevrolet
    General Motors Corp.

Beautiful beyond belief
    (*Hudson*) American Motors Corp.

Best bet's Buick
    (*Buick*) General Motors Corp.

Best built, best backed American cars
    (*Plymouth*) Chrysler Corp.

Best of all ... it's a Cadillac
    (*Cadillac*) General Motors Corp.

Best year yet to go Ford
    Ford Motor Co.

Body by Fisher
    (*Fisher automobile bodies*) General Motors Corp.

Built for the human race
    Nissan

Built tough for you
    Toyota Motor Distributors Inc.

Automobiles

Cars that make sense
　　Hyundai Motor America

Dedicated to excellence
　　American Motors Corp.

Driving in its purest form
　　(*Porsche*) Volkswagen of America Inc.

Engineered like no other car in the world
　　(*Mercedes–Benz*) Mercedes–Benz of North America Inc.

Escape from the ordinary
　　(*Oldsmobile*) General Motors Corp.

Everyday vehicles that aren't
　　American Suzuki Motor Corp.

Fahrvergnugen
　　(*Volkswagen* Volkswagen of America Inc.

First of the dream cars to come true
　　(*Chevrolet Corvette*) General Motors Corp.

Ford has a better idea
　　Ford Motor Co.

Ford trucks. The best never rest.
　　Ford Motor Co.

Get your hands on a Toyota ... you'll never let go
　　Toyota Motor Distributors Inc.

Have you driven a Ford ... lately?
　　Ford Motor Co.

Honda ... we make it simple
　　(*Honda*) American Honda Motor Co. Inc.

I love what you do for me
　　Toyota Motor Sales

It could change the way you think about American automobiles
　　(*Cadillac Seville*) General Motors Corp.

Inexpensive. And built to stay that way.
　　(*Subaru*) Subaru of America Inc.

It just feels right
　　Mazda Motor of America Inc.

It's not just a truck anymore
    (*GMC Truck*) General Motors Corp.

It's ugly, but it gets you there
    Volkswagen of America Inc.

Let yourself go ... Plymouth
    (*Plymouth*) Chrysler Corp.

Lincoln. What a luxury car should be.
    (*Lincoln–Mercury*) Ford Motor Co.

Live the dream
    De Lorean Motor Co.

Mark of excellence
    General Motors Corp.

Mercury. Where comfort and control come together.
    (*Lincoln–Mercury*) Ford Motor Co.

Nothing else is a Volkswagen
    (*Volkswagen*) Volkswagen of America Inc.

Nothing moves you like a Fiat
    Fiat

One drive is worth a thousand words
    (*Thunderbird*) Ford Motor Co.

Only in a Jeep
    (*Jeep CJ-7*) Jeep Corp.

On the road to civilization
    Mazda Motor of America Inc.

Our goal is to build the highest quality cars and trucks in the world
    Ford Motor Co.

People building transportation to serve people
    General Motors Corp.

Porsche 968: The next evolution
    Porsche Cars North America

Precision crafted performance
    (*Acura*) American Honda Motor Co. Inc.

Putting quality on the road
    General Motors Corp.

Putting you first, keeps us first
(*Chevrolet*) General Motors Corp.

Quality is Job 1
Ford Motor Co.

Rediscover American value
(*Dodge*) Chrysler Corp.

See the USA in your Chevrolet
(*Chevrolet*) General Motors Corp.

Simply the best motor car in the world
Rolls–Royce

Smart to be seen in, smarter to buy
(*Studebaker*) Studebaker Corp.

Socially, America's first motor car
(*Packard*) Studebaker–Packard Corp.

So new! So right! So obviously Cadillac!
(*Cadillac*) General Motors Corp.

Spend the difference
(*Ford*) Ford Motor Co.

Standard of the world
(*Cadillac*) General Motors Corp.

Stealing the thunder from the high-priced cars
(*Chevrolet*) General Motors Corp.

Strength, safety, style and speed
(*Hudson*) American Motors Corp.

Subaru. What to drive.
Subaru of America Inc.

Substance takes shape, Cadillac style
General Motors Corp.

The beauty and distinction of custom car styling
(*Kaiser*) Kaiser–Frazer Corp.

The best-built, best-selling American trucks are built Ford tough
Ford Motor Co.

The car of a thousand speeds
(*Owen Magnetic Motor Car*)

The car of no regrets
(*King Motor Car*)

The car of the year in eye appeal and buy appeal
(*Studebaker*) Studebaker Corp.

The car with a longer life
(*Westcott*) Westcott Motor Car Co.

The difference is valves
(*Datsun*) Nissan Motor Co.

The front-wheel-drive youngmobile from Oldsmobile
(*Toronado*) General Motors Corp.

The great highway performers
(*Corvair, Monza*) General Motors Corp.

The heartbeat of America
(*Chevrolet*) General Motors Corp.

The legendary marque of high performance
Alfa Romeo

The line is drawn for the future
(*Honda Civic Hatchback*) American Honda Motor Co. Inc.

The mini-brutes
(*Opel Kadett*) General Motors Corp.

The more you look, the more you like
Mazda Motors of America

The most intelligent car ever built
(*Saab*) Saab–Scania of America Inc.

The New England solution
(*Subaru*) Subaru of America Inc.

The new generation of Oldsmobile
General Motors Corp.

The new symbol for quality in America
(*Buick*) General Motors Corp.

The number one selling car in America the past three years running
(*Honda Accord*) American Honda Motor Co. Inc.

The one to watch
(*AMC/Renault*) Renault Inc.

Automobiles

The power of intelligent engineering
  (*Oldsmobile*) General Motors Corp.

There is a special feel in an Oldsmobile
  (*Oldsmobile*) General Motors Corp.

The relentless pursuit of perfection
  (*Lexus*) Toyota Motor Sales

There is no comparison
  Isuzu Motors of America

There's a Ford in your future
  Ford Motor Co.

There's only one Jeep
  (*Jeep-Eagle*) Chrysler Corp.

The rocket action car
  (*Oldsmobile*) General Motors Corp.

The room and ride Americans want. The size America needs.
  (*Pacer*) American Motors Corp.

The shape you want to be in
  (*Mercury*) Ford Motor Co.

The smart way to go places
  De Soto

The sportsman's car
  (*BMW*) Bavarian Motor Works

The style leader
  (*Lincoln Zephyr*) Ford Motor Co.

The "unstoppables"
  Kaiser Jeep Corp.

The word is getting around
  Mitsubishi Motors of America

They'll know you've arrived when you drive up in an Edsel
  Ford Motor Co.

Think small
  Volkswagen of America Inc.

This isn't your father's Oldsmobile
  (*Oldsmobile*) General Motors Corp.

Tomorrow's car today
(*Durant Star*)

Ugly is only skin-deep
(*Volkswagen Beetle*) Volkswagen of America Inc.

Watch the Fords go by
Ford Motor Co.

We are Dodge, an American Revolution
(*Dodge*) Chrysler Corp.

We are driven
(*Datsun*) Nissan Motor Corp.

We build excitement
(*Pontiac*) General Motors Corp.

We don't make compromises. We make Saabs.
Saab Cars USA Inc.

We just couldn't leave well enough alone
Toyota Motor Sales

Welcome home, America
(*Dodge*) Chrysler Corp.

We never forget who's driving
General Motors Corp.

When better cars are built, Buick will build them
(*Buick*) General Motors Corp.

Where better really matters
(*Buick*) General Motors Corp.

Where friend meets friend
(*Chevrolet*) General Motors Corp.

Where quality is built in, not added on
American Motors Corp.

Who could ask for anything more?
Toyota Motor Sales

Wide-track
(*Pontiac*) General Motors Corp.

Work horse of the world
(*Jeep*) Jeep Corp.

Automobiles

Wouldn't you really rather have a Buick?
> (*Buick*) General Motors Corp.

You get the good things first from Chrysler Corp.
> Chrysler Corp.

You'll step into a new automotive age when you drive your Tucker '48
> Tucker Corp.

Automotive Parts and Products

AUTOMOTIVE PARTS AND PRODUCTS
See also AUTOMOBILES, AUTOMOTIVE SERVICE, TIRES

All steel and a car wide
> (*bumpers*) Stewart–Warner Corp.

America's supreme ignition system
> Bosch Corp.

An eye for your gas tank
> (*Ford gas gauge*) Marquette Mfg. Co.

A real magnetic horn
> North East Electric Co.

As necessary as brakes
> (*windshield wipers*) Bosch Corp.

Assurance of quality
> National Automotive Parts Association

Because so much is riding on your tires
> Michelin

Best anti-freeze since mink
> (*Zerex*) Du Pont

Built stronger to last longer
> Powell Muffler Co.

Dependable spark plugs
> Champion Spark Plug Co.

Divides the road in half
> (*headlights*) Saf-De-Lite Sales Corp.

Eyes of the night
> (*Ilco headlight*) Indiana Lamp Corp.

Harrison cooled, the mark of radiator satisfaction
    Harrison Radiator Corp.

Ignition starts with P and D
    P and D Mfg. Co.

Made to stay brighter longer
    (*Mazda auto lamps*) General Electric Co.

Makes every road a boulevard
    (*shock absorbers*) E. V. Hartford Inc.

Means safety made certain
    (*brake linings*) Staybestos Mfg. Co.

Overcome skidding, nerve strain and muddy roads
    American Chain Co.

Performance as great as the name
    (*Edison–Splitdorf spark plugs*)

Puts the "go" in ignition!
    Tungsten Contact Mfg. Co.

Puts the steady hum in motordom
    Carter Carburetor Corp.

Simply say Delco
    (*storage batteries*) General Motors Corp.

Since 1921 ... the engine builders' source!
    Muskegon Piston Ring

Stop skidding around
    (*add-on anti-lock braking system*) ABSTrax

Temperatures made to order
    Harrison Radiator Division, General Motors Corp.

The aristocrat of auto jacks
    Duff Mfg. Co.

The heart of a tune-up
    Champion Spark Plug Co.

The perfect anti-freeze
    (*Prestone*) Du Pont

The world's most advanced radar detector
    (*Escort*) Cincinnati Microwave Inc.

Automotive Parts and Products

To feel new power, *instantly*, install new Champions now and every 10,000 miles
Champion Spark Plug Co.

World leader on highway and speedway
Monroe Auto Equipment Co.

World's largest maker of V-Belts
Gates Rubber Co.

World's largest producer of automotive wheels, hubs and drums
Kelsey–Hayes Co.

Automotive Service

AUTOMOTIVE SERVICE
See also AUTOMOBILES, AUTOMOTIVE PARTS AND PRODUCTS, PETROLEUM PRODUCTS

As you travel ask us
Standard Oil Division, American Oil Co.

At the sign of friendly service
Mobil Oil Corp.

Come to Shell for answers
Shell Oil Co.

Every ten minutes
Jiffy Lube

For more good years in your car
(*Goodyear service*) Goodyear Tire and Rubber Co.

It may be your car, but it's still our baby
(*Ford Quality Care*) Ford Motor Co.

Keep that great GM feeling
(*GM service*) General Motors Corp.

Stop by ... if you can
The Brake Shop

The sign of extra service
Esso

Trust the Midas touch
Midas Mufflers

TRUST YOUR CAR TO THE MAN WHO
WEARS THE STAR

Automotive Service

Trust your car to the man who wears the star
  Texaco Inc.

Uh-oh, better get Maaco
  (*body repair*) Maaco Enterprises Inc.

Why go anywhere else?
  (*transmission service*) Aamco Transmissions

Baby Products

BABY PRODUCTS
See also FOOD, MISCELLANEOUS; SOAP; TOYS AND GAMES

A friend of the family
  (*nurser, breast pads*) Evenflo Co.

Babies are our business ... our only business
  Gerber Products Co.

Baby's best bed builders
  Gem Crib and Cradle Co.

"Baby talk" for a good square meal
  (*Biolac*) Borden's Prescription Prods.

Because you only want the best for your baby
  Gerber Products Co.

Because you're only young once
  (*educational toys*) Fisher–Price Toys Inc.

Best for baby, best for you
  (*Johnson's baby powder*) Johnson & Johnson Baby Products Co.

Custom made for outstanding leakage protection
  (*disposable diapers*) Luvs Phases

Designed to fit better and help stop leaks every step of the way
  (*Huggies Baby Steps disposable diapers*) Kimberly–Clark Corp.

If babies were born trained, they wouldn't need Diaparene Baby Powder
  Breon Laboratories Inc.

If it doesn't come from you, shouldn't it come from Gerber?
  Gerber Products Co.

If they could just stay little 'til their Carter's wear out
  (*infant wear*) Carter's

I'm a big kid now!
     (*Huggies Pull-Ups disposable diapers*) Kimberly–Clark Co.

Quality is our main ingredient
     (*baby food*) Beech-Nut Stages

The food that builds bonnie babies
     (*Glaxo*) Jos. Nathan & Co., Ltd., London

The strained foods baby really likes
     (*Stokely*)

Wash easier, dry faster, absorb more, wear longer
     (*Curity diapers*) Textile Division, The Kendall Co.

We've learned a lot about food because we care a lot about babies
     Gerber Products Co.

Your baby's comfort begins with Luvs
     (*disposable diapers*)

BAKED GOODS AND BAKING SUPPLIES
See also FOOD, MISCELLANEOUS; KITCHEN PRODUCTS AND
UTENSILS

A sack of satisfaction
     (*Bewley's flour*)

As good as the best you ever ate
     (*Drake's cake*) Drake Bakeries Inc.

A whole grain different
     (*bread*) Nutri-Grain

Bakes right because it is made right
     (*Made-Rite flour*)

Balanced for perfect baking
     The Pillsbury Co.

Best by test
     Calumet Baking Powder Co.

Better taste makes the difference
     (*Duncan Hines Cookie Mix*) Procter & Gamble Co.

Bread is your best food, eat more of it
     Fleischmann Co.

Baked Goods and Baking Supplies

Chewy, gooey, homemade good
    (*Duncan Hines cookie mix*) Procter & Gamble Co.

Choose Crisco and put your money on good taste every time
    (*shortening*) Procter & Gamble Co.

Completes the feast
    (*National fruit cake*) National Biscuit Co.

Crisco'll do you proud every time
    (*shortening*) Procter & Gamble Co.

Every bite a delight
    Grennan Cake Co.

Favorite of housewives for 150 years
    (*Baker's cocoa*) General Foods Corp.

For fresher bread tomorrow, buy Taystee Bread today
    Purity Bakeries

Helps build strong bodies 12 ways!
    (*Wonder Bread*) Continental Baking Co. Inc.

It could be what's missing in your cooking
    Karo Corn Syrup

I'se in town, honey
    (*Aunt Jemima pancake flour*) Quaker Oats Co.

It raises the dough
    Codville Co. Ltd.

It splits in two
    (*Tak-hom-a-biscuit*) Loose-Wiles Biscuit Co.

It's what's inside that counts
    (*flour*) Roman Meal Co.

It tastes good to the last crumb
    (*pumpernickel*) Geo. F. Stuhmer Co.

It wouldn't be America without Wonder
    (*Wonder Bread*) ITT Continental Baking Co. Inc.

Made in the bakery of a thousand windows
    (*Sunshine Biscuits*) Sunshine Biscuits Inc.

Makes pancakes mother's way
    Armour Grain Co.

Mmm, Ahhh, Ohhh, Poppin' Fresh Dough
(*Poppin' Fresh Dough*) The Pillsbury Co.

Nobody doesn't like Sara Lee
Sara Lee Foods

Nothing tastes as good as Ritz, but RITZ
(*Ritz crackers*) National Biscuit Co.

One bowl brownies
(*Baker's Chocolate*) Kraft General Foods

Rich as butter, sweet as a nut
(*Franz Butter-Nut bread*) U. S. Bakery

Right in the mixing bowl, light from the oven
(*Clabber Girl baking powder*) Hulman & Co.

Something good always comes out of it
(*biscuit mix*) Bisquick

Southern cakes for southern tastes
Southern Biscuit Works

That ole southern flavor
Abilene Flour Mills

The aristocrat of package cocoa
E. & A. Opler Inc.

The freshest ideas are baking at Pillsbury
Pillsbury

The heart's in it
(*flour*) Elam Mills Inc.

The sweet snacks you can say yes to
(*Hostess Lights Twinkies*) Continental Baking Co.

They just don't wilt
(*Ritz crackers*) National Biscuit Co.

Trust Crisco. Because you're baking for your family.
Crisco oil

Use the wheat and spare the meat
Fisher Flouring Mills Co.

With every bite you know you're frying right
(*Wesson*) Beatrice Companies Inc.

Baked Goods and Baking Supplies

You and Betty Crocker can bake someone happy
General Mills Inc.

You can have your cake and drink it, too
(*ground chocolate*) Guittard Chocolate Co.

You sweet talker, Betty Crocker
General Mills Inc.

BANKS
See FINANCIAL SERVICES AND INSTITUTIONS

Bath Accessories

BATH ACCESSORIES
See also SHAVING SUPPLIES, SOAP, TOILETRIES

Coordinated fashions for bed and bath
Fieldcrest Mills Inc.

Correct in every weigh
(*Counselor bathroom scales*) The Brearley Co.

Royal family of home fashions
(*towels*) Cannon Mills Co.

The personal bathroom scale
(*Detecto*) Jacobs Bros. Co. Inc.

Twin names in quality towels
(*Martex, Fairfax*) West Point Pepperell

BATHING SUITS
See SWIMWEAR

BATTERIES
See ELECTRICAL PRODUCTS AND SERVICES

BEAUTY AIDS
See TOILETRIES

BEDS AND BEDDING
See also FURNITURE

A pillow for the body
Sealy Mattress Co.

Enjoy the rest of your life
(*Koolfoam pillows*) American Latex Products Corp.

Famous overnight
Eclipse Sleep Products Inc.

Fine combed, fine count percale sheets
(*Utica*) Stevens & Co. Inc.

First name in towels is the last word in sheets
(*Cannon towels & sheets*) Cannon Mills Co.

For controlled warmth
(*thermostatic blankets*) Fieldcrest Mills Inc.

For the best in rest
(*Southern Comfort mattress*) Charleston Mattress Mfg. Co.

Guest-room luxury for every bed in your house
(*Pepperell sheets*) West Point Pepperell

If you'd walk without a care do your sleeping on Spring-Air
(*mattresses*) The Spring Air Co.

Invest in rest
Better Bedding Alliance of America

Just everyday things for the home made beautiful by Stevens
Stevens & Co. Inc.

Like sleeping on a cloud
(*Sealy mattress*) Sealy Inc.

Makers of the world's only electronic blanket
Simmons U.S.A.

No sag in any WAY
Minneapolis Bedding Co.

Nothing warms you up like Ogallala down
(*comforters*)

One third of your life is spent in bed
Simmons U.S.A.

Beds and Bedding

Recline on Eclipse and the rest is easy
  Eclipse Sleep Products Inc.

Rest assured
  (*Marshall mattress*)

The bedspring luxurious
  Rome Co.

The mattress that feels so good
  (*Spring-Air*) The Spring Air Co.

The one bed frame people ask for by name
  Harvard Mfg. Co.

There is only one In-A-Dor bed, the Murphy
  Murphy Dor Bed Co.

Words to go to sleep by
  (*Perfect Sleeper*) Serta Inc.

Your morning is as good as your mattress
  Sealy Inc.

You sleep ON it, not IN it
  (*Serta Perfect Sleeper mattress*) Serta Inc.

Beer and Ale

BEER AND ALE
See also BEVERAGES, MISCELLANEOUS; LIQUORS; WINES

Add a Dutch of class to your next party
  (*Grolsch lager*) Grolsch Importers Inc.

Aged by Father Time himself
  Hyde Park Breweries Association

A Guinness a day is good for you
  (*Guinness Stout*) Guinness–Harp Corp.

America has gone Budweiser
  (*Budweiser*) Anheuser–Busch Inc.

America's beverage of moderation
  U. S. Brewers Association

America's oldest lager beer
  (*Schaefer*) F. & M. Schaefer Brewing Co.

ONE THIRD OF YOUR LIFE IS SPENT IN BED

Beer and Ale

America's original sparkling malt liquor
(*Champale*) Metropolis Brewery of New Jersey, Inc.

America's premium quality beer
Falstaff Brewing Corp.

Any time is STANDARD time
Standard Brewing Co.

Ask your doctor
(*All-American Premium Beer*)

As tonic as sunshine itself
Aetna Brewing Co.

A taste sells a case
Pacific Brewing & Malting Co.

Be ale-wise
Old Colony Brewing Co.

Beer is as old as history
(*Budweiser*) Anheuser–Busch Inc.

Beer that grows its own flavor
(*Edelbrew*)

Best beer by far at home, club, or bar
Jacob Hornung Brewing Co.

Born in Canada, now going great in the 48 states
(*Carling's ale*) Carling National Breweries Inc.

Brewed in the British manner
Connecticut Valley Brewing Co.

Brewed *only* in Milwaukee
(*Miller High Life*) Miller Brewing Co.

Brew that holds its head high in any company
(*Senate beer*) Heurich Brewing Co.

Brew with a head of its own
(*Krueger*) Narragansett Brewing Co.

Bring out your best
(*Bud Light*) Anheuser–Busch Inc.

Budweiser ... King of Beers
(*Budweiser*) Anheuser–Busch Inc.

Come to think of it, I'll have a Heineken
  (*Heineken*) Van Munching & Co. Inc.

Delicious, deLIGHTful, demand it
  (*Piel's*) Piel Bros. Inc.

Don't say beer, say Falstaff
  Falstaff Brewing Corp.

Everything you always wanted in a beer ... and less
  (*Lite*) Miller Brewing Co.

Experts pronounce it best
  (*Krueger*) Narragansett Brewing Co.

Famous for five generations
  Oil City Brewing Co.

Foaming with flavor
  (*Eichler*)

For all you do, this Bud's for you
  (*Budweiser*) Anheuser–Busch Inc.

From one beer lover to another
  (*Stroh's*) The Stroh Brewing Co.

From the land of sky blue waters
  (*Hamm's*) Theo. Hamm Brewing Co.

Get that golden glow with Rheingold
  Liebmann Breweries

Give me another Central Royal Beer
  Central Breweries Inc.

Good old Munich and it's good for you
  Buckeye Producing Co.

Guinness and oysters are good for you
  (*Guinness Stout*) Guinness–Harp Corp.

Have a glass of Guinness when you're tired
  (*Guinness Stout*) Guinness–Harp Corp.

Head for the mountains
  (*Busch*) Anheuser–Busch Inc.

If you've got the time, we've got the beer
  (*Miller*) Miller Brewing Co.

It's a dynamite taste
(*Colt 45 Malt Liquor*) Carling National Breweries Inc.

It's always Fehr weather
Frank Fehr Brewing Co.

It's beer as beer should taste
(*Rheingold*) Liebmann Breweries

It's better, not bitter
(*Carling's ale*) Carling National Breweries Inc.

It's better than it used to be, and it used to be the best
(*Horton Pilsener*)

It's blended, it's splendid
(*Pabst Blue Ribbon*) Pabst Corp.

It's it and that's that
(*Miller Lite*) Miller Brewing Co.

It's one of the three great beers
(*Krueger*) Narragansett Brewing Co.

It's the water
(*Olympia*) Olympia Brewing Co.

Just the kiss of the hops
Jos. Schlitz Brewing Co.

Keeps a head
General Brewing Corp.

King of bottled beer
(*Budweiser*) Anheuser–Busch Inc.

Light beer of Broadway fame
(*Trommers*) Piel Bros. Inc.

Lunch time is Guinness time
(*Guinness Stout*) Guinness–Harp Corp.

Makes every bite a banquet
(*Iron City Beer*) Pittsburgh Brewing Co.

Millions remember Doelger, a glass will tell you why
(*Doelger*)

Milwaukee's choice
(*Braumeister beer*) Huber Brewing Co.

Milwaukee's most exquisite beer
  (*Blatz*) Heileman Brewing Co. Inc.

Mountain water makes the difference
  (*Old Export beer*) Cumberland Brewing Co.

Preferred ... for mellow moments
  (*Hamm's beer*) Theo. Hamm Brewing Co.

Put a little weekend in your week
  (*Michelob*) Anheuser–Busch Inc.

Real gusto in a great light beer
  (*Schlitz*) Jos. Schlitz Brewing Co.

Retains all the esters
  Buckeye Producing Co.

Schaefer is the one beer to have when you're having more than one
  (*Schaefer*) F. & M. Schaefer Brewing Co.

Smooth sailing with Old Anchor Beer
  Brockenridge Brewing Co.

Some days are better than others. That's why there's Michelob.
  Anheuser–Busch Inc.

Some things speak for themselves
  (*Michelob*) Anheuser–Busch Inc.

Strength ... in a glass by itself
  (*Guinness Stout*) Guinness–Harp Corp.

Taste without waist
  (*Black Label beer*) Brewing Corp. of America

That Bud ... that's beer!
  (*Budweiser*) Anheuser–Busch Inc.

The all-American ale
  Cleveland–Sandusky Brewing Corp.

The beer of friendship
  Jax Brewing Co.

The beer that made Milwaukee famous
  Jos. Schlitz Brewing Co.

The beer that made the nineties gay
  Potosi Brewing Co.

Beer and Ale

The beer that made the old days good
    (*Jacob Ruppert*)

The beer that makes friends
    Lubeck Brewing Co.

The beer with the 4th ingredient
    Breidt Brewing Co.

The best has a taste all its own
    (*Bud Light*) Anheuser–Busch Inc.

The best tonic
    Pabst Corp.

The blond beer with the body
    (*Tecate*) Tecate Importers

The bottled beer with the draught beer flavor
    Globe Brewing Co.

The brew that brings back memories
    Pabst Corp.

The champagne of bottled beer
    (*Miller High Life*) Miller Brewing Co.

The head of the class
    Brewing Corp. of America

The most popular beer the world has ever known
    (*Budweiser*) Anheuser–Busch Inc.

The next one tastes as good as the first
    Central Breweries Inc.

The peer of beers
    Rubsam & Horrmann

The perfect glass
    (*Ballantine*) Narragansett Brewing Co.

The Prince of Ales
    (*Busch Pale Dry*) Anheuser–Busch Inc.

There is as much satisfaction in the brewing of a good beer as in
    the drinking of it
    (*Blatz*) Heileman Brewing Co. Inc.

The toast of the coast
    Aztec Brewing Co.

Thirst come, thirst served
    Erlanger Brewery

Unmistakably ... America's premium quality beer
    Falstaff Brewing Corp.

Weekends were made for Michelob
    (*Michelob*) Anheuser–Busch Inc.

Welcome to Miller time
    (*Miller*) Miller Brewing Co.

We'll rest our case on a case
    Liebmann Breweries

What beer drinkers drink when they're not drinking beer
    (*non-alcohol beer*) O'Doul's Malt Beverage

When you're out of Schlitz, you're out of beer
    Schlitz Brewing Co.

When you say Budweiser, you've said it all
    (*Budweiser*) Anheuser–Busch Inc.

Why ask why? Try Bud Dry.
    Anheuser–Busch Inc.

BEVERAGES, MISCELLANEOUS
See also BEER AND ALE; COFFEE; DAIRY PRODUCTS; FOOD, MISCELLANEOUS; LIQUORS; SOFT DRINKS; TEA; WINES

Adds 70% more nourishment to milk
    (*Cocomalt*) R. B. Davis Co.

A pippin of a drink
    Virginia Fruit Juice Co.

As long as they keep making kids, we'll keep making Ovaltine
    Wander Co.

Avoid teeter-totter vitality
    Horlick's Malted Milk Corp.

Builds brain, nerves and body
    (*Ovaltine*) Wander Co.

Children like it better than milk
(*Ghirardelli's hot chocolate*) Ghirardelli Chocolate Co.

Contains no caffeine or other harmful stimulants
(*Postum*) General Foods Corp.

Drink a bunch of quick energy
(*Welch grape juice*) Welch Grape Juice Co.

Drink your apple a day
S. Martinelli & Co.

Drink your prunes
California Prune & Apricot Growers Association

Even a child can tell the difference
Reichardt Cocoa & Chocolate Co.

Evian. The balance.
Evian Waters of France

Fagged? Drink a bunch of quick energy.
(*Welch grape juice*) Welch Grape Juice Co.

Feel fine, go alkaline
Saratoga Vichy Spring Co.

For that deep down body thirst
Gatorade

It beats the Dutch
(*Philips cocoa*)

It's good for you, America
(*Ocean Spray cranberry drinks*) Ocean Spray Cranberries Inc.

Keeps YOU sparkling, too
(*White Rock water*) White Rock Products Corp.

Nutrition in disguise
(*Tang Fruit Box*) General Foods Corp.

Picked with pride, packed with skill since 1869
(*Welch grape juice*) Welch Grape Juice Co.

See it made
(*Sunkist fresh fruit drinks*) Sunkist Growers Inc.

That marvelous mixer
(*Waukesha mineral water*)

The champagne of table waters
(*Perrier*) Health Waters Inc.

The earth's first soft drink
(*Perrier*) Great Waters of France Inc.

The fountain of youth
Horlick's Malted Milk Corp.

The *natural* lift
(*Instant Postum*) General Foods Corp.

The only one good enough to be called ReaLemon
(*lemonade*)

The prune juice with the fruit juice appeal
(*Del Monte*) California Packing Corp.

The real thing from Florida
(*orange juice*) Florida Citrus Commission

The world's best table water
(*White Rock water*) White Rock Products Corp.

We know what we CAN 'cause we can what we grow
(*Donald Duck orange juice*) Citrus World Inc.

Beverages,
Miscellaneous

BOATS AND BOATING EQUIPMENT
See also SEA TRAVEL AND CARGO

America's most popular boats
Starcraft Co.

Another carefree Johnson
(*Johnson*) Outboard Marine Co.

Cruiser of tomorrow
(*Richardson Ranger*) Richardson Boat Co.

Dependable in any weather
(*Baltzer boats*)

Evinruding is rowboat motoring
Evinrude Motor Co.

First in dependability
(*Johnson*) Outboard Marine Co.

Boats and
Boating
Equipment

Boats and Boating Equipment

First in marine propulsion
(*Keikhaefer Mercury*) Brunswick Corp.

It's a winner
(*PlastiCraft motorboat*)

Matchless in outdoor excellence
(*Mercury outboard motor*) Brunswick Corp.

Missing the boat? Own an Owens.
Owens Yacht Co.

Precision-built, water-tight
(*Johnson "sea-worthy" boats*)

Starts with a quarter turn
(*Elto outboard motors*)

BOOKS
See PUBLISHING

Broadcasting

BROADCASTING
See also RADIO EQUIPMENT, TELECOMMUNICATIONS, TELEVISIONS

Cable contributes to life
National Cable Television Association

Give us 20 minutes and we'll give you the world
WINS Radio

More than ever. The #1 network for kids.
Nickelodeon

Only one network will keep you in the race from start to finish
(*presidential campaign coverage*) Cable News Network

Parade of stars
National Broadcasting Co.

The heart of Country
The Nashville Network

The total sports network
ESPN Inc.

Twice a day, we mean the world to you
National Public Radio News

Weather you can always turn to
The Weather Channel

Where what you want to know comes first
(*CBS radio network*) Columbia Broadcasting System Inc.

Wide world of entertainment
American Broadcasting Co.

BUILDING SUPPLIES
See also HARDWARE, INTERIOR DECORATION, METALS
INDUSTRY, PAINT AND PAINTING SUPPLIES

Always one step ahead of the weather
(*Rusco windows*) R. C. Russell Co.

Amerock makes it authentic
Amerock Corp.

Anchors like a rock
Chicago Steel Post Co.

Asbestos cannot burn
Asbestos Shingle, Slate and Sheathing Co.

Back-bone of better plastering
Milwaukee Corrugating Co.

Beautiful birch for beautiful woodwork
Northern Hemlock Mfrs. Association

Beauty and economy burned in
Common Brick Mfrs. Association of America

Best way to close an opening
(*doors*) Cookson Co.

Building for the ages
Queenston Limestone

Build right, with Insulite
The Insulite Co.

Build the nation securely with the nation's building stone
Indiana Limestone

Built like fine furniture
    (*kitchen cabinets*) Coppes Bros. & Zook

Built to weather the years
    Rust Sash and Door Co.

Come home to quality. Come home to Andersen.
    (*Windows*) Andersen Corp.

Cork-lined houses make comfortable homes
    Armstrong Cork & Insulation Co.

Creative ideas in glass
    American Saint Gobain Corp.

Duraflake makes *only* particleboard and only the best
    Duraflake Co.

Easy to spread, hard to beat
    National Mortar & Supply Co.

Everything to build anything
    Dower Lumber Co.

First in epoxies ... in the age of ideas
    CIBA Products Co.

For the beautiful point of view
    (*windows*) Woodco Corp.

Gently as a whisper
    (*door checks*) Sargent & Co.

Home builders to the nation
    (*Readi-cut houses*) Aladdin Co.

Insulate as you decorate
    Certigrade Red Cedar Shingles

Just a "shade" better
    (*Thorpe awnings*)

Keep heat where it belongs
    Mason Fibre Co.

Keep the weather out
    Ceco Weatherstrip Co.

Leadclad fences make good neighbors
    Leadclad Wire Co.

Let the "kitchen maid" be your kitchen aid
   (*cabinets*) Wassmuth–Endicott Co.

Look to MFG for the shape of things to come
   Molded Fiber Glass Companies Inc.

Made by the mile, sold by the foot
   (*sectional steel buildings*) Liberty Prods.

Makes products better, safer, stronger, lighter
   Fiber Glass Division, PPG Industries Inc.

Make your windows avenues of health
   Vita Glass Corp.

Men who build America trust this trade mark
   (*Arro-lock shingles*)

Monarch out-strips them all
   Monarch Metal Weatherstrip Co.

More savings with Symons
   Symons Mfg. Co.

Never renew, yet ever new
   Associated Tile Mfrs.

Niedecken Showers give refreshing hours
   Hoffmann & Billings

No better built than Durabilt
   Durabilt Steel Locker Co.

Once in a lifetime
   New Jersey Zinc Co.

Only the rich can afford poor windows
   Andersen Corp.

PPG makes the glass that makes the difference
   PPG Industries Inc.

Put your house in the pink
   (*Fiberglas insulation*) Owens–Corning Fiberglas Corp.

Resists fire and rot
   California Redwood Association

Rightly put together to fight both time and weather
   Ohio Brass Co.

Slate—consider its uses
National Slate Association

Smooth as a kitten's ear
Hammond Cedar Co.

Step inside a Yankee Barn. You many never want to live in a
house again.
Yankee Barn Homes

The brightest name in aluminum
Nichols Aluminum Co.

The builder's selection for unfailing protection
American Tar & Chemical Co.

The cabinet-wood of the elect
American Walnut Mfrs. Association

The choice of the crew and the big boss, too
Ohio Brass Co.

The easiest way out
(*automatic treadle-operated door*) National Pneumatic Co.

The hardest hardwoods grow in the north
Northern Hard Maple Mfrs.

The home with the silver lining
(*insulation*) Reynolds Corp.

The mark of a good roof
Celotex Corp.

The mark of the well-built house
Flax-li-num Insulating Co.

The master wood of the ages
Mahogany Association Inc.

The material difference in building
(*Geon Vinyls*) B. F. Goodrich Co.

The most beautiful kitchens of them all
H. J. Scheirich Co.

The one-man, one-hand shingle
Bird & Son Inc.

The original masonry wall reinforcement with the truss design
(*Dur-O-Wal*) Cedar Rapids Block Co.

The pavement that outlasts the bonds
National Paving Brick Mfrs.

The paving that's saving
Jennison–Wright Co.

The pick o' the pines
Western Mfrs. Association

The post everlasting
Long–Bell Lumber Co.

The red nylon ring of reliability
Elastic Stop Nut Corp. of America

The roof of ages
(*red cedar shingles*) West Coast Lumbermen's Association

The roof without a regret
Hawthorne Roofing Tile Co.

The silent servant with a hundred hands
(*kitchen cabinets*) Hoosier Mfg. Co.

The sun never sets on Hammond tanks
Hammond Iron Works

The superior interior
(*Upson Board*) The Upson Co.

The wood eternal
Southern Cypress Mfrs. Association

Use redwood, it LASTS
California Redwood Association

Walls of character
Hachmeister Lind Chemical Co.

We fool the sun
Indianapolis Tent & Awning Co.

When you think of asbestos, think of Johns–Manville
Johns–Manville Corp.

Where your sealing is unlimited
Standard Products Co.

Building Supplies

Window beauty is Andersen
    Andersen Corp.

Withstands the test of time
    Barber Asphalt Co.

Wood that nature armed against decay
    Red Cedar Lumber Mfrs. Association

Wood that weathers every storm
    National Oak Lumbermen's Association

Your windows are the lamps which light your rooms by day
    Columbia Mills Inc.

Bus Lines

BUS LINES
See also TRAVEL

Easiest travel on earth
    Continental Trailways Bus System

Leave the driving to us
    Greyhound Lines Inc.

Only by highway you meet the real America
    Greyhound Bus Lines

Roll south into summer this winter
    Greyhound Lines Inc.

Trailways serves the nation at "scenery level"
    Continental Trailways Bus System

BUSINESS MACHINES
See COMPUTER EQUIPMENT, OFFICE EQUIPMENT AND SUPPLIES

CAMPAIGN SLOGANS
See PRESIDENTIAL CAMPAIGNS

CAMPING EQUIPMENT
See RECREATIONAL EQUIPMENT

60

A breathless sensation
>(*Pioneer mints*) Strong, Cobb & Co.

A delicious health confection
>(*Post's Bran Chocolates*) Postum Cereal Co. Inc.

After every meal
>(*Wrigley's gum*) William Wrigley Jr. Co.

A gift to remember
>(*Princesse de Conde chocolates*)

A grand slam favorite
>American Chewing Products Corp.

Aids digestion
>(*Beech-nut gum*) Life Savers Inc.

All you can eat for a nickel
>(*Baby Ruth candy bar*) Curtis Candy Co.

Always refreshing
>(*Beech-nut gum*) Life Savers Inc.

An agreeable chewing digestant
>Bi-Car Gum Co.

As sweet as love songs
>(*butterscotch*) Kerr Bros.

A woman never forgets the man who remembers
>(*Whitman's chocolates*) Pet Inc.

Be Chic—Chew Chicks
>American Chewing Products Corp.

Best nickel candy there iz-z-z
>(*Whiz*) Paul F. Beich

Candy has energy and taste
>(*Rebbor candies*)

Confections that win affections
>(*Funke*)

Cut to fit the mouth
>(*salt water taffy*) James Bros.

Candy and Gum

Dandy candy
   (*Yankee Toffee*) Brown & Haley

Double your pleasure, double your fun
   (*Doublemint Gum*) William Wrigley Jr. Co.

Eat candy for energy
   National Confectioners' Association

For beauty exercise
   (*Wrigley's gum*) William Wrigley Jr. Co.

Freedent's the one that took the stick out of gum, and put the fresh
   in your breath
   (*Freedent chewing gum*) William Wrigley Jr. Co.

Good to chew and fight's cavities too
   (*Trident gum*) Warner–Lambert Co.

Happiness in every box
   United Retail Candy Stores

Have you had your fruit today?
   (*SunKist Fruit Rolls*) Sunkist Growers Inc.

High as the Alps in quality
   Peter Cailler Kohler Swiss Chocolate Co.

It's pure chewing satisfaction
   (*Wrigley's Spearmint chewing gum*) William Wrigley Jr. Co.

Leaves you breathless
   (*gum*) L. P. Larson, Jr. Co.

Life Savers ... a part of living
   (*Life Savers*) Life Savers Inc.

Love at first bite
   (*Suchard chocolate bars*) Wilbur–Suchard Choc. Co.

Make it a habit, take "her" a bar
   Mary Lincoln Candies Inc.

Making the world sweeter
   (*Nut Tootsie Rolls*) Sweets Co. of America

Nestle's makes the very best
   (*Nestle's chocolates*) Nestle Co. Inc.

Old England's finest chocolates
        Cadbury's Ltd.

Only natural flavors last longer, naturally
        (*Topps gum*) Topps Chewing Gum Inc.

Packed with good taste
        (*Clark's Teaberry gum*) Philip Morris Inc.

Perfection in a confection
        Confections Inc.

Satisfies you
        (*Snickers candy bar*) Mars Inc.

Served by modern hostesses
        American Chewing Products Corp.

That good Pittsburgh candy
        Reyner & Bros. Inc.

The butter in Bamby makes it better
        Cushman's Sons Inc.

The candy mint with the hole
        (*Life Savers*) Mint Products Co.

The chocolates with the wonderful centres
        (*Liggett's chocolates*)

The confection of the fairies
        Liberty Orchards Co.

The gum with the fascinating artificial flavor
        (*Wrigley's gum*) William Wrigley Jr. Co.

The handy candy
        (*mints*) Beechnut Packing Co.

The milk chocolate melts in your mouth. Not in your hands.
        (*M & M Candies*) Mars Candy Company

The more you eat, the more you want
        (*Crackerjacks*) Rueckheim Bros. & Eckstein

The nickel lunch
        Planter's Nut & Chocolate Co.

The one and only one cocktail gum
        (*Warren's chewing gum*)

63

Candy and Gum

The perfect candy for smart entertaining
  (*Brach*) B.J. Brach & Sons

The perfect little "Thank Me"
  Andes Candies

The South's most famous confection
  (*Creole pralines*) Hotel Grunewald

Unexpectedly moist. Unexpectedly chewy. Unexpectedly delicious.
  (*Quaker chewy granola bars*) Quaker Oats Co.

Untouched by human hands
  (*Sweet Message chocolates*)

When you crave good candy
  Milky Way Co.

Wholesome sweets for children
  (*Laura Secord candy*) Laura Secord Candy Shops Ltd.

You bet your Life Savers
  (*Life Savers*) Life Savers Inc.

CARGO
See AIR TRAVEL AND CARGO, RAIL TRAVEL AND CARGO, SEA TRAVEL AND CARGO

CARPETS
See FLOOR COVERINGS

CARS
See AUTOMOBILES

CASSETTES
See RECORDINGS

CERAMICS
See GLASS AND CERAMICS

Cereals

CEREALS
See also FOOD, MISCELLANEOUS

A full meal in two biscuits
  Shredded Wheat Co.

A hot weather hot cereal
  (*Zoom*) Fisher Flouring Mills Co.

America's best-liked cereal assortment
    The Kellogg Co.

America's new breakfast banquet of shredded whole wheat
    (*Cubs cereal*) National Biscuit Co.

America's popular year 'round breakfast
    Quaker Oats Co.

An ounce of prevention for everybody, everyday
    (*Post's Bran Flakes*) General Foods Corp.

Best because it's pan-dried
    (*Robin Hood*) Rapid Oats

Breakfast of champions
    (*Wheaties*) General Mills Inc.

Delicious and nutritious
    (*Frosted mini-wheats*) Kellogg Co.

Food shot from guns
    (*Puffed Wheat, Puffed Rice*) Quaker Oats Co.

For bracing up digestion, nerves, and appetite
    Quaker Oats Co.

Fresh as the morning
    (*Campbell's corn flakes*)

Fresh from the mill to you
    (*Livingstone's oats*)

Fresh to you each morning
    The Kellogg Co.

Had your Wheaties today?
    General Mills Inc.

Health without hazard
    (*Kellogg's All-Bran*) The Kellogg Co.

Here's a thrill for breakfast
    (*Grape Nuts Flakes*) General Foods Corp.

Join the "regulars" with Kellogg's All-Bran
    The Kellogg Co.

Keep going with Pep
    (*Pep Bran Flakes*) The Kellogg Co.

Kid-tested, mother-approved
    (*Kix*) General Mills

Life is swell when you keep well
    (*Post's Bran Flakes*) General Foods Corp.

Makes kids husky
    (*Three Minute cereals*) The National Oats Co.

New to look at, new to taste
    (*Corn Kix*) General Mills Inc.

Quaker Oats. It's the right thing to do.
    Quaker Oats Co.

Stay crisp in milk or cream
    (*Post Toasties*) General Foods Corp.

Tastes so good and so good for you
    (*Cream of Rice*) Grocery Store Products Co.

The best to you each morning
    The Kellogg Co.

The great American family cereal
    (*Cream of Wheat*) Nabisco Inc.

The plus food for minus meals
    (*Kellogg's All-Bran*) The Kellogg Co.

They're Grrrr-eat!
    (*Kellogg's Sugar Frosted Flakes*) The Kellogg Co.

Top of the morning
    (*Cream of Wheat*) Nabisco Inc.

Two Scoops!
    (*Raisin Bran*) Kellogg Co.

What the big boys eat!
    (*Wheaties*) General Mills Inc.

Yours for a good morning
    (*Carnation Albers cereals*) Albers Bros. Milling Co

CHARITABLE ORGANIZATIONS
See PUBLIC SERVICE

SPECIALISTS IN MAKING WATER BEHAVE

CHEMICAL INDUSTRY
See also CLEANING AND LAUNDRY PRODUCTS, PEST
CONTROL

Anticipating tomorrow's needs today ...
Enjay Chemical Co. Division, Humble Oil and Refining Co.

Basic producers from mine to finished product
Tennessee Corp.

Basic to America's progress
Allied Chemical Corp.

Best-selling aerosols are powered with Freon propellents
(*Freon*) Du Pont

Better things for better living through chemistry
Du Pont

Houdry means progress ... through catalysis
Houdry Process and Chemical Co.

In home, health, farm and industry, science in action for you
American Cyanamid Co.

Let us help put Armour idea chemicals to work for you
Armour and Co.

Look for more from Morton
Morton Chemical Co.

Putting the "push" in America's finest aerosols
(*Genetron*) Allied Chemical Corp.

Specialists in making water behave
Anderson Chemical Co. Inc.

The bright new silicates for industry
Allegheny Industrial and Chemical Co.

The chemistry's right at Amoco
Amoco Chemical Co.

To gladden hearts and lighten labor
Dow Chemical Co.

Where flame technology creates new products
Cabot Corp.

Where what's happening gets its start
    Amoco Chemicals Corp.

CHINA AND CRYSTAL
See also GLASS AND CERAMICS, KITCHEN PRODUCTS AND
UTENSILS

A world apart. Let it express your world.
    Lenox China

Born of the breath of man, Waterford is life's child
    (*Waterford crystal*)

China by Iroquois for the hosts of America
    Iroquois China Co.

Don't wait to inherit Spode
    Spode Inc.

Fine dinnerware
    (*Vernonware*) Vernon Division, Metlox Mfg. Co.

Fine French crystal you can afford to enjoy
    Cristal d'Arques

Finest in china since 1735
    (*Richard Ginori*) Pasmantier Inc.

Know the best by this mark
    Jackson China Co.

Steadfast in a world of wavering demands
    Waterford Crystal

The beginning of taste
    Syracuse China Corp.

The crystal for America
    Fostoria

The living crystal
    Orreforo

The morning, noon and night crystal
    Ittala Finland

The world's most beautiful china
    Meakin & Ridgway

When the name says Gorham, the gift says everything
Gorham

CIGARETTES
See TOBACCO PRODUCTS

CIGARS
See TOBACCO PRODUCTS

CLEANING AND LAUNDRY PRODUCTS
See also CHEMICAL INDUSTRY, SOAP

America's favorite bleach and household disinfectant
(Clorox bleach) Clorox Co.

A shine in every drop
Black Silk Stove Polish Works

Avoid "tattletale gray"
(Fels Naphtha soap) Purex Corp.

A wipe and it's bright
(porcelain cleaner) B. T. Babbitt Inc.

Breaks the static barrier
(Fab) Colgate–Palmolive Co.

Cascade eliminates drops that spot
(Cascade) Procter & Gamble Co.

Chases dirt
(Old Dutch cleanser) Cudahy Packing Co.

Cleans as it polishes
(O-Cedar polish) Channel Chemical Co.

Cleans easier, works faster, won't scratch
(Sunbrite cleanser) Swift & Co.

Cleans in a jiff
(washing powder) Dif Corp.

Cleans like a white tornado
(Ajax) Colgate–Palmolive Co.

Cleans the impossible washload
(Dynamo detergent) Colgate–Palmolive Co.

Clean up with S. O. S. It's easy.
　　(*S. O. S. Magic scouring pads*) Miles Laboratories Inc.

Complete household soap
　　(*Oxydol*) Procter & Gamble Co.

Cuts dishpan time in half
　　(*Washington powder*) Dif Corp.

Doesn't scratch
　　(*Old Dutch cleanser*) Cudahy Packing Co.

Don't be bullied by your bowl, Bully your bowl instead
　　(*Bully toilet bowl cleaner*)

Duz does everything
　　(*Duz washing powder*) Procter & Gamble Co.

Eats everything in the pipe
　　(*drain pipe cleaner*) John Sunshine Chemical Co.

Faultless starch lightens laundry labor
　　Faultless Starch Co.

Get brighter windows with Windex
　　(*Windex window cleaner*) The Drackett Co.

Gets out what America gets into
　　(*Spray 'n' Wash*) Dow Brands

Give your dishwasher the best
　　(*Cascade*) Procter & Gamble Co.

Gleaming armor for your floors
　　(*Old English No Rubbing Wax*) A. S. Boyle Co.

Good soap is good business
　　Procter & Gamble Co.

Good washing wins good will
　　Cowles Detergent Co.

Grease just vanishes from pots, pans, dishes
　　(*Rinso*) Lever Bros. Co.

Hasn't scratched yet
　　(*Bon Ami cleanser*) Bon Ami Co.

Home-care know-how ... at your doorstep!
　　Amway Corp.

Hurts only dirt
(*Kitchen Klenzer*) Fitzpatrick Bros.

If it's lovely to wear it's worth Ivory Flakes care
(*Ivory Flakes*) Procter & Gamble Co.

If it's safe in water, it's safe in Lux
(*Lux soap*) Lever Bros. Co.

Isn't it worth it?
(*Lysol disinfectant spray*) Lehn and Fink Consumer Products

It makes a dust magnet of your dust mop or cloth
(*Endust*) The Drackett Co.

It's always a shade better
(*Bulldog Venetian blind cleaner*)

It's sudsy
Gold Dust Corp.

It's the tops for kitchen tops
(*asbestos pads*) Weiss & Klau Co.

Keep your floors beautiful always
Raynorshyne Products

Kindness to hands, speed in the dishpan
(*Ivory Snow*) Procter & Gamble Co.

Makes cotton look and feel like linen
(*Linit laundry starch*) CPC International Inc.

Makes hard water soft
(*Gold Dust soap powder*) N. H. Fairbank Co.

Makes old things new, keeps new things bright
(*polish*) Britelite Co.

Makes water wetter
(*PN-700 washing powder*) Service Industries

Mar-VEL-ous for dishes, stockings, lingerie, woolens
(*Vel soap*) Colgate–Palmolive Co.

Of paramount importance to the housewife
Arcraft Broom Co.

Old floors look new in six to nine minutes
(*Aerowax*) Midway Chemical Co.

Out of the blue comes the whitest wash
　　　(*Reckitt's blue*) Reckitt & Colman Ltd.

Pearline keeps white things white and bright women bright
　　　Pearline

Rougher on dirt, easiest on clothes
　　　(*Oxydol soap*) Procter & Gamble Co.

Scours the pan, not your hands
　　　(*GLO soapy scouring pads*) J. H. Rhodes Co.

Scratches disappear as you polish
　　　(*Old English scratch removing polish*) Boyle–Midway

Sheeting action
　　　(*Cascade*) Procter & Gamble Co.

Sombre silver dulls more than the dinner
　　　(*Wright's silver cream cleaner*) Caswell–Massey Co.

Spray that cleans windows without water
　　　(*Windex window cleaner*) The Drackett Co.

Spreads like good news
　　　(*Satinwax*) Economics Laboratory Inc.

Static is stuck on you
　　　(*Static Guard*) Alberto–Culver Co.

Stronger than dirt
　　　(*Ajax detergent*) Colgate–Palmolive Co.

Suds in a jiffy
　　　(*Jif soap flakes*)

Sunbrite, the cleanser with a spotless reputation
　　　Swift & Co.

Sure is strong
　　　(*lye*) Wm. Schield Mfg. Co.

Takes TOIL out of toilet cleaning
　　　Globe Laboratories

The finest dye that money can buy
　　　(*dye*) Rit Products Corp.

The meanest chore is a chore no more
　　　(*Sani-flush*) Boyle–Midway

Cleaning and Laundry Products

The shine shines through
　　　(*Ajax all-purpose cleaner*) Colgate–Palmolive Co.

The washday miracle
　　　(*Tide*) Procter & Gamble Co.

The white line is the Clorox line
　　　(*Clorox bleach and disinfectant*) Clorox Co.

The woman who uses it, knows
　　　(*E-Z polish*) Martin & Martin

This is a good place for a Stickup
　　　(*Stickup room deodorant*)

Thoughtfully designed with a woman in mind
　　　(*Bowlene*) The Climalene Co.

Tide's in, dirt's out
　　　(*Tide*) Procter & Gamble Co.

We cut it when they can't
　　　(*Dawn dishwashing liquid*)

Wisk, strong enough to get ring around the collar and the whole
　　wash clean
　　　Lever Brothers Co.

You cook, we'll clean
　　　Palmolive

You'll find the woman's touch in every Purex product
　　　Purex Corp.

Cleaning Services

CLEANING SERVICES

And away go troubles down the drain
　　　Roto-Rooter Corp.

Send it to the dry cleaner
　　　Amercian Laundry Machine Co.

CLOCKS
See WATCHES AND CLOCKS

74

CLOTHING, MISCELLANEOUS
See also FOOTWEAR, HOSIERY, SWIMWEAR, UNDERWEAR,
WARDROBE ACCESSORIES

A hat for every face
  Sam Bonnart Inc.

Always virgin wool
  Pendleton Woolen Mills

America's only known-priced clothes
  (*Styleplus*) Henry Sonneborn & Co.

A miracle in the rain
  (*Koroseal raincoat*) Goodrich General Products Co.

A "must" for every wardrobe
  (*Sportleigh briefer coat*)

Apparel without parallel
  (*Ellesse clothing*) Ellesse U.S.A. Inc.

A 'round the year coat
  (*Alligator rainwear*)

As western as the setting sun
  (*Frontex shirts*)

Because it might rain
  (*Harbor Master*) Jonathan Logan

Because you don't stop being a junior when you become a woman
  College Town

Belcraft Shirts, your bosom friend
  Belcraft Shirt Co.

Berkley Ties the world
  Berkley Knitting Co.

Be Scotch, get your money's worth
  Doniger & Co.

Big thinking in little sizes
  (*kids' shoes and clothing*) Reebok

Born in America. Worn round the world.
  John B. Stetson Co.

Brilliant as the sun
(*Lustray shirts*) Lustberg–Nast Co.

Business wear that's not all business
(*women's clothing*) Barrie Pace Ltd. Shops

By this sign you shall know them
Currick, Leiken & Bandler

Clothes in the New York manner
Weber & Heilbroner

Clothes that enhance your public appearance
House of Worsted-Tex

Cut out for a long career
(*Washwear*) Elder Mfg. Co.

Danskins are not just for dancing
Danskin Inc.

Designed to be lived in
(*sweaters*) Irwill Knitwear Corp.

Designs for the world's best dressed
Mr. John

Does something for you
(*Style-Mart suit*) Merit Clothing Co.

Don't forget that Koveralls Keep Kids Klean
Levi Strauss & Co.

Don't get wet, get Palmer
Palmer Asbestos & Rubber Corp.

Dry back or money back
(*outdoor clothing*) Lewis M. Weed Co.

Expensive shirts ought to look it
(*Excello*) Kayser–Roth Corp.

Fashion in action
(*ranch togs*) Wrangler's

Feel the fabric and you'll feel the difference
(*Botany shirts*)

Follow the ARROW and you follow the style
(*shirts*) Cluett, Peabody & Co. Inc.

A HAT FOR EVERY FACE

Clothing, Miscellaneous

For goodness sake wear Buckeye Shirts
    Buckeye Shirt Co.

For men who dress for women
    Curlee

For that good-looking feeling
    Doris Miller Clothes

For the man on the move
    McGregor–Doniger Inc.

For the nicest youngsters you know
    Mason Clothes

For the rest of the night
    (*pajamas*) Steiner & Son

For those confident few who have acquired a taste for simplicity
    (*jeans*) Lee

For those friskie years
    (*Spree Togs for children*) Tri-Parel Corp.

For younger young men
    Leopold, Solomon & Eisendrath

Fur goodness sake try Kruskal
    (*furs*) Kruskal and Kruskal

Guaranteed, the hardest working workwear
    H. D. Lee Co. Inc.

Help build personality
    (*Stadium clothes*) Woodhull, Goodale & Bull Inc.

If you think clothes don't make a difference, try walking down the street without any
    Wolf Tailoring

It's in the fit
    Schwartz Bros. Dress Co.

It's not Jockey brand if it doesn't have the Jockey boy
    Jockey Menswear Division, Coopers Inc.

Jeans for the way you live and love
    Sergio Valente

Just wear a smile and a Jantzen
        Jantzen Inc.

Just what works
        GAP Kids

Lead the Ship 'n Shore life
        (*blouses*) Ship 'n Shore Inc.

Learn about little women from us
        Schwartz Bros. Dress Co.

Let them grow up in Kaynee
        The Kaynee Co.

Let us tan your hide
        (*furs*) Crisby Frisian Fur Co.

Made in America for little Americans
        R. Solomon Knitting Mills

Make yourself comfortable
        (*apparel, footwear, accessories*) The Cherokee Group

Mix 'em and match 'em
        Buster Boy Suit Co.

Neatness lasts from breakfast to bedtime
        Essley Shirt Co.

"Never wear a white shirt before sundown," says Hathaway
        C. F. Hathaway Co.

Official tailors to the West
        H. D. Lee Co. Inc.

Oshkosh, b'gosh
        (*overalls*) Oshkosh Overall Co.

Quality never goes out of style
        (*blue jeans*) Levi Strauss & Co.

Soft as kitten's ears
        (*Melbroke ties*) Spiegel Neckwear Co. Inc.

So-o soft, so-o smooth, so-o comfortable
        Eclipse Sleep Products Inc.

Sportswear for sportsmen
        Jantzen Inc.

Takes the guessing out of dressing
Wembley Ties Inc.

The aristocrat of polyester neckwear
Wembley Ties Inc.

The brand that fits
Lee

The finest habit a man can have
Merchant Tailors Society

The kind of clothes gentlemen wear
Kahn Tailoring Co.

The kind real boys wear
(*Perfection clothes*) H. A. Seinsheimer Co.

The mark of modern pajamas
(*Dot snappers*) United–Carr Inc.

The mystique of France. The energy of America.
pierre cardin

The name in New York for men's better clothing
Moe Ginsburg

The name to remember in rainwear
(*Weatherbee*) Triangle Raincoat Co.

The national summer suit for men
(*Keep-Kool*) Snellenburg Cloth Co.

The pattern people
Simplicity Patterns Co. Inc.

The rage of the college age
(*Sidley cords*)

There are no dudes in our duds
(*Man-O-West slacks and pants*) Freeman Mfg. Co.

There's a Lee for every job
(*Lee work clothes*) H. D. Lee Co. Inc.

There's something about them you'll like
(*Fleurette frocks*) Einhorn Bros.

The secret of California casualness
(*men's sportswear*) H. & L. Black

The skier's tailor since 1929
>   White Stag Mfg. Co.

The signature of American style
>   Lord & Taylor

The world's smartest collar
>   Phillips–Jones Corp.

They hold their shape
>   (*Travelo knit jackets and vests*) Peckham–Foreman

They must make good or we will
>   Oshkosh Overall Co.

Tropical suit that "breathes" fresh air
>   (*Northcool suits*) Sagner Inc.

We are what others pretend to be
>   Izod Lacoste

Wears like a pig's nose
>   (*men's overalls*) W. M. Finck & Co.

We don't insure status ... only quality
>   (*Hang Ten clothing*) Ram Knitting Mills

When in Broderick suits your class is dressed, each girl's inspired to
play her best
>   Tom Broderick Co.

Wherever you go you look better in Arrow
>   Cluett, Peabody & Co. Inc.

You can't knock the crease out
>   (*Digby slacks*) Digby Inc.

Younger by design
>   (*Van Heusen*) Phillips–Van Heusen Corp.

COFFEE
See also BEVERAGES, MISCELLANEOUS; TEA

Always in good taste
>   (*Royal Blend*) Granger & Co.

Always the same, always good
>   (*Old Reliable*) Dayton Spice Mills Co.

Coffee

America's No. 1 mountain grown coffee
(*Folger's*) Folger and Co.

A mountain of flavor in every spoonful
(*Folger's*) Folger and Co.

A Swedish obsession
Gevalia Kaffe

Celebrate the moments of your life
(*General Foods International Coffees*) General Foods Corp.

Chock Full O' Nuts is that heavenly coffee
(*Chock Full O' Nuts*) Chock Full O' Nuts Corp.

Coffee rich enough to be served in America's finest restaurants
(*Folger's instant*) Procter & Gamble Co.

Coffee, the American drink
Joint Coffee Trade Publicity Committee

Colombian Coffee. The richest coffee in the world.
National Federation of Coffee Growers of Colombia

Drink it and sleep
(*Sanka*) General Foods Corp.

Enjoy your coffee and enjoy yourself
(*Sanka instant*) General Foods Corp.

Fall in love with coffee all over again
(*High Point decaffeinated*) Procter & Gamble Co.

Fill it to the rim with Brim
(*Brim decaffeinated*) General Foods Corp.

For people who love coffee, but not caffeine
(*Sanka decaffeinated*) General Foods Corp.

Get more out of life with coffee
Pan-American Coffee Bureau

Good to the last drop
(*Maxwell House*) General Foods Corp.

It more than satisfies, it agrees
Coffee Products of America

Life begins at breakfast with McLaughlin's Coffee
(*McLaughlin's*)

Look for the date on the tin
(*Chase & Sanborn*) Standard Brands Inc.

Morning's first thought
(*Royal Blend*) Granger & Co.

One good cup deserves another
(*Beechnut*)

Roaster-fresh coffee made in the cup
(*Nescafe*) Nestle Co. Inc.

So good you want a second cup
(*Savarin*) S. A. Schonbrunn & Co. Inc.

The choice for taste
(*Taster's Choice*) Nestle Foods Corp.

The coffee-er coffee
(*Savarin*) S. A. Schonbrunn & Co. Inc.

The coffee that lets you sleep
Kaffee Hag Corp.

The coffee without a regret
(*Barrington Hall*) Baker Importing Co.

The cup of southern hospitality
Duncan Coffee Co.

The first taste tells you it's good to the last drop
(*Maxwell House*) Cheek-Neal Coffee Co.

The guest coffee
(*Yuban*) General Foods Corp.

The only instant coffee that's caffeine-free
(*Instant Sanka*) General Foods Corp.

We roast it, others praise it
(*Big Horn*)

Wings of the morning
(*Schilling coffee*) McCormick and Co. Inc.

Without grounds for complaint
Alexander Balart Co.

You never had coffee like this before
(*Borden's instant*) Borden Inc.

Computer Equipment and Software

COMPUTER EQUIPMENT AND SOFTWARE

Addressing society's major unmet needs
>   Control Data Corp.

A little IBM can mean a lot of freedom
>   IBM General Systems Division

Announcing the state of the smart
>   (*personal computers*) IBM

A small computer can make a big difference
>   IBM General Systems Division

A tool for modern times
>   (*personal computers*) IBM

Automation is economical
>   Fusion Inc.

Because ˆ is the way you want to go
>   (*laptop computers*) NEC

Brains & Beauty
>   (*Olivetti M20 personal computer*) Olivetti Corp.

Building on the theory of productivity
>   Mokawk Data Sciences

Building small business the power and strength of the triangle
>   (*BusinessVision II software*) BusinessVision Management Systems Inc.

Business to business. Person to person.
>   ComputerLand Corp.

Command the powers of Adam
>   (*Adam Computers*) Coleco

COMPAQ PLUS, the first high-performance portable personal
computer
Compaq Computer Corporation

Computers for people
Atari

Computers for the advancement of society
Vector Graphic Inc.

Data General. A Generation ahead.
Data General Corp.

Designers of innovative systems for the information worker
(*terminals*) Lee Data Corp.

Discover the Dysan difference
(*disks*) Dysan Corp.

Everybody makes terminals. Only we make Lear Sieglers.
(*terminals*) Lear Siegler Inc.

Everything a computer's supposed to be. Except expensive.
Alpha Micro

Everywhere you look
Integraph Co.

Family computer history is about to be written
Coleco

Glare/Guard: A difference you can see
(*anti-glare panels*) Optical Coating Laboratory Inc.

High performance matrix printers
(*printers*) Datasouth Computer Corporation

ICOT ... the data communications company
(*terminals*) ICOT Corp.

Information. Not automation.
Sperry Corp.

It's the next thing
(*PowerBook laptop computer*) Apple Computer

Leader in computer graphics
(*Cal Comp*) California Computer Products Inc.

Machines that make data move
> Teletype Corp.

Make the Wyse decision
> Wyse Technology

Making good connections
> (*PC connectors*) Western Telematic Inc.

Making the world more productive
> Wang

Maxell. It's worth it.
> (*disks*) Maxell Corp.

MicroComputers for DataCommunications
> Micom Systems Inc.

NEC and me
> (*printers*) NEC Information Systems Inc.

Never forgets
> (*disks*) Elephant Memory Systems

Nothing is better than a Verbatim response
> (*disks*) Verbatim Corp.

Now's the perfect time
> (*software*) WordPerfect Corp.

Now that the world relies on computers it needs a computer it can
rely on
> (*software*) Stratus

One language. One solution.
> (*FOCUS software*) Information Builders Inc.

Our business is the intelligent use of computers
> Electronic Data Systems

Our technology has the computer world talking. More than ever.
> (*modems*) Hayes

Our windows reflect the way you work
> (*Desq software*) Quarterdeck Office Systems

Powerful software solutions
> Software AG of North America Inc.

SAS saves time
(*software*) SAS Institute Inc.

Setting you free
(*Hewlett–Packard personal computers*) Hewlett–Packard Co.

Simply powerful software
Claris Corp.

Software superior by design
Computer Associates International Inc.

Specialists in digital technology
(*Cal Comp*) California Computer Products Inc.

Standard of the plotting industry
(*Cal Comp*) California Computer Products Inc.

Strategic solutions to storing, sharing and moving data
(*data storage*) Masstor Systems Corp.

Take advantage of change
Electronic Data Systems Corp.

Tandem. NonStop transaction processing.
Tandem Computers Inc.

The accounting education software publisher
(*CPA exam review*) MicroMash

The automated answer to the paper explosion
Remington Office Systems Division, Sperry Rand Corp

The best monitors you never heard of
Sampo America

The computer inside
(*chips*) Intel

The computer superstore
Comp USA

The data compression experts
(*PKLite file compressing software*) PKWARE Inc.

The dawn of a new era in personal computing
(*Tandy personal computers*) Radio Shack

The fastest way to find the right word
(*Random House Webster's Electronic Dictionary and Thesaurus*)
Reference Software International

The first computer
(*Univac*) Sperry Rand Corp.

The friendly computer
Commodore

The future ... without the shock
(*Exxon office systems*) Exxon Corp.

The hardest working software in the world
(*Lotus software*) Lotus Development Corp.

The image of the future
(*computer-output microfilm*) AnaComp Inc.

The industrial bar code experts
(*terminals*) Intermec

The information service you won't outgrow
CompuServe

The ingenuity of people, the power of computers
Honeywell

The lifeblood of business
(*software*) Dow Jones Information Services

The most complete software company in the world
University Computing Co.

The natural language query system
(*Intellect software*) Artificial Intelligence Corp.

The network you can control
(*networks*) M/A-COM Linkabit Inc.

The office automation computer people
(*Wang VS computers*) Wang Laboratories Inc.

The other computer company
Honeywell

The power is within your reach
Timex/Sinclair

The power of choice
   (*computers*) AST Research Inc.

The power to be your best
   Apple Computer

The Smart Desk from IBM
   (*personal computers*) IBM

The standard on the streets
   (*mapping software*) MapInfo

The user friendly company
   (*software*) Sterling Software Marketing

The world's #1 selling financial software
   (*Quicken*) Intuit

Together, we can find the answers
   Honeywell

Tomorrow's software. Here today.
   Hogan Systems

Univac is saving a lot of people a lot of time
   Sperry Rand Corp.

We connect people and the computers they use
   Dayna Communications

We don't just design it to work. We design it to work wonders.
   (*printers*) Okidata

We don't make computers. We make them better.
   (*Quadram System*) Texas Instruments Inc.

We make networks work
   (*networks*) Interlan Inc.

We make the addition easy
   (*computer systems*) PHAZE Information Machines Corp.

We make the right decisions
   (*printers*) Decision Data Computer Corporation

We put computing in the palm of your hand
   MSI Data Corp.

We put computing within everyone's reach
   Texas Instruments Inc.

We sparked the revolution
(*networks*) Datapoint Corp.

We take care of our own
Data General

When performance must be measured by results
Hewlett–Packard

Where imagination leads
(*Lasergrafix 1200 printer*) Quality Micro Systems Inc.

Where miracles never cease
Casio

Where the data movement started and startling moves are made
Teletype Corp.

Where the solutions come first
Perkin–Elmer

Working to improve your image
(*Bubble jet printers*) Canon

Why every kid should have an Apple after school
Apple Computer

You're not just playing, you're learning
Texas Instruments Inc.

You see one. You want one.
(*printers, copiers*) Canon

CONDIMENTS AND SPICES
See also FOOD, MISCELLANEOUS

America's favorite for thick, rich catsup
(*Heinz catsup*) H. J. Heinz Co.

Bring out the Hellmann's and bring out the best
(*Hellmann's mayonnaise*) Best Foods

Come rain or fog there's no shaker-clog
International Salt Co.

First aid for clever cooks
(*Derby steak sauce*) Derby Foods Inc.

Flavor so delicious only your figure knows they're low calorie
(*Wish Bone salad dressing*) Thos. J. Lipton Inc.

For the well-dressed salad
Seidner's Mayonnaise

Free running
(*Regal salt*)

Good things to eat come from 1 Mustard St.
The R. T. French Co.

Health in every jar
(*Blue Ribbon mayonnaise*) Richard Hellman Inc.

It's in the bag
(*rock salt*) International Salt Co.

It stays on the salad
(*French dressing*) A. E. Wright Co.

Made in the home-made way
(*mayonnaise*) Richard Hellman Inc.

Make good foods taste better
(*tomato catsup*) H. J. Heinz Co.

Makes every meal an event
(*Premier salad dressing*) F. H. Leggett

Mellowed in wood to full strength
(*vinegar*) H. J. Heinz Co.

New Orleans' most famous sauce
(*Remoulade*)

Salt of the Covenant
(*kosher salt*) Ohio Salt Co.

Silent partners in famous foods
(*coloring, flavoring*) Stange Co.

The added touch that means so much
(*Lee & Perrin's sauce*)

The catsup with the big tomato taste
(*catsup*) Hunt–Wesson Foods Inc.

The dash that makes the dish
(*A-1 sauce*) Heublein Inc.

Condiments and Spices

The house of flavor
McCormick and Co. Inc.

The one and only sunshine
(*French's mustard*)

The pick of pickles
(*pickles*) Crosse & Blackwell

There *are* imitations—be sure the brand is *Tabasco*
(*Tabasco sauce*) McIlhenny Co.

The salt of the earth
Morton Salt Co.

The way to a man's heart
(*Log Cabin syrup*) General Foods Corp.

When it rains, it pours
Morton Salt Co.

When it's wet it's dry
Worcester Salt Co.

Word to the wives is sufficient
Carey Salt Co.

You know it's fresh, it's dated
Dated Mayonnaise Inc.

Ze dash zat makes za dish
(*A-1 sauce*) Heublein Inc.

COOKWARE
See BAKED GOODS AND BAKING SUPPLIES, KITCHEN PRODUCTS
AND UTENSILS

COPYING EQUIPMENT
See also OFFICE EQUIPMENT AND SUPPLIES

Copies for communication throughout the world
      American Photocopy Equipment Co.

Electro-Copyst, a photo-copying machine for every office
      (*Electro-Copyst*)

For imagination in communication, look to 3M business
  product centers
      Minnesota Mining and Manufacturing Co.

New advances in office copying keep coming from Kodak
      Eastman Kodak Co.

Now everybody can have Xerocopies
      Xerox Corp.

Quickest way to duplicate
      (*Ditto duplicator*) Duplicator Manufacturing Co.

You can't buy a multigraph unless you need it
      Multigraph Co.

CORPORATIONS, MISCELLANEOUS

American Express. The power to move you.
      (*financial services, travelers checks*)

And you thought you knew us
      Amway Corp.

An eye to the future, an ear to the ground
      General Motors Corp.

A step ahead of tomorrow
      Zurn Industries Inc.

Building business is our business
      Tenneco Inc.

Diversified—worldwide
Singer Co.

Does a lot for you
Scovill Manufacturing Co.

Giving shape to imagination
Lockheed

... Helping people communicate
Addressograph–Multigraph Corp.

Imagine what we can do together
Corning

In metals, plastics and paper Budd works to make
tomorrow ... today
Budd Co.

Innovation working for you
3M Corp.

Lincoln Logs ... The country living experts
(*Log home communities*) Lincoln Logs Ltd.

North American Rockwell and the future are made for you
North American Rockwell Corp.

Progress for industry worldwide
Combustion Engineering Inc.

Progress is our most important product
General Electric Co.

Putting ideas to work ... in machinery, chemicals, defense, fibers
and films
FMC Corp.

Reliability in rubber, asbestos, sintered metal, specialized plastics
Raybestos–Manhattan Inc.

Technology that delivers
United Parcel Service

The company of champions
General Mills

The discovery company
Union Carbide Corp.

The Foodpower people
    Central Soya Co. Inc.

The great engineers
    Borg–Warner Corp.

The *name* is Crane
    Crane Co.

The people movers
    Budd Co.

The power is on
    GTE Corp.

We're not playing games
    (*IndyCar racing*) Championship Auto Racing Teams Inc.

We're synergistic
    Sperry Rand Corp.

We're the neighborhood professionals
    Century 21 Real Estate Corp.

We run the tightest ship in the shipping business
    United Parcel Service

We understand how important it is to listen
    Sperry Corp.

What's new for tomorrow is at Singer today
    Singer Co.

Where ideas unlock the future
    Bendix Corp.

You can be sure if it's Westinghouse
    Westinghouse Electric Corp

COSMETICS
See also HAIR CARE,   TOILETRIES

A beautiful skin is adored
    Nu-Art Laboratories

Adds life to years rather than years to life
    (*face cream*) B. S. Boss

A fountain of youth for your skin
    (*Balm-o-Lem*) Jean Jordeau Inc.

America's number one nail protection
    (*Hard-As-Nails nail polish*) Sally Hansen

A personalized service that comes to your home
    (*Avon cosmetics*) Avon Products Inc.

Beautiful skin begins with Noxema
    (*Noxema Skin Cream*) Noxell Corp.

Beauty in every box
    (*face powder*) Celebrated Products Sales

Beauty *is* only skin deep; Luminiere controls the skin
    En-Ve Inc.

Because I'm worth it
    (*L'Oreal*) Cosmair Inc.

Because lips that feel lifeless aren't worth a look
    (*Blistex lip balm*) Blistex Inc.

Be kind to your skin
    Beaver–Remmers–Graham Co.

Don't be a pale face
    The Coppertone Corp.

Doubles your face value
    (*Dreskin cosmetics*) Campana Corp.

Enchanting ladies choose Dorothy Gray
    Lehn and Fink Consumer Products

Ends that painted look
    (*Tangee lipstick*) Luft–Tangee Inc.

Eyes of youth
    (*eye creams*) Gertrude Shyde

Filters sun, speeds tan
    (*Sutra lotion*)

For all important occasions, wear Dura-Gloss
    Lorr Laboratories

For "dream hands," cream your hands
    (*Paquins hand cream*)

For matching lips and fingertips
    (*lipstick, nail polish*) Revlon Inc.

For smooth white hands tomorrow use Thine Hand Creme tonight
    Frailey Prods

For that "come hither" look
    (*Angelus lipstick*)

For that smart sun-tan look
    (*Max Factor make-up*) Max Factor & Co.

For the difference it makes
    (*skin cream, cleansers*) Neutrogena

For women whose eyes are older than they are
    John Robert Powers Products Co.

Guard your youth with Youth Garde
    (*Youth Garde Moisturizer*)

It can help you look younger too
    (*Oil of Olay*) Olay Corp.

Just to show a proper glow
    (*Ingram's rouge*) F. F. Ingram Co.

Keep kissable with Flame-Glo Lipstick
    Flame-Glo Cosmetics

Keeps your face fit
    (*Aqua Velva cream*) J. B. Williams Co. Inc.

Keep the stars in your eyes
    (*eye lotion*) Sales Affiliates Inc.

Lash out
    (*L'Oreal mascara*) Cosmair Inc.

Liquid jewelry
    (*nail polish*) Lorr Laboratories

Living face make-up and living face cosmetics
    (*Marinello*) Sales Affiliates Inc.

Makes dull faces shine
    Keystone Emery Mills

Makes the skin like velvet
    Mystic Cream Co.

Make up your mind before you make up your face
   (*hypo-allergenic cosmetics*) Almay

Maybe she's born with it. Maybe it's Maybelline.
   Maybelline Inc.

More than mascara
   (*Moisture-Binding Formula Mascara*) Estée Lauder

Personality face powder
   Celebrated Products Sales

Powdered perfume for the complexion
   (*Velveola Souveraine face powder*)

P. S. And it's especially great as a hand lotion
   (*Dermassage*) S. M. Edison Chemical Co.

Redefining beautiful
   (*Cover Girl products*) Noxell Corp.

Refresh, revive that sleepy skin
   Dorothy Gray

Removes the freckles, whitens the skin
   Stillman Co.

Screens out burn and makes you brown
   (*sun oil*) Dorothy Gray

Sheer make-up for sheer beauty
   (*Houbigant*) Houbigant Inc.

She has it made
   Clairol Inc.

Sifted through silk
   (*Pussywillow face powder*) Henry Tetlow Co.

So advanced ... it's simple
   Matrix SkinCare

... So glamorous you have to be *told* they're hypo-allergenic
   (*Almay*) Schieffelin and Co.

Stays on till you take it off
   (*Coty 24 Hour lipstick*) Chas. Pfizer and Co. Inc.

The body cosmetic
   (*Cashmere Bouquet talcum*) Colgate–Palmolive Co.

The eye make-up in good taste
      Maybelline Co.

The girl with the beautiful face
      Clairol Inc.

The lipstick without the dye
      Ar-ex Products Inc.

The most prized eye cosmetics in the world
      Maybelline Co.

The most unforgettable women in the world wear Revlon
      Revlon Inc.

There is beauty in every jar
      (*milkweed cream*) F. F. Ingram Co.

The smartest shop in town
      Avon Products Inc.

We know how beautiful can be
      Merle Norman Cosmetic Studios

When a Studio Girl enters your home a new kind of beauty
brightens your life
      Helene Curtis Industries Inc.

Why most European women don't look 30 til they're 40
      (*Face First*) Elizabeth Grady

You make me smile
      Avon Products Inc.

Your face never had it so clean!
      (*1006 lotion*) Bonne Bell Inc.

CRUISE SHIPS
See SEA TRAVEL AND CARGO

CUTLERY
See HARDWARE

DAIRY PRODUCTS
See also BEVERAGES, MISCELLAENOUS; FOOD,
MISCELLANEOUS

Always churned from sweet cream
      (*butter*) June Dairy Products Co.

Baby's milk must be safe
      (*Challenge milk*) Challenge Foods Co.

Calcium the way nature intended
      National Dairy Board

Cheese; zest at its best
      American Dairy Association

Churned from sweet (not sour) cream
      Land O' Lakes Creameries Inc.

Cream's rival
      Sego Milk Products Co.

Digestible as milk itself
      (*Velveeta*) Kraft Inc.

Don't forget the cheese
      National Dairy Board

Fresh milk; have you had your glass today?
      Fresh Milk Industry

From contented cows
      Carnation Co.

Get a little taste of French culture
      (*yogurt*) Yoplait

Gives cream and butter flavor
      Pet Milk Co.

Have more milk 'cause milk's got more
      American Dairy Association

How to make a muscle
      National Dairy Products

Ice cream for health
      National Association of Ice Cream Mfrs.

KNOW YOUR MILKMAN

If it's Bordens, it's got to be good
Borden Inc.

Know your milkman
Twin City Milk Producers Association

Look for this famous name in the oval
(*Philadelphia Brand Cream Cheese*) Kraft Inc.

Made in the milky way
Ohio Butterine Co.

Milk is the fresher refresher
American Dairy Association

Mother's first thought for every milk need
(*White House evaporated milk*)

Nature forgot vitamin D, but Dean's didn't
Dean Milk Co.

No artificial anything
(*yogurt*) The Dannon Co. Inc.

No matter how diluted, it is never skimmed milk
Pet Milk Co.

Pure country milk with the cream left in
(*evaporated milk*) Borden Inc.

Taste that stands out in a crowd
Sealtest

Taste the difference
(*Breyer's ice cream*) Kraft Inc.

The cheese most people like
(*Brookfield*) Swift & Co.

The cheese with the paper between the slices
N. Dorman and Co.

The first hands to touch it are yours
(*Elkhorn cheese*) J. L. Kraft & Bros.

The milk every doctor knows
Carnation Milk Products Co.

We wrote the book on unsalted butter
Land-O-Lakes Butter

You eat it with a smile
(*ice cream*) Seale-Lilly Ice Cream Co.

You'll fall in love with Jersey Maid
(*ice cream*) Jersey Maid Ice Cream Co.

DENTAL CARE
See also TOILETRIES

A clean tooth never decays
(*Pro-phy-lac-tic toothbrush*) Pro-phy-lac-tic Brush Co.

A massage for the gums
(*Gum-rub*) Dental Lab. Prods. Co.

Aren't your kids worth Crest?
(*toothpaste*) Procter & Gamble

Beauty bath for your teeth
(*Listerine tooth paste*) Lambert Pharmacal Co.

Be good to your gums
(*Pro-phy-lac-tic toothbrush*) Pro-phy-lac-tic Brush Co.

Bent like a dentist's mirror to reach more places
(*Squibb toothbrush*) Squibb Corp.

Be true to your teeth or they'll be false to you
(*Medisalt*) Carey Salt Co.

Beware *Of Smokers* Teeth
(*tooth paste*) Bost Inc.

Cleans as it fizzes
(*denture cleanser*) Fizzadent Corp.

Colgate helps stop cavities before they start
(*Colgate toothpaste*) Colgate–Palmolive Co.

Double protection fights cavities and freshens breath
(*Aqua-fresh toothpaste*) Beecham Products

Fighting cavities is the whole idea behind Crest
(*toothpaste*) Procter & Gamble

For lazy people
(*Listerine tooth paste*) Lambert Pharmacal Co.

Dental Care

For the smile of beauty
  (*Ipana*) Bristol–Myers Co.

Good for tender gums
  (*Ipana*) Bristol–Myers Co.

Good habits that last a lifetime
  (*Aim toothpaste*) Lever Bros. Co.

It cleans your breath while it cleans your teeth
  (*Colgate dental cream*) Colgate–Palmolive Co.

It tastes as good as it tests
  (*Crest toothpaste*) Procter & Gamble

Just rub it on the gums
  (*Dr. Hand's teething lotion*) Colorado Chemical Co.

Keeps breath pure and sweet 1 to 2 hours longer
  (*Pepsodent antiseptic*) Lever Bros. Co.

Kids love the flavor. Moms love the fight.
  (*Crest gel*) Procter & Gamble

Lovely to look at, pleasant to use
  (*Tek toothbrush*) International Playtex Corp.

Makes your teeth feel smooth as silk
  Otis Clapp & Son

More dentists use Lavoris than any other mouthwash. Shouldn't you?
  (*Lavoris*) Vick Chemical Co.

Now, no bad breath behind his sparkling smile
  (*Colgate dental cream*) Colgate–Palmolive Co.

Prescription for your teeth
  (*Listerine tooth paste*) Lambert Pharmacal Co.

Recommended by dentists surveyed 9 to 1 over all toothpastes
  combined
  (*Polident*) Block Drug Co. Inc.

Removes the dingy film
  (*Pepsodent*) Lever Bros. Co.

Take Aim against cavities
  (*Aim toothpaste*) Lever Bros. Co.

THE SAFE MODERN WAY TO CLEAN
PLATES AND BRIDGES

Dental Care

The *green* cleans in-between ... the *white* polishes bright
Pro-phy-lac-tic Brush Co.

The powder that penetrates between the teeth
McKesson & Robbins

The safe modern way to clean plates and bridges
(*Polident*) Block Drug Co. Inc.

The toothsome paste
Red Gum Products Co.

Tooth powder in paste form
Sunny Smile Products Co.

Twice a day and before every date
(*Colgate Ribbon dental cream*) Colgate–Palmolive Co.

Use BOST, and get a good paste in the mouth
Bost Inc.

Wake up lazy gums with Ipana and massage
Bristol–Myers Co.

We're working to make cavities a thing of the past
(*Crest toothpaste*) Procter & Gamble

Your mouth will sing its praises
(*Worcester Salt tooth paste*)

Your strongest line of defense against gum disease
(*Johnson & Johnson dental floss*) Johnson & Johnson

DEODERANTS
See TOILETRIES

DETERGENTS
See CLEANING AND LAUNDRY PRODUCTS

DISHES
See CHINA

Acutrim helps you beating your cheating hours
Acutrim

Advanced medicine for pain
(*Advil analgesic*) Whitehall Laboratories

Ah, there's the rub
Somerville Co.

All you need is Bayer
(*Bayer aspirin*) Glenbrook Laboratories

America's home remedy
(*Alka-Seltzer*) Miles Laboratories Inc.

A precious bit more than a laxative
(*Alonzo*) Bliss Medical Co.

At the first sneeze, Vick's VapoRub
(*VapoRub*) Vick Chemical Co.

Bayer works wonders
(*Bayer aspirin*) Glenbrook Laboratories

Be as regular as a clock
(*Serutan laxative*) Healthaids Inc.

Because you're not just treating a fever. You're treating a child.
(*Tempra 2 baby aspirin*) Mead Johnson & Co.

Better care for better kids
(*Junior Strength Tylenol analgesic*) McNeil Consumer
Products Co.

Better than a mustard plaster
(*Musterole*) Plough Inc.

Better than whisky for a cold
Dr. Miles Medical Co.

Birth control that you control
(*Semicid vaginal contraceptive inserts*) Whitehall Laboratories

Birth control you can trust
(*Encare*) Thompson Medical Co.

Casco kills colds
    Casco Co.

Children cry for it
    (*Fletcher's Castoria*) Glenbrook Laboratories

Chlorine ointment, better than iodine
    Minox Chemical Corp.

Corn-free happy feet
    (*corn salve*) Kohler Mfg. Co.

Cures most vaginal yeast infections
    (*Monistat 7*)

Does not harm the heart
    (*Bayer aspirin*) Glenbrook Laboratories

Drixoral—the 12-hour advantage
    Schering–Plough Health Care Products

Early treatment, early cure
    (*Gyne-lotrimin*) Schering–Plough Health Care Products

Easy doses, no fishy taste, no bad after-taste
    (*Caritol*) S. M. A. Corp.

Easy to read, unmistakable result
    (*Fact Plus home pregnancy test*) Ortho Pharmaceutical Corp.

Easy to use, just shake in your shoes
    (*Allen's Foot Ease*)

Everything will come out all right
    (*laxative*) The Dill Co.

Feel it heal
    (*Noxema skin cream*) Noxell Corp.

Fights colds and sore throats
    (*Listerine*) Lambert Pharmacal Co.

First choice for patients in pain
    (*Tylenol Extra Strength Gel Caps*) McNeil Consumer
    Products Co.

For a good night's sleep
    (*Nytol*) Block Drug Co. Inc.

For FAST headache help
    (*Bromo Seltzer*) Warner–Lambert Pharmaceutical Co.

For fast relief, it's second to none. Primatene Mist.
    (*asthma inhaler*) Whitehall Laboratories

For her greater stimulation and pleasure
    (*Arouse condoms*) Protex Division

For natural feeling and sensitivity
    (*Fourex lambskin condoms*) Schmid Laboratories

For penetrating relief get Hall's Vapor Action
    (*Hall's Mentho-Liptus*) American Chicle Co.

For relief you can trust
    (*Tylenol pain reliever*) McNeil Consumer Products Co.

For the anemia of RETROVIR-treated HIV-infected patients
    (*Procrit Epoetin Alfa*) Amgen Inc.

For the committed quitter, membrane controlled
    (*Nicoderm nicotine skin patches*) Marion Merrell Dow Inc.

... for the period before your period
    (*Premsyn PMS*) Chattem Consumer Products

For these symptoms of stress that can come from success
    (*Alka-Seltzer*) Miles Laboratories Inc.

For the tummy
    (*Tums*) Norcliff Thayer Inc.

Get at that corn today, forget that ouch tomorrow
    (*corn salve*) Kohler Mfg. Co.

Gets the red out
    (*Visine eye drops*) Leeming/Pacquin

Give us a week, we'll take off the weight
    (*Ultra Slim-Fast*) Slim-Fast Foods Co.

Give your cold to Contac. Real medicines for real colds.
    (*Contac cold medicine*) Menley & James Laboratories

Great aches from little corns grow
    (*Blue Jay corn plaster*) The Kendall Co.

Handiest thing in the house
    (*Vaseline*) Chesebrough–Pond's Inc.

Helps nature cure your cough
(*Pertussin*) Chesebrough–Pond's Inc.

How do you spell relief?
(*Rolaids antacid*) American Chicle Co.

If you've got the will, now you've got the power
(*Habitrol nicotine skin patch*) Basel Pharmaceuticals

I'm stuck on Band-Aid because Band-Aid is stuck on me
Johnson & Johnson

Instant relief of feminine itching
(*Vagisil creme medication*) COMBE Inc.

It happens in two seconds
(*Bayer aspirin*) Glenbrook Laboratories

It's the easiest
(*Clearblue Easy home pregnancy test*) Whitehall Laboratories

It's the little daily dose that does it
(*Krushen salts*)

Join the regulars
(*Ex-Lax*) Ex-Lax Distributing Co. Inc.

Keep fighting, keep working, keep singing, America
E. R. Squibb & Sons

Keeps you going
(*Contac cold capsules*) Menley & James Laboratories

K-Y Jelly. The safer choice.
(*lubricant*) Johnson & Johson

Laugh it off with a "Jest"
(*alkalizer*) Jests Inc.

Makes milk and dairy products more digestible
Lactaid Inc.

Medically proven to help you lose weight
(*Dexatrim*) Thomas Medical Co.

More than just a great antacid
(*Tums*) Norcliff Thayer Inc.

Never neglect a break in the skin
Newskin Co.

GETS THE RED OUT

Never neglect the tiniest cut
　　(*Band-Aid*) Johnson & Johnson

Never upset an upset stomach
　　(*Pepto-Bismol*) Norwich–Eaton Pharmaceuticals

Next to safety first, first aid
　　Johnson & Johnson

Nip-it with Sip-It
　　(*Sip-It cough remedy*)

Nothing gives you more relief than Bayer. Nothing.
　　(*aspirin*) Glenbrook Laboratories

Nothing you can buy is stronger or works harder on your headache.
　Absolutely nothing.
　　Extra Strength Excedrin

NR tonight, tomorrow all right
　　(*Nature's Remedy laxative*) Norcliff Thayer Inc.

Nupe it with Nuprin
　　(*analgesic*) Bristol–Myers Co.

Pat it on the face, wop it on the body
　　(*Pat-&-Wop*) Allied Drug Products

Prolong sexual pleasure for both partners
　　(*Maintain condoms*) Schmid Laboratories

Put one on, the pain is gone
　　(*Zono pads*)

Real medicine for throats too sore to ignore
　　(*Chloraseptic*) Norwich–Eaton Pharmaceuticals

Recommended by "Dr. Mom"
　　(*Robitussin cough medicine*) A.H. Robins Co.

RELy on REL for real RELief
　　Maryland Pharmaceutical Co.

Revive with Vivarin
　　(*stimulant tablets*)

Rolaids spells relief
　　(*Rolaids antacid*) American Chicle Co.

Safe for the little folks, too
> The New-Syn Co.

Serutan spelled backwards spells "Nature's"
> (*Serutan laxative*) Healthaids Inc.

Sharing the goal of good health
> The Upjohn Co.

So gentle for children, so thorough for grown-ups
> (*Phillips' Milk of Magnesia*) Glenbrook Laboratories

Soothes. Cleanses. Refreshes.
> (*eye drops*) Murine Co. Inc.

Speedy is its middle name
> (*Alka-Seltzer*) Miles Laboratories Inc.

Take two, pain's through
> Neo-Syn Co.

Taste as good as they make you feel
> (*Tums*) Lewis–Howe Co.

That's all. Nothing else.
> (*Comtrex Cold Reliever*) Bristol–Myers Co.

The antidiarrheal patients solidly prefer
> (*Imodium A-D*) McNeil Consumer Products Co.

The art and science of hair transplantation
> Bosley Medical Group

The bandage that breathes
> (*Sealtex*)

The beauty laxative
> (*Dr. Edward's Olive tablets*) Oakhurst Co.

The best in tapes has "Able" on the label
> Arno Adhesive Tapes Inc.

The candy-mint alkalizer
> (*Alkaid*) F. & F. Laboratories Inc.

The cheapest health insurance in the world
> (*cough drops*) Smith Bros.

The criminal within
> (*Eno laxative*)

The doctor's prescription
(*Father John's medicine*) Medtech Laboratories Inc.

The European way to slim
Fibre Trim

The first real improvement since the spoon
(*Contac cough capsules*) Menley & James Laboratories

The first thought in burns
(*Unguentine*) Norwich–Eaton Pharmaceuticals

The gentle laxative more women prefer
(*Correctol*) Schering–Plough Health Care Products

The great regulator
(*Beecham's pills*) Beecham Products Inc.

The moisture so important to a woman's body
(*Gyne-Moistrin*) Schering–Plough Health Care Products

The more you know, the better you'll feel
(*vitamins*) Nature Made Pharmavite Corp.

The one more pediatricians give their own children
(*Children's Tylenol*) McNeil Consumer Products Co.

The one that coats is the only one you need
(*Pepto-Bismol*) Norwich Pharmacal Co.

The original chocolate laxative
(*Ex-Lax*) Ex-Lax Distributing Co. Inc.

There's no beating deep heating
(*Mentholatum Deep Heating Rub*) The Mentholatum Co.

The ovulation kit OB/GYN doctors recommend most
(*First Response home pregnancy test*) Carter–Wallace Inc.

The premenstrual relief specialist
(*Midol*) Glenbrook Laboratories

The salve with a base of old-fashioned mutton suet
(*Penetro*) Plough Inc.

The science of success
Schering–Plough Health Care Products

The sniffling, sneezing, coughing, aching, stuffy head, fever, so you
can rest medicine
(*Nyquil cold medicine*) Vick Chemical Co.

The successor to the tranquilizers
(*Librium*) Roche

The tested treatment for infectious dandruff
(*Listerine*) Lambert Pharmacal Co.

Time it when you take it
(*Pasmore's 2-minute aid*)

Today's choice in birth control
(*Today sponge*) Whitehall Laboratories

Today sponge. The 24-hour contraceptive.
Whitehall Laboratories

To fly high in the morning, take Phillips at night
(*Phillips' Milk of Magnesia*) Glenbrook Laboratories

Touches the spot
(*ointment*) Homocea, Ltd., England

Trust Band-Aid brand to cover you better
(*Band-Aid*) Johnson & Johnson

Trust Tylenol. Hospitals do.
(*non-aspirin analgesic*) McNeil Consumer Products Co.

Vivarin keeps you going
(*stimulant tablets*)

Wake up your liver
(*Carter's pills*) Carter–Wallace Inc.

When nature won't, Pluto will
(*Pluto Water*) French Lick Springs Co.

Will cure a cold in one night
(*Carter's Compound Extract*) Brown Medicine Co.

Works like a penetrating massage
(*Deep Heating Rub*) Mentholatum Co.

Worth a guinea a box
(*Beecham's pills*) Beecham Products Inc.

DRY GOODS
See SEWING AND KNITTING SUPPLIES

EARTHMOVERS
See MACHINERY

ECONOMIC DEVELOPMENT
See also TRAVEL

A great state in which to live and work
  Rhode Island

Better yet, Connecticut
  Connecticut Department of Economic Development

Birthplace of the nation
  Virginia Department of Conservation and Economic Development

Come to Kentucky! It's a profitable move!
  Kentucky Department of Commerce

Dallas is the door to Texas
  Dallas, Texas

Discover the new in New York State
  New York State Department of Commerce

Growing city within a growing city
  W. Seattle Community Adv.

Industrious Maine, New England's big stake in the future
  Maine Department of Economic Development

Industry is on the move to Iowa
  Iowa Development Commission

Industry's friendliest climate
  Public Services of Indiana Inc.

Isle of June
  Nassau Development Board, Nassau, Bahamas

It is profitable to produce in Massachusetts
  Commonwealth of Massachusetts

Jersey City has everything for industry
  Jersey City, New Jersey

Keep Missouri in the center of your thinking
>Missouri Commerce and Industrial Development Commission

Land of enchantment
>Department of Development, New Mexico

Land of perpetual prosperity
>Oklahoma City

Logical locale for new business
>Massachusetts Development & Industry Comm.

Make the capital choice
>Port Authority of the City of St. Paul

Michigan, state of happiness for everyone
>Michigan

Minnesota brainpower builds profits
>Minnesota Department of Business Development

Mix fun and history in Virginia
>Virginia Department of Conservation and Economic Development

Now's the time to get away *to* it all!
>Southwest Sun Country Association

Now that you've conquered the world, separate yourself from it
>Fisher's Island

Ship from the center, not from the rim
>St. Louis, Missouri

Speaking the language of global business
>Singapore

The city that does things
>Norfolk, Virginia

The dynamo of Dixie
>Chattanooga, Tennessee

The land of elbow room and elbow grease
>Omaha Public Power District

The port of personal service
>Wilmington, Delaware

Economic Development

"We like it here"
    Wisconsin Division of Economic Development

Where big things are happening
    Commonwealth of Kentucky

Where free enterprise is still growing
    Indiana Department of Commerce

Where good government is a habit
    North Carolina Department of Conservation

Where nature helps industry most
    Los Angeles, California

Electrical Products and Service

ELECTRICAL PRODUCTS AND SERVICE
See also ELECTRONICS INDUSTRY, HEATING AND AIR
CONDITIONING, HOME APPLIANCES AND EQUIPMENT,
LIGHTING PRODUCTS, PUBLIC UTILITIES

Battery with a kick
    (*Prest-O-Lite*) The Prestolite Co.

Cook electrically and enjoy the difference
    (*Reddy Kilowatt*) Reddy Communications

From the tiniest to the mightiest
    (*electric motors*) General Electric Co.

Give Red Bands your hard job
    Howell Electric Motors Co.

In electricity, it's Edison from start to finish
    Edison–Splitdorf Corp.

Instantly known when blown
    (*Royal Crystal fuse plug*) Royal Electric Co.

Live better electrically
    Edison Electric Institute

Longest life by owners' records
    Gould Storage Battery Co.

More than horse-power
    (*electric motors*) Louis Allis Co.

Name that means everything in electricity
    Westinghouse

No damp amps
    Cincinnati Elec. Prods. Co.

Nothing lasts longer
    (*batteries*) Duracell Inc.

Off when it's on, on when it's off
    Gould Storage Battery Co.

Plug in, I'm Reddy
    (*Reddy Kilowatt*) Reddy Communications

Portable power for progress
    Battery Division, Sonotone Corp.

Power to spare
    (*Eveready batteries*) Union Carbide Corp.

Responsiveness of a well-trained servant
    North East Electric Co.

Stay fresh for years
    (*Ray-O-Vac batteries*) ESB Inc.

Still going ...
    (*Eveready Energizer batteries*) Eveready Batter Co. Inc.

The motor's the thing
    Herschell–Spillman Motor Co.

They keep a-running
    (*electric motors*) Century Electric Co.

They show when they blow
    (*Trico fuse*) Trico Mfg. Co.

Wherever wheels turn or propellers spin
    (*Delco battery*) Delco Products

You can't top the copper top
    (*batteries*) Duracell Inc.

ELECTRICITY
See PUBLIC UTILITIES

ELECTRONICS INDUSTRY
See also AEROSPACE, AUDIO EQUIPMENT, BROADCASTING, COMPUTER EQUIPMENT AND SOFTWARE, CORPORATIONS, ELECTRICAL PRODUCTS AND SERVICE, RADIO EQUIPMENT, TELECOMMUNICATIONS, TELEVISIONS, VIDEO EQUIPMENT

America's technology store
(*Radio Shack*) Tandy Corp.

A world of experience
Collins Radio Co.

Builders of the tools of automation
Reliance Electric and Engineering Co.

Creating a new world with electronics
Hughes Aircraft Co.

Engineered to fit your life
Sansui USA Inc.

From sharp minds come Sharp products
Sharp Electronics Corp.

Go with the sound America's truckers trust
(*Whistler radar detectors*)

Helping you control your world
Honeywell

In touch with tomorrow
Toshiba America Inc.

Just slightly ahead of our time
(*Panasonic*) Matsushita Electric Corp. of America

Manning the frontiers of electronic progress
Autonetics Division, North American Rockwell Corp.

New ideas in automation control
Photoswitch Division, Electronics Corp. of America

New leader in the lively art of electronics
Motorola Inc.

The brightest star in electronics
GoldStar Electronics International Inc.

The first and greatest name in electronics
General Electric Co.

The intelligent choice
      (Bell 966W radar detector) Beltronics Ltd.

The "light" touch in automation and control
      Clairex Corp.

The most trusted name in electronics
      RCA Corp.

The one and only
      Sony Corp. of America

The world's most advanced radar detectors
      (Escort, Passport, Solo) Cincinnati Microwave Inc.

We get the message
      (answering machines) Phone-Mate

ELEVATORS

From pit to penthouse
      Otis Elevator Co.

Morning uplift
      Otis Elevator Co.

The safe, swift, silent "lift"
      Turnbull Elevator Co.

EMPLOYMENT AGENCIES

Good people
      Olsten Temporary Services

Kelly can do
      Kelly Services Inc.

Kelly helps America work
      Kelly Services Inc.

Office help—temporary or permanent
      American Girl Service

One source, one standard—nationwide
      Kelly Services Inc.

Employment Agencies

The right people for the job
    Dunhill Personnel System

The very best in temporary help
    Manpower Inc.

When you need the best, call the best
    Dunhill Temporaries

ENERGY
See HEATING AND COOKING FUELS

ENTERTAINMENT
See MOVIES AND ENTERTAINMENT

Eyeglasses

EYEGLASSES
See also WARDROBE ACCESSORIES

Acuvue. The first disposable contact lens.
    Vision Products Inc.

Better vision for better looks
    Better Vision Institute

Don't say sunglasses—say C'Bon
    Polaroid Corp.

For better eyesight
    American Optical Co.

Glasses in about an hour
    NuVision

Glasses in about 60 minutes or less
    D.O.C.

Grace the face and stay in place
    (*glasses*) E. Kirstein & Sons

Isn't that you behind those Foster Grants?
    (*sunglasses*) Foster Grant Co.

Life looks brighter
    (*Univis glasses*)

Like pearl temples behind the ears
    (*spectacles*) No-Ease Co.

Precription lenses that change
Corning Glass Works

Seeing is believing
(*Oculens sunglasses*) Comptone Co.

Since 1833 ... better vision for better living
American Optical Co.

Style, protection, quality, warranty. After Vuarnet, you'll choose
nothing else.
(*sunglasses*) Vuarnet France

That eyes may see better and farther
Bausch & Lomb Optical Co.

Wear them for up to a week and then just throw them away
(*Acuvue Disposable Contact Lenses*) Vision Products Inc.

We make you look good
(*sunglasses*) Foster Grant

FABRICS INDUSTRY
See SEWING AND KNITTING SUPPLIES

FARMING SUPPLIES AND EQUIPMENT
See also MACHINERY, TRUCKS AND TRUCKING INDUSTRY

A better yield in every field
York Chemical Co.

An American legend caring for the land
(*Junior Tomahawk Chipper-Shredder*) Troy-Bilt

As necessary as the rain
Buhner Fertilizer Co.

Beware where you buy your bee-ware
G. B. Lewis Co.

Bred, not just grown
Associated Seed Growers

Can lay their weight in gold
(*baby chicks*) Ken-La Farms

Consistently good year after year
(*corn seeds*) Funk G. Hybrids

Don't just fertilize ... Spencerize
Spencer Chemical Division, Gulf Oil Corp.

Easier to handle, lighter draft, more durable
(*plow*) E. B. Foot Lift Plow

Farm Implements with a future—yours!
Brillion Iron Works Inc.

Feeds and seeds to meet your needs
Crabbs Taylor Reynolds Elevator Co.

First in grassland farming
New Holland Division, Sperry Rand Corp.

First to serve the farmer
International Harvester Co.

From the tractor people who make the big ones
(*tractors*) Allis–Chalmers Mfg. Co.

Good enough to eat
(*poultry feed*) American Agricultural Chemical Co.

Hen's only rival
103 Degree Incubator Co.

If Purina chows won't make your hens lay, they are roosters
Ralston Purina Co.

In garden or in fields, Schell's seeds produce best yields
(*Schell's seeds*)

Keeps cows contented from sunrise to sunset
Usol Fly Spray

Makes every acre do its best
(*Armour's fertilizer*)

Man, that's corn
Pfister Associated Growers

More acres of corn, more corn per acre
Pfister Associated Growers

More corn, less cob; it's bred that way
Pfister Associated Growers

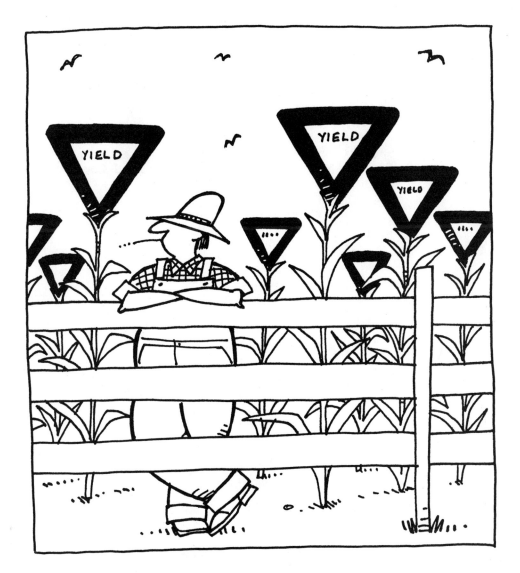

A BETTER YIELD IN EVERY FIELD

Farming Supplies and Equipment

Serving the businessman in the blue denim suit
    (*Master Mix feeds*) Central Soya Co. Inc.

So easy, a child can steer it
    (*tractors*) Cleveland Tractor Co.

Something to crow about
    American Agricultural Chemical Co.

Southern Fertilizers for the southern farmer
    The Barrett Co.

Specialists in farmstead mechanization
    New Holland Division, Sperry Rand Corp.

Team of steel
    (*tractors, threshers*) Minneapolis Steel & Machinery Co.

The courage to change. The strength to grow.
    International Harvester Co.

The feeder's silent partner
    (*Tuxedo feeds*) Early & Daniel Co.

The national soil sweetener
    Kelley Island Lime & Transport Co.

The people who bring you the machines that *work*
    International Harvester Co.

The second best nurser in the world
    Eveready Nurser

They moo for more
    (*cottonseed meal*) Ashcraft–Wilkinson Co.

Where bold new ideas pay off for profit-minded farmers
    New Idea Farm Equipment Co.

World's first mass produced tractor
    (*tractors*) Ford Tractor Division, Ford Motor Co.

Your way of life depends upon your day of work
    (*tractors*) Morrison Tractor

FASHION ACCESSORIES
See CLOTHING, COSMETICS, WARDROBE ACCESSORIES

FEED
See FARMING SUPPLIES AND EQUIPMENT

FERTILIZER
See FARMING SUPPLIES AND EQUIPMENT

FILM
See PHOTOGRAPHIC EQUIPMENT

FINANCIAL INSTITUTIONS AND SERVICES
See also INSURANCE, INVESTMENT

A bank of personal contact
> Interstate Trust Co.

A concern for your future
> Kemper Financial Services Inc.

A distinguished banking connection
> Bank of the United States

All the bank you'll ever need in Texas
> Texas National Bank of Commerce of Houston

All your banking under one roof
> Mellon National Bank

America's First Family of no-load funds
> Scudder Development Fund

A tower of strength
> Bankers Trust Co.

A tradition of trust
> Merrill Lynch

Bank of personal service
> First Trust & Deposit Co.

Behind the enduring institution, successful customers
> Farmers Deposit Bank

Be SURE you save at a savings bank
> Savings Bank Association

Be thrifty and be happy
> Baldwin National Bank & Trust Co.

Better banking, better service, better join us
Reliance State Bank

Better than money
(*travelers checks*) First National City Bank

Common sense. Uncommon results.
Fidelity Investments

Constantly building for community usefulness
New First National Bank

Courtesy, efficiency, service
Manufacturers Trust Co.

Distance is no barrier to our service
Citizens Trust Co.

First in banking
Bank of America

First in loans to business and industry
Chase Manhattan Bank

For people who'd rather invest money than time
(*Selected Funds*) Selected Financial Services Inc.

Forward with Miami's oldest bank
Bank of Bay of Biscayne

For Wilmington, the Carolinas, and the South
Murchison National Bank

Founded by merchants for merchants
Merchants National Bank

Get the First National habit
First National Bank at Pittsburgh

Good for money wherever money means anything
Bankers Trust Co.

Helping investors help themselves
Charles Schwab & Co.

Help yourself financially without financial help
Illinois National Bank

It pays to Discover
(*Discover credit card*) Greenwood Trust Co.

... It's good to have a great bank behind you
  Manufacturers Hanover Trust Co.

Investing with a sense of direction
  Van Kampen Merritt

Invest with confidence
  T. Rowe Price Investment Services Inc.

Keep your income coming in
  American National Bank

Master the moment
  Master Card International Inc.

Membership has its privileges
  American Express

Not just banking, Citibanking
  Citicorp Financial Services

Oldest trust company in Connecticut
  Hartford Conn. Trust Co.

Partners in progress around the world
  First National City Bank

People's Trust is the people's bank
  People's Trust & Guaranty Co.

Quality tax-free investing since 1898
  Nuveen

Save as you spend with Christmas Club Thrifties
  Christmas Club

Save for a sunny day
  First National Bank, Boston

Security with no ifs
  America's Banks

Service is the difference between our money and other money
  Barclays American

Small-business people helping each other
  The Kessler Exchange

Solutions for business
  (*accounting*) Coopers & Lybrand

Spendable everywhere
(*travelers checks*) American Express Co.

Strength, safety, service
National City Savings Bank & Trust Co.

Systematic saving spells success
Old Colony Co-operative Bank

The bank for bankers and businessmen
Irving Trust Co.

The bank that works hardest for you
Chemical Bank, New York

The bank where you feel at home
Central Trust & Savings Co.

The bank with the international point of view
Bank of the Southwest

The little bank with a large circle of friends
1st National Bank of Pleasanton

The nation's largest futures discount firm
Lind–Waldock

The Oil Bank of America
National Bank of Tulsa

The place where you keep your checking account
Foundation for Commercial Banks

The power to make a difference
NationsBank

Thinking ahead to stay ahead
Incorp

Thrift brings happiness
Roosevelt Savings Bank

We're making it hard to bank anywhere else
The Bank of New York

Where all street cars meet
Utica Trust & Deposit Co.

Where people make the difference
Toronto–Dominion Bank

Where you save *does* make a difference
      The Savings and Loan Foundation Inc.

Where we go from here
      (*Andersen Consulting*) Arthur Andersen & Co.

Working for your success
      Texas Commerce Bank

Working to get the right information first
      Paine Webber

You can get there from here
      Shearson Lehman Brothers

You have a friend at Chase Manhattan
      Chase Manhattan Bank

FINISHES
See PAINT AND PAINTING SUPPLIES

FIREARMS

A gun for every American shooting need
      Marlin Firearms Co.

A load for every purpose and a shell for every purse
      U. S. Cartridge Co.

As easy as pointing your finger
      Colt Patent Fire Arms Mfg. Co.

Favorite shells satisfy good shooters
      Federal Cartridge Corp.

First in sporting arms
      Browning Arms Co.

For clean hits and clean barrels
      (*Remington shells*) Du Pont

Hits where you aim
      United States Cartridge Co.

Largest manufacturer of shotguns in the world
      Savage Arms Corp.

Firearms

Power without powder
> Crosman Arms Co.

Proven best by government test
> Colt Patent Fire Arms Mfg. Co.

The arms that protect American farms
> Iver–Johnson Arms and Cycle Works

The gun that knows no closed season
> Crosman Arms Co.

They better your aim
> Lyman Gun Sight Corp.

When you get a shot, you get a duck, with Super X
> Western Cartridge Co.

World's largest producer of non-powder guns and ammo
> Daisy/Heddon Division, Victor Comptometer Corp.

Fishing Supplies

FISHING SUPPLIES
See also RECREATIONAL EQUIPMENT, SPORTING GOODS

Adds science to fisherman's luck
> True Temper Corp.

"Bait of champions"
> Fred Arbogast Co., Inc.

First in world records
> Ashaway Line and Twine Mfg. Co.

First on famous waters
> Johnson Reels Inc.

If Weber makes it, a fish takes it
> Frost Fishing Tackle Co.

Make your own luck with Heddon
> James Heddon's Sons

Put a Burke where they lurk!
> Flexo-Products Division, McClellan Industries

Right in shape, temper and finish
> (*fish hooks*) O. Mustad & Sons

132

The fish hook people
O. Mustad & Sons

The most respected name in fishing tackle
Zebco Division, Brunswick Corp.

The river-runt does the stunt
(*fishing tackle*) James Heddon's Sons

The rod with the fighting heart
James Heddon's Sons

Veteran reel for veteran fisherman
Meiselbach Mfg. Co. Inc.

Where the action is!
Zebco Division, Brunswick Corp.

World's largest exclusive fly line manufacturer
Scientific Anglers Inc.

FITNESS
See HEALTH AND FITNESS

FLATWARE
See CHINA, JEWELRY AND SILVER

FLAVORINGS
See CONDIMENTS AND SPICES

FLOOR COVERINGS
See also BUILDING SUPPLIES, INTERIOR DECORATION

Artistry in carpets
Painter Carpet Mills, Inc., Division of Collins and Aikman

A rug for every room
Bird & Son Inc.

A shining example of what a floor should be
Mannington Gold

A title on the door rates a Bigelow on the floor
Bigelow–Sanford Inc.

Beauty basis for your home
(*Mohawk rugs and carpets*) Mohasco Corp.

Floor Coverings

Brighten your home at little expense
   (*Congoleum rugs*) Congoleum Corp.

Burlington, the scatter rug of beauty
   Lack Carpet Co.

Carpets of distinction
   Patcraft Mills Inc.

Fashion loomed to last
   Magee Carpet Co.

Feels like walking on velvet
   Clinton Carpet Co.

For every floor in the house
   (*linoleum*) Armstrong Cork Co.

Holmes rugs for artistic homes
   Archibold Holmes & Son

Loomed by American labor to beautify American homes
   Magee Carpet Co.

Originators of prefinished hardwood flooring
   The Cromar Co.

Outlast the factory
   (*Kreolite floors*) Jennison–Wright Co.

People who know buy Bigelow
   Bigelow–Sanford Inc.

So nice to come home to
   Armstrong World Industries Inc.

Styled in California, applauded by all America
   (*Pabco linoleums*) Fibreboard Corp.

The floor of enduring beauty
   Congoleum Corp.

They wear and wear and wear
   Armstrong Cork Co.

Those heavenly carpets by Lees
   James Lees and Sons Co.

Woven with a warp of honesty and a woof of skill
   Magee Carpet Co.

Years of wear in every yard
        (*Congoleum*) Congoleum Corp.

FOOD, MISCELLANEOUS
See also BABY PRODUCTS; BAKED GOODS AND BAKING
SUPPLIES; BEVERAGES, MISCELLANEOUS; CANDY AND GUM;
CEREALS; CONDIMENTS AND SPICES; DAIRY PRODUCTS;
FRUITS AND NUTS; MEATS; PET FOOD AND PRODUCTS;
RESTAURANTS

A cube makes a cup
        (*Steero cubes*) Schieffelin and Co.

All fresh-fruit good!
        (*jellies, preserves*) Kraft Foods

America is cookin' with Holly Farms
        (*chicken*)

America's first, finest and favorite pork and beans
        Stokely–Van Camp Inc.

America's first name for ham
        Hormel and Co.

America's most famous dessert
        (*Jell-o*) General Foods Corp.

A pip of a chip
        (*Jays potato chips*) Jays Foods Inc.

Aristocrat of the breakast table
        (*marmalade*) Chivers & Sons Ltd.

As a change from potatoes
        (*macaroni*) C. F. Mueller Co.

As good as can be
        Stouffer Foods

As they eat 'em in New England
        (*brick-oven beans*) Burnham & Morrill Co.

A treasure for eating pleasure
        (*canned vegetables*) Country Gardens Inc.

Best cooks know foods fried in Crisco don't taste greasy!
        Procter & Gamble Co.

Better buy Birds Eye
> Birds Eye Division, General Foods Corp.

Bring home the Bac-Os
> (*bacon flavor bits*)

Canned food is grand food
> American Can Co.

Catch them yourself or buy Fowler's
> Fowler Sea Products Co.

Chocolate bar flavor you can eat with a spoon
> Hershey's Pudding

Choosey mothers choose Jif
> (*Jif peanut butter*) Procter & Gamble Co.

Close. But no lumps.
> (*Heinz Home Style gravy*) H. J. Heinz Co.

Cooks in nine minutes
> (*macaroni, noodles*) C. F. Mueller Co.

Different, delicious, digestible
> Doughnut Corp. of America

Each grain salutes you
> (*rice*) Uncle Ben's Foods

Energy eggs from happy hens
> New Jersey Egg Market Committee

Every bite a rarebit
> (*Chicken of the Sea tuna*) Ralston Purina Co.

Everything's better with Blue Bonnet on it
> (*margarine*) Standard Brands Inc.

Everything you've ever wanted in a fish fillet
> (*Mrs. Paul's fish fillets*) Mrs. Paul's Kitchens

Feels like it's time, Cup-A-Soup time
> (*Cup-A-Soup*) Lipton Inc.

57 Varieties
> H. J. Heinz Co.

Food of the gods
> (*honey*) Arthur W. Hoffman

For good food and good food ideas
>Kraft Foods

For the lightest, fluffiest popcorn there's only one, Orville Redenbacher
>(*Orville Redenbacher Gourmet Popping Corn*) Hunt–Wesson Foods Inc.

Fresh as dewy dawn
>Pacific Egg Producers

From flower to bee to you
>(*Airline honey*) A. I. Root Co.

Homemade taste. It's in there!
>(*Prego spaghetti sauce*) Campbell Soup Co.

If it says Ore-Ida, it's got to be alrighta
>(*frozen potatoes*)

If you like peanuts, you'll like Skippy
>(*Skippy peanut butter*) CPC International Inc.

It's all in this little yellow box
>(*Velveeta*) Kraft Inc.

It's like homemade
>(*Soup Di Pasta*)

It's love at first bite
>(*canned ham*) Spam

It's not just any snack
>(*Nacho Cheese Doritos*) Frito–Lay Inc.

It's uncanny
>(*Knorr soups*) CPC International Inc.

Just form and fry
>(*codfish cakes*) J. W. Beardsley's sons

Like grandma's, only more so
>General Foods Corp.

Like little meat pies in sauce
>(*ravioli*) American Home Foods Inc.

Look-alikes aren't cook-alikes
>Idaho Potato Growers Inc.

Look to Libby's for perfection
　　Libby, McNeil & Libby

Make it as hearty as you are hungry
　　(*Tomato soup*) Campbell Soup Co.

Makes eyes sparkle and mouths water
　　(*Mazola salad oil*) CPC International Inc.

Makes fish day a red letter day
　　(*Chicken of the Sea tuna*) Ralston Purina Co.

Man's greatest food
　　(*potato*) Maine Development Commission

Mazola makes good eating sense
　　(*margarine*) Corn Products Co.

Moist as homemade
　　(*Duncan Hines cake mixes*) Procter & Gamble Co.

More Ummm, Ummm after every crunch
　　(*Planters Cheese Balls*) Planters Peanuts

Move over, bacon
　　(*Sizzlean*) Swift & Co.

M'm! M'm! Good!
　　Campbell Soup Co.

Nothing to do but fry
　　(*Gorton's codfish cakes*) The Gorton Corp.

Once you pop, you can't stop
　　Pringle's Potato Chips

Packed with the wiggle in its tail
　　New England Fish Co.

Picked at the fleeting moment of perfect flavor
　　(*Green Giant peas*) Green Giant Co.

Pick of the pack, picked at the peak of perfection
　　(*Polar Frosted Foods*)

Reach for the Campbell's. It's right on your shelf.
　　Campbell Soup Co.

Set yourself free. With Stouffer's.
　　(*frozen dinners*) Stouffer Foods Corp.

Seven cents a glass
        (*jelly*) La Vor Products Co.

Short lengths, easy to eat
        (*macaroni, noodles*) C. F. Mueller Co.

Shrimply elegant
        (*shrimp*) Treasure Isle Inc.

Some like 'em big, some like 'em little
        (*peas*) Bozeman Canning Co.

Soup it up with Lipton
        (*soup mixes*) Lipton Inc.

Soup so big, it eats like a meal
        (*Chunky soup*) Campbell Soup Co.

Start with—stay with Knox
        Chas. Knox Gelatine Co.

Stir up the Campbell's ... soup is good food
        Campbell Soup Co.

Sugar's got what it takes
        Sugar Information Inc.

Sweeten it with Domino
        American Sugar Refining Co.

Taste you can love for life
        Stouffer Foods Corp.

Thank goodness for Chef Boyardee
        American Home Food Products

That's Italian
        (*Ragu Spaghetti Sauce*) Ragu Foods Inc.

The better spread for our daily bread
        (*Interstate cotton oil*)

The big cheese of potato chips
        (*Pringle's Cheesum*) Procter & Gamble Co.

The brand that always puts flavor first
        (*Del Monte fruit cocktail*) Del Monte Corp.

The economical energy food
        (*macaroni, spaghetti, noodles*) Quaker Maid Co.

The famous family of Gorton's sea foods
Gorton–Pew Fisheries Co.

The most experienced food processor in the world
Libby, McNeill & Libby

The name you can trust in margarine
(*Mazola*) Best Foods Division, Corn Products Co.

There's a name for food this good
Hormel and Co.

The San Francisco style snack thins
(*Better Cheddars*) Nabisco Inc.

The San Francisco treat
Rice-a-roni

The tender-textured gelatin
(*Royal*) Standard Brands Inc.

The way America likes beans
(*pork and beans*) Campbell Soup Co.

They always eat better when you remember the soup
Campbell Soup Co.

They're not just breadcrumbs
(*4C Breadcrumbs*)

This is living
(*diet foods*) Weight Watchers International Inc.

Too good to be just a sandwich
(*tuna*) Chicken of the Sea

Trim is in
(*Trim Cup-A-Soup*) Lipton Inc.

What you really want for breakfast
Aunt Jemima Waffles

When only the best will do, say Uncle
(*Uncle Ben's rice*) Uncle Ben's Foods

With a name like Smucker's, it's got to be good
(*jelly and jam*)

Why Fry?
(*Shake & Bake*)

Young America spreads it on thick
(*marmalade*) Welch Grape Juice Co.

FOOTWEAR
See also CLOTHING, MISCELLANEOUS; WARDROBE
ACCESSORIES

Absorb shocks and jars
(*Massagic air cushion shoes*) Weyenberg Shoe Mfg. Co.

Action shoes for boys and girls
(*Red Goose shoes*) International Shoe Co.

A foot nearer perfection
G. R. Kinney Co.

A foot of comfort means miles of happiness
Ault Williamson Shoe Co.

Always a step ahead in style
Connolly Shoe Co.

American gentlemen shoes designed for the American man
Hamilton Brown Shoe Co.

America's No. 1 heel
O'Sullivan Rubber Co.

America's smartest walking shoes
(*Enna Jetticks*) Dunn & McCarthy Inc.

A million Americans can't be wrong
(*Father & Son shoes*) Endicott Johnson Corp.

A more intelligent approach to building shoes
(*New Balance*) Athletic Shoe Inc.

Ankle-fashioned shoes
Nunn-Bush Shoe Co.

Any Palizzio is better than no Palizzio
Palizzio Inc.

Anything goes with Hush Puppies
Hush Puppies

Art in footwear
Laird, Schober & Co.

A shoe with a talking point
    Teeple Shoe Co.

Beauty treatment for your feet
    (*Red Cross shoes*) Krohn Feckheimer Co.

Bends with your foot
    (*Red Cross shoes*) Krohn Feckheimer Co.

Best for rest
    (*house slippers*) S. Rauh & Co.

Better little shoes are not made
    Mrs. Day's Ideal Baby Shoe Co.

Boots that never say die
    Herman Survivors

Breathin' brushed pigskin
    (*Hush Puppies*) Wolverine World Wide Inc.

Built for your body
    (*athletic shoes*) Avia

Built so you can last
    (*athletic shoes*) Etonic

Cushion every step
    Weyenberg Shoe Mfg. Co.

Designed for going places in style, in comfort
    (*Pediforme shoes*)

Every pair made to wear
    (*Gutta Percha rubbers*) PPG Industries Inc.

Every pair shows the care of the shoemaker's hand
    (*Bostonian*) The Commonwealth Shoe & Leather Co.

Faithful to the last
    Nunn, Bush & Weldon Shoe Co.

Fashion-over-the-shoe
    (*U. S. Gaytees rubbers*) Uniroyal Inc.

Fashion's favored footwear
    Washington Shoe Mfg. Co.

Fit right, feel right, they're walk-fitted
    Bostonian Shoe Co.

Fits on the foot like a glove on the hand
    F. Blumenthal Co.

Fit to be tried
    Musebeck Shoe Co.

Flexible where you want it, rigid where you need it
    United States Shoe Co.

Florsheims afoot mean comfort ahead
    Florsheim Shoe Co.

Foot insurance for the future
    Julian & Hokenge Co.

For any wear and everywhere
    Florsheim Shoe Co.

For every walk in life
    Melville Shoe Corp.

For people who have other things to spend their money on
    Sam & Libby Inc.

For the active woman of today
    F. Mayer Shoe Co.

For the winning edge
    (*Dr. Scholl's Odor Eaters*) Scholl Inc.

For those who dress from the ground up
    Durango Boot

Friendly to the feet
    Jarman Shoe Co.

From first step to fourteen years
    Fargo–Hallowell Shoe Co.

Gives joy complete to women's feet
    Dunn & McCarthy Inc.

Give your feet young ideas
    Weyenberg Shoe Mfg. Co.

Good feet are the foundation of good health
    Burns Cuboid Co.

Great shoes for little Americans
    (*Little Yankee*)

Half the fun of having feet
(*Red Goose shoes*) International Shoe Co.

He won't change from shoes to slippers because he's enjoying
Massagic comfort
Weyenberg Shoe Mfg. Co.

Honest wear in every pair
Marston & Brooks Co.

In step with fashion
Lampe Shoe Co.

It takes leather to stand weather
J. Edwards & Co.

Just do it.
(*athletic shoes*) Nike

Keep children's feet as nature made them
Shaft–Pierce Shoe Co.

Keep in step with Paris
Enzel-of-Paris Inc.

Keep in step with youth
Burdett Shoe Co.

Kiddies' feet are safe in Kinney's hands
G. R. Kinney Co.

Kid flatters the foot
(*Kid Group*) Tanners Council of America

Like walking on air
Weyenberg Shoe Mfg. Co.

Little shoes for little devils
Faust Shoe Co.

Look at your shoes, others do
Florsheim Shoe Co.

Made stronger to wear longer
Fargo–Hallowell Shoe Co.

Made-to-measure fit in ready-to-wear shoes
W. B. Coon Co.

Makes life's walk easy
      L. A. Crossett Co.

Make you want to walk
      Nature-Tread Mfg. Co.

Men wear them everywhere
      Florsheim Shoe Co.

Mighty good shoes for boys
      Teeple Shoe Co.

Miles ahead
      Converse Rubber Co.

More by the pair, less by the year
      Stetson Shoe Co.

More quality than you may ever need
      Timberland Co.

Not the price per pair, but the cost per mile
      Stacy-Adams Co.

Praise for Biltrite comes from the heart but the comfort and long
    wear come from the sole
      Biltrite Rubber Co.

Prince of soles
      Alfred Hale Rubber Co.

Put your feet on easy street
      Weyenberg Shoe Mfg. Co.

Quality at your feet
      Brown Shoe Co.

Rockports make you feel like walking
      Rockport Co. Inc.

Shaped to fit like your stockings
      (*Foot Saver shoes*) Shortback's

She walks in beauty
      Brauer Bros. Shoe Co.

Shoes that often leave everyone natty
      (*Koorc Spat shoes*)

Smart shoes for beautiful feet
    Julian & Hokenge Co.

Soft shoes for hard wear
    Jumping-Jacks Shoes Inc.

Soft shoes for tender feet
    J. J. Grover's Sons Co.

Sole of fashion
    (*Neolite soles*)

Stay put
    Tweedie Boot Top Co.

Sticks like a barnacle
    Sperry Footwear

Stronger than the law
    (*shoes*) Roberts, Johnson & Rand

Sturdy to the last
    Merriam Shoe Co.

Take comfort in our quality
    (*Nine West*) Fisher Comula Corp.

The boot with the muscles
    Beacon Falls Rubber Co.

The easiest kind because skeleton lined
    Florsheim Shoe Co.

The future is here. In sizes 6 to 15.
    (*running shoes*) Nike Air

The great American shoe store
    Kinney Shoe Corp.

The heel that won't peel
    F. W. Mears Heel Co.

The heel with nine lives
    (*Cat's Paw*) Foster Rubber Co.

The jewel of patent leather
    Lawrence Leather Co.

The last fits, the fit lasts
        Goding Shoe Co.
        Stacy Adams Co.

The look that never wears out
        Bass

The man's styleful shoe on a real chassis
        E. T. Wright & Co.

The most powerful shoe in America
        Theo. Bergman

The next level
        (*athletic shoes*) Asics GEL

The prettiest thing on two feet
        Carlisle Shoe Co.

There's double wear in every pair
        Dryden Rubber Co.

The shoe everybody knows, and almost everybody wears
        Melville Shoe Corp.

The shoe of champions
        Keds Corp.

The shoe that understands children
        Stride Rite

The shoe with a memory
        (*Johnston and Murphy*) Genesco Inc.

The shoe with the mileage
        W. H. Walker & Co.

The walk of the town
        Simon Bros.

The washable shoes
        Keds Corp.

They feel good
        Keds Corp.

They'll take you as far as you want to go
        (*Men's shoes*) Bostonian

Footwear

They neither crimp your roll nor cramp your style
Bob Smart Shoe Co.

They're tops for the bottoms
Musebeck Shoe Co.

They walk with you
Melville Shoe Corp.

Time will tell, wear Sundial Shoes
Morse & Rogers

Today's most scientific shoes
W. B. Coon Co.

Turns sidewalks into soft carpets
(*Air Step shoes*) Brown Shoe Co.

Two feet of comfort in every step
W. H. Walker

Uncovered performance
Teva Sport Sandals

Watch your feet
(*foot health aids*) Scholl Inc.

Wear tested for your comfort
(*Jarman*) Genesco Inc.

We're in the shoe business, not show business
Saucony

When you're out to beat the world
(*tennis shoes*) Converse Rubber Co.

World's Fair feet
Selby Shoe Co.

You can't wear out their looks
J. P. Smith Shoe Co.

Your feet are worth Fortunes
Richland Shoe Co.

Your friend
Thom McAn Shoe Co.

Your personal pedestal
(*Adler elevator shoes*)

FRAGRANCES
See PERFUMES AND FRAGRANCES

FRUIT DRINKS
See SOFT DRINKS .

FRUITS AND NUTS
See also FOOD, MISCELLANEOUS

All good things come in pears
> Oregon–Washington–California Pear Bureau

All they're cracked up to be
> (*walnuts*) California Walnut Growers Association

An apple a day is Doc Apple's way
> Pacific Northwest Fruits Inc.

Awful fresh
> MacFarlane Nut Co.

Best for juice and every use
> (*oranges*) Sunkist Growers Inc.

Come on over to the right light
> (*Del Monte Light fruit*) Del Monte Corp.

Crackin' good walnuts
> (*walnuts*) California Walnut Growers Association

Eat more apples, take less medicine
> (*apples*) Virginia Horticultural Society

Every day in some way
> (*prunes*) United Prune Growers of California

Flavor first
> (*fruits*) Del Monte Corp.

Full of sunshine and good health
> California Prune & Apricot Growers

Good to the core
> Pacific Northwest Fruits Inc.

How'd you do your Dole today?
> Dole Food Co.

If you could see inside oranges, you'd buy Sunkist every time
(*oranges*) Sunkist Growers Inc.

Keep regular the healthful way
(*lemons*) Sunkist Growers Inc.

Life's a little fresher with Dole
(*Dole*) Castle & Cooke Inc.

Make Sunsweet your daily good health habit
Sunsweet Growers Inc.

Mott's. It's a good thing.
Mott's Apple Sauce

Nature's candy
California Raisins Advisory Board

One taste is worth a thousand words
MacFarlane Nut Co.

Only three calories a squeeze
(*Sunkist oranges*) Sunkist Growers Inc.

Quite possibly the world's perfect food
Chiquita Bananas

Red apples for red cheeks
Hood River Apple Growers Association

The snack bar from Dole
Dole Bananas

The nuts that get noticed
(*walnuts*) Diamond Walnut Growers

The way the best lemons sign their name
(*lemons*) Sunkist Growers Inc.

They make ordinary occasions special
(*dry roasted peanuts*) Planters Peanuts

They must be good
(*prunes*) Sunsweet Growers Inc.

We grow better snacks
Del Monte Co.

We grow variety
Del Monte Co.

We take the nut very seriously
>> (*packaged nuts*) Fisher Nut Company

When you take cold, take lemons
>> (*lemons*) Sunkist Growers Inc.

FUEL
See AUTOMOTIVE SERVICE, HEATING AND COOKING FUELS,
PETROLEUM PRODUCTS, PUBLIC UTILITIES

FURNITURE
See also BEDS AND BEDDING, INTERIOR DECORATION

A handy kitchen means living room leisure
>> Marsh Furniture Co.

A living tradition in furniture
>> Heritage Furniture Inc.

America's largest sofabed specialist
>> Jennifer Convertibles

Another fine creation by Krueger
>> Krueger Metal Products Co.

At home with your young ideas
>> Bassett Furniture Industries Inc.

At White, fine furniture making is a lost art we never lost
>> White of Mebane

A world of furniture made in a way that makes a world of
difference
>> Kroehler Mfg. Co.

Better your home, better your living
>> Drexel Heritage Furnishings

Built to sustain a reputation
>> Handy Chair & Table Co.

Built to take it ... beautifully
>> Daystrom Furniture Division, Daystrom Inc.

Buy Castle Furniture for your castle
>> Castle Furniture Co.

Carefree furniture
    Viko Furniture

Chairs for all business
    Boling Chair Co.

Classics in their own time
    Scandinavian Gallery

Craftsmen of fine solid wood furniture
    Davis Cabinet Co.

Definitive modern furniture
    Founders Furniture Inc.

Enduring masterpieces
    Kiel Furniture Co.

For the REST of your life
    (*Slumber Chair*) C. F. Streit Mfg. Co.

Furniture of timeless beauty
    Romweber Industries

Furniture that's fun to live with
    H. T. Cushman Mfg. Corp.

If it folds ... ask Howe
    Howe Folding Furniture Inc.

In a word ... it's Selig
    Selig Mfg. Co. Inc.

It's a big country. Someone's got to furnish it.
    IKEA

... Keeping tradition alive
    Meldan Co. Inc.

Leather: An investment in pleasure
    Roche–Bobois Furniture

Making the world safe for baby
    Trimble Nurseryland Furniture Inc.

More than a cedar chest, a piece of fine furniture
    Tennessee Furniture Corp.

Oak for charm and livable character, furniture for your children's children
>Oak Service Bureau, Hardwood Institute

One if by day, two if by night
>(*Sofa-niter*) Charlton Co.

One name in furniture everybody knows
>Kroehler Mfg. Co.

Prevent schoolroom slouch
>American Seating Co.

Push the button back—recline
>Royal Easy Chair Co.

Replete with hidden values, free from hidden dangers
>Snyder's Sani-Bilt Furniture

Sag Pruf will never let you down
>(*Sag Pruf furniture foundation*)

Solid and true, walnut clear through
>(*Gibbard furniture*)

Solid comfort seating
>Hampden Specialty Products Co.

Strong enough to stand on
>(*Samson folding table*)

The chair of amazing comfort
>Jamestown Upholstery Co.

The chair that stands by itself
>Stakmore Co. Inc.

The convertible sofa with accordion action
>(*Sofa-niter*) Charlton Co.

The costume jewelry of the home
>Mersman Tables

The folding furniture with the permanent look
>Stakmore Co. Inc.

The line with the go
>Conewango Furniture Co.

Furniture

The more living you do, the more you need Samsonite
    Samsonite Corp.

The present with a future
    (*West Branch cedar hope chest*)

The South's oldest makers of fine furniture
    White Furniture Co.

Tomorrow is a friend of Dunbar
    Dunbar Furniture Corp.

We help you make beautiful rooms
    Ethan Allen Galleries

GAMES
See TOYS AND GAMES

GARDEN PRODUCTS
See LAWN AND GARDEN PRODUCTS

GARTERS
See HOSIERY

GASOLINE
See PETROLEUM PRODUCTS

GAUGES
See INTSRUMENTS AND GAUGES

GEMS
See JEWELRY AND SILVER

Gifts and Greetings

GIFTS AND GREETINGS

America's best-loved greeting cards
    Norcross Inc.

Greeting cards of character
    Rust Craft Greeting Cards Inc.

Helping you say it right
    Florists Transworld Delivery

It's as easy as FTD
    Florists Transworld Delivery

154

Make a lasting impression
    Teleflora

Replace fear with cheer. Send Christmas cards this year.
    Greeting Card Association

Say it with flowers
    Society of American Florists

Say it with flowers, by wire
    Florists Telegraph Delivery Association

Scatter sunshine with greeting cards
    Greeting Card Association

Send your thoughts with special FTD care
    Florists Transworld Delivery Association

The world's neighborhood florist
    1-800-FLOWERS

What I'm really giving you is a part of me
    (*greeting cards*) Hallmark Cards Inc.

When you care enough to send the very best
    (*greeting cards*) Hallmark Cards Inc.

GLASS AND CERAMICS
See also CHINA AND CRYSTAL

A famous brand in glass
    Latchford Glass Co.

Everyday good ... glass with flair
    Anchor Hocking Glass Corp.

Get it in glass
    Glass Containers Manufacturers Institute

Glassware of distinction
    Czechoslovak Glass Products Co.

Pioneers in colored glass technology
    Houze Glass Corp.

Treasured American glass
    Viking Glass Co.

Glass and Ceramics

Vitrified pottery is everlasting
    Franklin Pottery

GLASSES
See EYEGLASSES

GLOVES
See WARDROBE ACCESSORIES

GLUE
See ADHESIVES

Government Services

GOVERNMENT SERVICE
See also PUBLIC SERVICE

A great way to serve
    U.S. Air Force Reserve

Americans at their best
    U.S. Army National Guard

Be a man and do it
    U.S. Navy

Be all that you can be
    U.S. Army

I Want You
    U.S. Army

Our business is knowing the world's business
    Central Intelligence Agency

Stand up, stand out
    U.S. Armed Forces

The Few. The Proud. The Marines.
    U.S. Marine Corps

The smartest college course you can take
    U.S. Army ROTC

The toughest job you'll ever love
    Peace Corps

You and the Navy. Full speed ahead.
    U.S. Navy

GREETINGS
See GIFTS AND GREETINGS

GUM
See CANDY AND GUM

GUNS
See FIREARMS

HAIR CARE
See also COSMETICS, TOILETRIES

A little dab will do ya
　　(*Brylcreem*) Beecham Products Inc.

Approved by professional hair colorists
　　(*Nestle Color Tint*) Nestle–LeMur Co.

... because it's nice to look younger than you are
　　(*Miss Clairol*) Clairol Inc.

Beautiful hair
　　John H. Breck Inc.

Beautiful hair is as easy as HQZ
　　(*hair preparations*) HQZ Laboratories

Beauty insurance
　　(*cocoanut oil shampoo*) R. L. Watkins Co.

Beauty through science
　　Redken Laboratories

Brush the cobwebs from your beauty
　　(*Kent brushes*)

Clairol is going to make someone beautiful today
　　(*hair color*) Clairol Inc.

Clean hair means a healthy scalp
　　(*Ace combs*) American Hard Rubber Co.

Colors hair inside, as nature does
　　Inecto Inc.

Come alive ... Revive
　　(*Dark & Lovely*) Carson Products Co.

Hair Care

Does she ... or doesn't she
Clairol Inc.

Europe's answer to thinning hair
(*Foltene*) Minnetonka Inc.

Final Net holds up longer than you do
(*hair spray*)

For the fullest, thickest, fluffiest hair you can have
(*Prell*)

Hair color so natural only her hairdresser knows for sure
Clairol Inc.

If I've only one life ... let me live it as a blonde
(*Ultra-blue Lady Clairol*) Clairol Inc.

If you don't look good, we don't look good
(*Vidal Sassoon*) Richardson Vicks Inc.

I'm worth it
(*Preference by L'Oreal hair color*) Cosmair Inc.

Is it true ... blondes have more fun?
(*Lady Clairol Creme Hair Lightener*) Clairol Inc.

It puts the sunshine in your hair
(*Pine Tree shampoo*)

It's the only way to handle a perm
(*PermaSoft*) Dow Brands Inc.

Keep hair-conditioned
The Nawa Co.

Keep it under your hat
(*shampoo, hair cream*) Lan-O-Tone Products

Keeps your color alive
(*L'Oreal Colorvive Technicare*) Cosmair Inc.

Keep your bob at its best
(*bobby pins*) Marcus–Lesoine Inc.

Lets your hair shine like the stars
(*Drene shampoo*)

Makes your husband feel younger, too ... just to look at you!
(*Loving Care*) Clairol Inc.

Never let your hair down
    (*Scoldy Lox bobby pin*) Scolding Locks Corp.

Now that you know you're worth it, aren't you ready for Ultress?
    Clairol Inc.

Only your hairdresser knows for sure
    (*Clairol hair color*) Clairol Inc.

Prell's freshness lasts even the day after you shampoo
    (*Prell*)

Ready to be the Ultimate Blonde
    Clairol Inc.

Reveals all your hair's natural beauty
    (*Alberto VO5 hairspray*) Alberto–Culver Co.

Reveals the hidden beauty of your hair
    (*Halo shampoo*) Colgate–Palmolive Co.

Show off your hair, not the itch of dandruff
    (*shampoo*) Head & Shoulders

Sometimes you need a little Finesse, sometimes you need a lot
    (*shampoo/conditioner*) Helene Curtis Inc.

Sparkling hair that thrills men
    (*Lustre-Cream shampoo*) Colgate–Palmolive Co.

Style has beautiful hair down to a science
    (*Style conditioner*)

The body-building no-lye relaxer
    (*Dark & Lovely Excelle*) Carson Products Co.

The closer he gets ... the better you look!
    (*Nice'n'Easy*) Clairol Inc.

The colorfast shampoo
    Clairol Inc.

The deliciously perfumed hair lacquer
    (*Nestle Hairlac*) Nestle–LeMur Co.

The hair net that sits true
    Sitroux Importing Co.

There's no telling who uses it
    (*Grecian Formula 16*) Combe Inc.

Hair Care

Trade secret of beautiful hair
        Jhirmack

Used by more men today than any other hair tonic
        (*Vaseline*) Chesebrough–Pond's Inc.

Venida rules the waves
        (*hair net*) Roser Co.

Wakes up your hair
        (*Admiration soapless shampoo*)

What's in a name
        Sebastion International Inc.

When you want gorgeous hair
        (*Isuplus*) J.M. Products Inc.

HANDBAGS
See WARDROBE ACCESSORIES

HANDKERCHIEFS
See WARDROBE ACCESSORIES

Hardware

HARDWARE
See also BUILDING SUPPLIES, TOOLS

Are you annoyed by a drip?
        Peerless Plumbers Corp.

Ask for K-V ... it's a *k*nown *v*alue!
        Knape & Vogt Mfg. Co.

Be seated by ... Bemis
        (*plumbing fixtures*) Bemis Mfg. Co.

Built like a bank vault door
        (*laminated padlocks*) Master Lock Co.

Built to wear without repair
        (*plumbing fixtures*) H. Mueller Mfg. Co.

Cammillus has the edge
        (*cutlery*) Cammillus Cutlery Co.

Crane beauty in the open; Crane quality in all hidden fittings
        (*plumbing fixtures*) Crane Co.

ARE YOU ANNOYED BY A DRIP?

... Creating better ways to hold things together
National Screw and Mfg. Co.

Everything hinges on Hager
Hager Hinge Co.

Famous for their razor-sharp edges
(*cutlery*) Remington Arms Co.

Faucets without a fault
H. Mueller Mfg. Co.

Genie keeps you in the driver's seat!
(*garage-door openers*) Alliance Mfg. Co. Inc.

Hardware is the jewelry of the home
McKinney Mfg. Co.

Helps you do things right
(*Stanley hardware*) The Stanley Works

Locks recommended by the world's leading lock experts
(*locks*) Yale & Towne

Mac-It endurance, your best insurance
(*screws*) Strong, Carlisle & Hammond Co.

No sash hardware installs faster than Grand Rapids Hardware
Grand Rapids Hardware

Serving the nation's health and comfort
(*plumbing fixtures*) American Standard

Stop that leak in the toilet tank
Ross Mfg. Co.

The best seat in the house
(*plumbing fixtures*) C. F. Church Division, American Standard Inc.

The safe way out
Von Duprin Division, Vonnegut Hardware Co. Inc.

The shovel with a backbone
Union Fork & Hoe

The silent drapery track
Silent Gliss Inc.

The Tiffany of the bolt and nut business
        R. I. Tool Co.

We took the splash out of the kitchen
        (*Union brass faucet*) Union Brass & Metal Manufacturing

Where quality is produced in quantity
        Sterling Faucet Co.

World's strongest padlocks
        (*locks*) Master Lock Co.

HEALTH AND BEAUTY AIDS
See COSMETICS, TOILETRIES

HEALTH AND FITNESS
See also DRUGS AND REMEDIES, RECREATIONAL EQUIPMENT,
SPORTING GOODS

Body by Soloflex
        (*Soloflex home fitness system*) Soloflex Inc.

Body made in America
        United Health Spa

Consult your doctor about your weight problems
        (*Sego*) Milk Products Division, Pet Inc.

Keep your health in tune
        (*Harmony vitamins*) A. S. Boyle Co.

Life is short. Play hard.
        Reebok

Look for the label with the Big Red "1"
        (*One-a-Day vitamins*) Miles Laboratories Inc.

More precious than gold for good health
        (*Z-Bec Vitamins*) Robins Co. Inc.

No appetite control capsule works harder to help you lose weight
        (*Dexatrim weight loss capsules*) Thompson Medical Co. Inc.

Rational Recovery means never having to say, "I'm sick"
        (*sobriety seminars*) Rational Recovery Systems Inc.

Health and Fitness

The best friend your willpower ever had
(*Slim-Mint Gum*) Thompson Medical Co. Inc.

The HMO choice
(*health maintenance organization*) MCARE

The modern aid to appetite control
(*Slim-Mint Gum*) Thompson Medical Co. Inc.

The most successful weight loss program in the world
Weight Watchers International Inc.

The sugar free taste of sugar
(*Nutrasweet*) G. D. Searle & Co.

The world's best aerobic exerciser
Nordic Track Inc.

Twice the results. Half the time.
(*NordicRow TBX*) Nordic Track Inc.

Your health deserves the best—HAP
(*health maintenance organization*) Health Alliance Plan

Hearing Aids

HEARING AIDS

Better hearing longer
(*Mini-Max hearing-aid devices*)

Hear more, carry less
(*Otarion singlepack hearing aid*)

There IS a difference in hearing aids
Western Electric

Heating and Air Conditioning

HEATING AND AIR CONDITIONING
See also ELECTRICAL PRODUCTS AND SERVICES, HOME
APPLIANCES AND EQUIPMENT

America's fireplace specialists
Heatilator

An above-the-floor furnace
(*parlor furnace*) Allen Mfg. Co.

A single match is your year's kindling
  Bryant Heater Co.

Beauty and warmth
  National Radiator Co.

Brings a touch of the tropics
  (*Flamingo gas heaters*) Jackes–Evans Mfg. Co.

Chases chills from cold corners
  Perfection Stove Co.

Come home to comfort
  Bryant Heater Co.

Cozy comfort for chilly days
  American Gas Machine Co.

Cradled silence
  (*Doe Oil Burner*) Oil-Elec-Tric Engineering Corp.

Don't be satisfied with less than Lennox
  Lennox Industries Inc.

For *any* air conditioning
  Trane Co.

For comfort and pleasure all through the house
  (*heaters*) Arvin Industries Inc.

Furnace freedom
  Penn Electric Switch Co.

Guardian of the nation's health
  (*water heater*) A. O. Smith Corp.

Heat alone is not comfort
  Holland Furnace Co.

Heat, how and when you want it
  Home Appliance Corp.

Heat like the rays of the sun
  American Gas Machine Co.

Heats every room, upstairs and down
  Estate Stove Co.

Hot water all over the house
  (*gas water heaters*) Ruud Mfg. Co.

Hot water at the turn of a faucet
    Humphrey Co.

Kalamazoo, direct to you
    Kalamazoo Stove Co.

Keeps step with the weather
    (*oil burners*) Northern Machinery Co.

Keeps you in hot water
    Humphrey Co.

Lets your pup be your furnace man
    Bryant Heater Co.

Makes its own gas, use it anywhere
    (*radiant heater*) Coleman Lamp Co.

Making houses into homes
    (*stokers, heaters*) Rheem Mfg. Co.

Modern heat with oldtime fireside cheer
    (*parlor furnace*) Allen Mfg. Co.

More people put their confidence in Carrier air conditioning than in any other make
    Carrier Corp.

Nothing to shovel, nothing to explode
    Motorstoker Corp.

Pioneers in smokeless combustion
    Utica Heater Co.

Round the calendar comfort
    Lennox Industries Inc.

See what air-conditioning is doing now ... See Gardner–Denver
    Gardner–Denver Co.

Silent as the rays of the sun
    Silent Glow Oil Burner Corp.

The hotter the water, the whiter the wash
    (*gas water heaters*) Ruud Mfg. Co.

HEATING AND COOKING FUELS
See also PETROLEUM PRODUCTS

A bear for heat
    Fraker Coal Co.

Always 2000 pounds to the ton
    Apex Coal Corp.

America's fastest growing fuel
    Thermogas Inc.

Chief of West Virginia high volatile coals
    Red Jacket Coal Sales Co.

For heating and cooling ... gas is good business
    American Gas Association

Hard soft coal
    Lumaghi Coal Co.

If it's done with heat, you can do it better with gas
    American Gas Association

It's always coal weather
    Stearns Coal & Lumber Co.

Keep the home fire burning
    (*coal*) American Ice Co.

Laugh at winter
    Kopper Gas & Coke Co.

No long waits, no short weights
    North Memphis Coal Co.

Solution of the power problem
    (*white coal*) Wellman–Seaver–Morgan Co.

Stays dustless until the last shovelful
    Giese Bros. Coal Co.

The anthracite that serves you right
    Deering Coal & Wood Co.

The clean, convenient fuel
    Sterno Corp.

The fuel without a fault
    (*coke*) Semet–Solvay Co.

To heat right, burn our anthracite
      Anthracite Mining Association

HERBS
See CONDIMENTS AND SPICES

HOME APPLIANCES AND EQUIPMENT
See also HEATING AND AIR CONDITIONING, KITCHEN
PRODUCTS AND UTENSILS

A bright new world of electric housewares
      (*Norelco*) North American Philips Corp.

A choice of over a million women
      (*stoves*) The Moore Corp.

A cup for two or two for you
      (*percolator*) Metal Ware Corp.

A life preserver for foods
      Alaska Refrigerator Co.

A million in service ten years or longer
      (*refrigerators*) General Electric Co.

A roller rolls and there's ice
      (*refrigerators*) Norge Co.

As simple as touching the space-bar of a typewriter, quick as the
      action of a piano key
      (*Savage ironer*) Savage Arms Corp.

Banishes ironing drudgery
      Proctor Electric Co.

Better because it's gas ... best because it's Caloric
      Caloric Corp.

Better products for a better world
      (*refrigerators*) Norge Co.

Bright ideas from Sunbeam
      (*small appliances*)

Brings happiness to homework
      (*washer*) Bluebird Appliance Co.

168

Build-in satisfaction ... build-in Frigidaire
     (*Frigidaire*) General Motors Corp.

Built for connoisseurs of refrigeration
     Kelvinator Co.

Built like the finest automobile
     (*Whirlpool washer*) 1900 Washer Co.

Buy your last refrigerator first
     Jewell Refrigerator Co.

Change work to play three times a day
     Standard Electric Stove Co.

Cleans without beating and pounding
     (*vacuum cleaners*) United Electric Co.

Cold and silent as a winter night
     (*Sparton refrigerator*)

Come on, breeze, let's blow
     (*electric fans*) Wagner Electric Corp.

Cooking is just a SNAP in an Estate electric range
     Estate Stove Co.

Cook into the future with electronics from Farberware
     (*Farberware Ultra Chef*) Farberware

Cooks with the gas turned off
     (*stoves*) Chambers Corp.

Defrosts itself, saves shut-downs
     (*refrigerators*) Belding–Hall Electric Corp.

Designed by women for women
     (*Hotpoint ranges*) General Electric Co.

Discover the built-in advantages of Kenmore
     Sears, Roebuck & Co.

Even the collars and cuffs are clean
     (*Coffield washer*)

First with the features women want most
     (*Hotpoint*) General Electric Co.

Gets the dirt, not the carpet
     (*Eureka vacuum cleaner*) The Eureka Co.

GE ... We bring good things to life
General Electric Co.

Give her a Hoover and you give her the best
(*Hoover vacuum cleaner*) The Hoover Co.

Ice cubes instantly, tray to glass
(*refrigerators*) Inland Mfg. Co.

Ideas at work
Black & Decker

If it doesn't say Amana, it's not a Radarange oven
(*microwave oven*) Amana Refrigeration Inc.

Irons while it steams
Elder Co. Inc.

Is your refrigerator a Success?
Success Mfg. Co.

It beats, as it sweeps, as it cleans
(*Hoover vacuum cleaner*) The Hoover Co.

It's the woman-wise range
Estate Stove Co.

Jet action washers
(*Frigidaire*) General Motors Corp.

Kelvination, cold that keeps
(*refrigerators*) Kelvinator Co.

Kitchenaid. For the way its made.
(*Kitchenaid appliances*) Hobart Manufacturing Co.

Make it yourself on a Singer
(*Singer sewing machine*) Singer Co.

Making your world a little easier
(*Whirlpool appliances*) Whirlpool Corp.

Matchless cooking
(*Norge ranges*) Norge Co.

Mighty monarch of the Arctic
(*refrigerators*) Grisby–Grunow

Millions of women have their hearts set on a new Maytag
(*washer*) Maytag Co.

CLEANS WITHOUT BEATING AND POUNDING

New ideas for happier homemaking
The West Bend Co.

Nobody knows more about microwave cooking than Litton
(*Litton Microwave ovens*) Litton Systems Inc.

No watching, no turning, no burning
(*toaster*) Waters–Genter Co.

Originator and perfecter of the garbage disposer
In-Sink-Erator Mfg. Co.

Peak of quality for more than 30 years
(*Apex vacuum cleaner*)

Put your sweeping reliance on a Bissell appliance
Bissell Carpet Sweeper Co.

Rigid as an oak
(*Sturdee folding ironing table*) Tucker & Dorsey Mfg. Co.

'Round and 'round and over and over
(*Whirlpool washer*) 1900 Washer Co.

Rubbermaid means better made
Rubbermaid Inc.

Sanitize your dishes sparkling clean!
(*Frigidaire*) General Motors Corp.

Servants for the home
(*Hotpoint appliances*) General Electric Co.

Set it and forget it
(*refrigerators*) Kelvinator Co.

Since 1876, the servant of the well-dressed woman
(*White sewing machine*) White Consolidated Industries Inc.

So beautifully practical
(*ranges*) Jenn-Air Corp.

Takes the burns out of broiling
(*Moore's Hi-Lo broiler*) The Moore Corp.

The crisp dry cold of a frosty night
Iroquois Electric Refrigeration Co.

The dependability people
Maytag Co.

The Eden cleans by gentle means
    (*washer*) Brokaw–Eden Mfg. Co.

The finest cooking system ever created
    Jenn-Air Corp.

The gas range you want
    Caloric Corp.

The house of magic
    General Electric Co.

The iron with the cool blue handle
    Coleman Lamp Co.

The modern bed of coals
    (*electric range*) Tampa Electric Co.

The name that means everything in electricity
    Westinghouse

The original drawer type freezer
    Portable Elevator Mfg. Co.

The professionals in home and family protection
    (*smoke detector*) First Alert

The ranges that bake with fresh air
    Estate Stove Co.

The record is trouble-free
    (*refrigerators*) Kelvinator Co.

The silent servant
    National Refrigerating Co.

The store that never closes
    (*Coldspot freezers*) Sears, Roebuck & Co.

To lighten the burden of womankind
    (*Crystal washer*)

Washes and dries without a wringer
    Laundryette Mfg. Co.

We haven't compromised. Neither should you.
    (*food processor*) Cuisinart

We'll sweep you off your feet
    (*vacuum cleaners*) The Eureka Co.

Home Appliances and Equipment

We're cooking at the table now
(*table appliances*) Chase Brass & Copper

When the mercury soars, keep happy
(*Arctic electric fan*)

Where the nicest people meet the nicest things
Stanley Home Products Inc.

World's oldest and largest manufacturer of electric blankets
Northern Electric Co.

Year in, year out, the perfect servant
(*refrigerators*) Copeland Products

Years from now you'll be glad it's Norge
(*Norge*) Borg–Warner Corp.

You live better automatically with Tappan
Tappan Co.

You never have to lift or tilt it
(*electric iron*) Proctor Electric Co.

Yours for leisure
(*Eureka vacuum cleaner*) The Eureka Co.

HOME MAINTENANCE
See CLEANING AND LAUNDRY PRODUCTS, PEST CONTROL

Hosiery

HOSIERY
See also CLOTHING, MISCELLANEOUS; FOOTWEAR;
UNDERWEAR; WARDROBE ACCESSORIES

All that its name implies
True Shape Hosiery Co.

A mile of silk, inspected inch by inch
Berkshire Knitting Mills

As you like it
J. R. Baston Co. Inc.

Because you love nice things
(*silk stockings*) Van Raalte Co. Inc.

Finer seamless stockings
     Oleg Cassini Inc.

For every walk in life
     (*socks*) Monarch Knitting Co., Ltd.

For good and FITTING reasons
     (*Kayser gloves and hosiery*) Kayser–Roth Glove Co. Inc.

For sheer loveliness wear Chatelaine Silk Hosiery
     St. Johns Silk Co.

Hanes knows how to please him
     (*hosiery*) Hanes Corp.

It lox the sox
     Pittsburgh Garter Co.

Knit to fit with the comfort foot
     Burson Knitting Co.

Long mileage hosiery
     Phoenix Hosiery Co.

Miles of wear in every pair
     (*Rollins Runstop*) Rollins Hosiery

No metal can touch you
     (*Paris garters*) A. G. Stein Co.

Nothing beats a great pair of L'eggs!
     (*L'eggs pantyhose*) L'eggs Products Inc.

Sheer, sheer, Berkshire
     Berkshire Knitting Mills

She's got L'eggs
     (*Sheer Elegance*) L'eggs Products Inc.

Sings its own praise
     Rosenberg & Brand

Take to water like a duck
     (*Adler socks*) Burlington Industries Inc.

The lady prefers Hanes
     Hanes Corp.

The leg of nations, before the court of the world
     (*men's garters*) Sidley Co.

The new air-rolled garter
Novelty Rubber Sales Co.

The smartest thing on two feet
(*Esquire socks*) Kayser–Roth Hosiery Co. Inc.

The sock America wears to work
Nelson Knitting Co.

The support of a nation
(*Paris garters*) A. G. Stein Co.

They do things for your legs
Rollins Hosiery Mills

They fit
(*Round-the-Clock*) National Mills Division, U. S. Industries

To uphold your sox, trousers and dignity
(*Barrthea garters and suspenders*)

Try them on for sighs
(*Strutwear nylons*) Kayser–Roth Hosiery Co. Inc.

Wash them any way you like, we guarantee the size
(*Adler socks*) Burlington Industries Inc.

Wear Kayser, you owe it to your friends
(*gloves and hosiery*) Kayser–Roth Corp.

You can fool Mother Nature
(*hosiery*) Donna Karan New York

You just know she wears them
McCallum Hosiery Co.

You're asking for a good sock
(*Westminster socks*)

Your legs will thank you
(*Brighton Wide-Web garters*) Pioneer Suspender Co.

HOTELS AND MOTELS
See also TRAVEL

Aglow with friendliness
Hotel Fort Shelby, Detroit, Michigan

A home away from home
   Park Central Hotel, New York, New York

All that is best
   Biltmore Hotel, New York, New York

America's business address
   Hilton Hotels Corp.

America's smartest resort hotel
   Ritz–Carlton, Atlantic City, New Jersey

An hotel of distinction
   Mayfair House, New York, New York

At the crossroads of the world
   Hotel Astor, New York, New York

A welcome change
   Radisson Hotel Pontchartrain, Detroit, Michigan

Boston's most convenient hotel
   The Midtown Hotel, Boston, Massachusetts

Boston's most famous hotel
   Parker House, Boston, Massachusetts

Carnival's Crystal Palace. Go for the fun!
   Crystal Palace Resort and Casino, Nassau, the Bahamas

Coast to coast, we give the most
   Milner Hotels

Convenient to everywhere
   Rittenhouse Hotel, Philadelphia, Pennsylvania

Downtown St. Louis at your doorstep
   Hotels Mayfair and Lennox, St. Louis, Missouri

Exotic by nature. Civilized by choice.
   Ocean Reef Club, Key Largo, Florida

Feel the Hyatt touch
   Hyatt Hotels & Resorts

First class service. With room to enjoy it.
   Guest Quarters Suite Hotels

Front door to the Back Bay
   The Westin Hotel Copley Place, Boston, Massachusetts

Hotels and Motels

Get treated like one of a kind, not one of the crowd
Fallswview Resort & Country Club, Ellenville, New York

Holiday Inn is Number One in people pleasin'
Holiday Inns of America Inc.

House of hospitality
Hotel Lincoln, New York, New York

In keeping with a fine old tradition
The Coronado Hotel, St. Louis, Missouri

In San Francisco it's the Palace
Palace Hotel, San Francisco, California

Live in the atmosphere of an exclusive club
Hotels Mayfair and Lennox, St. Louis, Missouri

One of the world's great hotels
Bellevue Stratford, Philadelphia, Pennsylvania

Plump on the Boardwalk
Alamac Hotel, Atlantic City, New Jersey

Register socially
Hotel Delmonico, New York, New York

Right where you want to be in New York
Helmsley Hotels, New York, New York

Service. The ultimate luxury.
Marriott

South's supreme hotel
Atlanta Biltmore, Atlanta, Georgia

Stay with someone you know
Holiday Inns of America Inc.

That enchanting small hotel in Old Santa Fe
Inn on the Almeda, Santa Fe, New Mexico

The antidote for civilization
Club Med

The big hotel that remembers the little things
New Yorker, New York, New York

The desert resort by the sea
Playa de Cortes, Guaymas, Mexico

The elegant place to play
Boca Raton Resort & Club, Boca Raton, Florida

The Enchanted Garden. A place to refresh the soul.
Enchanted Garden Resort, Ocho Rios, Jamaica

The hotel with a duck in every tub
The Colonnade, Boston, Massachusetts

The most dreamed-of spot on Earth
Kona Village Resort, Hawaii

The nation's innkeeper
Holiday Inns of America Inc.

The natural choice
ITT Sheraton

The only small luxury hotel on San Francisco Bay
Waterfront Plaza Hotel, California

The Plaza pleases
Plaza Hotel, New York, New York

This is living ... this is Marriott
Marriott Motor Hotels Inc.

Today's Palm Beach
The Ocean Grand, Palm Beach, Florida

What price Paradise?
(*Acapulco Princess and Pierre Marquis hotels*) Princess Hotels
International Inc., Acapulco, Mexico

Where love comes to stay
Sandals Jamaica Resorts, Jamaica

Where people really care if you have a good time
(*Marriott hotels, resorts, suites*)

Where your "resort dollar" buys more
Stardust Hotel and Golf Club

Why get a room when you can get a Radisson?
Radisson

INSECTICIDES
See PEST CONTROL

INSTRUMENTS AND GAUGES

Always accurate
> Guarantee Liquid Measure Co.

Always on the level
> The Liquidometer Corp.

It will tell your eyes before your eyes tell you
> (*sight meter*) Tampa Electric Co.

Laboratory accuracy at a toolroom price
> (*Hoke gauges*) Pratt & Whitney

Longest lived micrometer that can be bought
> J. T. Slocomb Co.

No springs, honest weight
> Toledo Scale Co.

Tell the truth
> (*scientific measuring instruments*) A. E. Moeller Co.

The right way to weigh right
> Stimpson Computing Scale Co.

The weigh to profits
> Stimpson Computing Scale Co.

Watches your weight
> (*scale*) Jarcons Bros. Inc.

Weigh the loads and save the roads
> Black & Decker Mfg. Co.

INSURANCE
See also FINANCIAL INSTITUTIONS AND SERVICES,
INVESTMENT

Aetna, I'm glad I met ya
> Aetna Life & Casualty

A man who can't remember his last hailstorm is likely to get one he
> will never forget
> Rain & Hail Insurance Bureau

An idea whose time has come!
Harlan Insurance Co.

A policy to do more
Aetna Life & Casualty

As solid as the granite hills of Vermont
National Life Insurance Co. of Vermont

Because there *is* a difference
The Northwestern Mutual Life Insurance Co.

Be sure, insure in INA
Insurance Co. of North America

Build your future on The Rock
The Prudential Co. of America

Burglars know no season
Standard Accident Insurance Co.

Buy protection, not policies
"America Fore" Insurance & Indemnity Group

Call your Investors man—today!
Investors Diversified Services Inc.

Cheaper insurance is easier to purchase but harder to collect
Standard Accident Insurance Co.

Enduring as the mountains
Western Life Insurance Co.

Ensuring the future for those who shape it
Teachers Insurance and Annuity Association College Retirement Equities Fund

Everyone needs the Sun
Sun Insurance Co.

First in life, first in death
Detroit Life Insurance Co.

For all kinds of insurance in a single plan, call your Travelers man
Travelers Insurance Co.

For doctor bills
Blue Shield

Insurance

Get a piece of the Rock
    Prudential Insurance Co.

Guardian will enrich and safeguard your retirement years
    Guardian Life Insurance Co.

Industry-owned to conserve property and profits
    Factory Mutual Insurance Co.

Inspection is our middle name
    Hartford Steam Boiler Inspection and Insurance Co.

Insure today to save tomorrow
    Rain & Hail Insurance Bureau

Inventor and scientist make dreams come true; the insurance man
    keeps nightmares from happening
    Fireman's Fund Insurance Co.

It is better to have it and not need it than to need it and
    not have it
    Columbia Casualty Co.

It pays to know when to relax
    Metropolitan Life Insurance Co.

It pays to think about it
    Savings Bank Life Insurance

Keep a roof over your head
    North British & Mercantile Insurance Co.

Light that never fails
    Metropolitan Life Insurance Co.

Like a good neighbor, State Farm is there
    State Farm Insurance Co.

Live and die with Assurance
    Maryland Assurance Corp.

Looks out for you
    Sentry Insurance Co.

Make insurance understandable
    Employers Mutual of Wausau

MONY men care for people
    Mutual of New York

More than you expect or pay for
>Auto Owners Insurance Co.

Nationwide is on your side
>Nationwide Insurance Co.

No man's debts should live after him
>Morris Plan Insurance Society

Our business is insuring people's dreams
>Trans America Insurance Company

Our savings are your profits
>American Mutual Liability Insurance Co.

Policies "Good as Gold"
>London Life Insurance Co.

Procrastination is the highest cost of life insurance. It increases both your premium and your risk.
>The Union Central Life Insurance Co.

Protecting the nation—through hometown agents
>Great American Insurance Co.

Protect what you have
>Insurance Co. of North America

Provident Mutual for stability, safety, security
>Provident Mutual Life Insurance Co.

P. S.—Personal Service
>Aetna Life & Casualty

Safe and sound
>Peoples Fire Insurance Co.

Serving you around the world ... around the clock
>The St. Paul Insurance Co.

Six and a half billion dollars of protection for our policyholders
>Great West Life Assurance Co.

Solid as the continent
>North American Life

The Aetna-izer, a man worth knowing
>Aetna Life & Casualty

Insurance

The Blue Chip company
    Connecticut Mutual Life Insurance Co.

The financial company that gives you an edge
    Principle Mutual Life Insurance Co.

The fourth necessity
    Metropolitan Life Insurance Co.

The future belongs to those who prepare for it
    Prudential Insurance Co.

The "good hands" people
    Allstate Insurance Co.

The greatest name in health insurance
    Mutual of Omaha Insurance Co.

The man with the plan
    Employers' Group Insurance

The name again ... Nationwide Life
    Nationwide Insurance Co.

The New York Agent in your community is a good man to know
    New York Life Insurance Co.

The older we get, the younger we think
    AFIA Worldwide Insurance

The power of the pyramid is working for you
    Trans America Insurance Company

The Prudential has the strength of Gibraltar
    Prudential Insurance Co.

There's no obligation ... except to those you love
    Metropolitan Life Insurance Co.

The seal of certainty upon an insurance policy
    Hartford Fire Insurance Co.

We aim to humanize the science of insurance
    Manufacturers Liability Insurance Co.

We can help you here and now. Not just hereafter.
    John Hancock Companies

We help you keep your promises
    MassMutual

We want you with us
Transamerica Occidental Life

When you do business with a conscience, everyone benefits
Consumers United Insurance Co.

Where people and ideas create security for millions
Connecticut General Life Insurance Co.

Wise men seek wise counsel
Employers Liability Assurance Corp.

With everything American, tomorrow is secure
American Insurance Co.

World leaders in insurance and financial services
AIG Insurance Cos.

You can bank on Bankers
Bankers Accident Insurance Co.

You can count on what we know
UNUM

You can get all types of insurance under the Travelers umbrella
Travelers Insurance Co.

You're in good hands with Allstate
Allstate Insurance Co.

Your guardian for life
Guardian Life Insurance Co.

Your peace of mind is worth the premium
National Surety Co.

INTERIOR DECORATION
See also BUILDING SUPPLIES, FLOOR COVERINGS, FURNITURE,
PAINT AND PAINTING SUPPLIES

A shade is only as good as its rollers
Stewart Hartshorn Co.

Dare you move your pictures?
(*Sunworthy wallpapers*) Reed Ltd.

For connoisseurs by connoisseurs
Mottahedeh and Sons

Interior Decoration

For the decorator touch
> (*Best Pleat Nip-tite*) Conso Products Co., Consolidated Foods Corp.

Oldest in permanent type wall coverings
> Frederic Blank and Co. Inc.

Quality-made by Illinois Shade
> Illinois Shade Division, Slick Industrial Co.

The look of quality
> La Barge Mirrors Inc.

The surprise of Formica products
> Formica Corp.

The wipe-clean wall covering
> Columbus–Union Oil Cloth Co.

Tone the sunlight with window shades just as you tone the electric light with lamp shades
> (*window shades*) Columbia Mills Inc.

Tops everything for lasting beauty
> (*Nevamar*) National Plastics Products Co.

Wipe off the dust
> (*Sanitas wall covering*) Standard Textile Products Co.

Investment

INVESTMENT
See also FINANCIAL INSTITUTIONS AND SERVICES, INSURANCE

Bonds that grow in security
> Baker, Frentress & Co.

Complete brokerage service in the world's markets
> Fenner, Beane, & Co.

Depression spells opportunity for the real investor
> Sloat & Scanlon

... Helping people and business help themselves
> Commercial Credit Co.

Help yourself as you help your country
> United States Savings Bonds

Instant news service
Dow Jones and Co.

Lots of satisfaction
Miami Realty Co.

Merrill Lynch is bullish on America
Merrill Lynch Pierce Fenner and Smith

Minds over money
(*Shearson/American Express*) American Express Co.

Own your share of American business
New York Stock Exchange Members

Safe as America
United States Savings Bonds

Smith Barney. They make money the old-fashioned way ...
they earn it.
Smith Barney

Take stock in America
U.S. Savings Bonds

The growth fund
National Investors Corp.

Trust us to make it work for you
(*Sears Financial Network*) Sears, Roebuck & Co.

When E. F. Hutton talks, people listen
E. F. Hutton

Where your dollar works harder ... grows bigger!
Insured Savings and Loan Associations

Working funds for industry
Walter E. Heller and Co.

You look like you just heard from Dean Witter
Dean Witter Reynolds

Your investment success is our business
Francis I. duPont and Co.

JETS
See AEROSPACE, AIR TRAVEL AND CARGO

JEWELRY AND SILVER
See also WARDROBE ACCESSORIES

A diamond is forever
     DeBeers Consolidated Mines Ltd.

America's leading silversmiths since 1831
     Gorham Division, Textron Inc.

Art in diamond rings
     B. & E. J. Gross Co.

Bejeweled by Gaylin
     Gaylin Jewelry Co.

Beloved by brides for almost a century
     (*ArtCarved rings*) ArtCarved Inc.

Could it be the real thing?
     (*pearls*) Marvella Inc.

Diamonds win hearts
     Loftis Bros. & Co.

Express your individuality
     Continental Jewelry Co.

Fine fashion Jewelry
     Sarah Coventry Inc.

For that breath-taking moment
     (*Lady Crosby diamond rings*)

From generation to generation
     (*Heirloom Sterling*) Oneida Ltd.

Give the girl of your choice the ring of her choice
     A. H. Pond Co.

Grows more beautiful with use
     Wallace Silversmiths

It's smart to choose the finest sterling
     Reed and Barton

Jewelers to the sweethearts of America for three generations
     Loftis Bros. & Co.

Jewelry of tradition for the contemporary man
     Swank Inc.

Let's make it for keeps
      (*Community silver*) Oneida Ltd.

Modern silver with the beauty of old masterpieces
      (*Watson sterling*) Wallace Silversmiths

Never a love so true, never a ring so cherished
      (*Keepsake diamond ring*) Lenox Inc.

Serve it in silver
      Benedict Mfg. Co.

Silver with a past, a present, and a future
      International Silver Co.

Sterling of lasting good taste
      (*Lunt silverware*) Lunt Silversmiths

The choice you make once for a life-time
      (*sterling*) Wallace Silversmiths

The originator of cultured pearls
      K. Mikimoto Inc.

There is no finer sterling silver than Fine Arts
      (*Fine Arts sterling silver*)

The world's best way to wear gold
      Krugerrand Coin Jewelry

The world's most precious simulated pearls
      Majorca

When it looks this good ... it's got to be DANSK
      Dansk International Design

JOB PLACEMENT
See EMPLOYMENT

JUICES
See BEVERAGES, MISCELLANEOUS

KITCHEN PRODUCTS AND UTENSILS
See also BAKED GOODS AND BAKING SUPPLIES, CHINA,
HOME APPLIANCES AND EQUIPMENT

Better meals by the minute
(*pressure cooker*) Landers, Frary & Clark

Built to be the last cookware you'll ever buy
Calphalon

For better and faster cooking
(*Pyrex cookware*) Corning Glass Works

From generation to generation
(*aluminum ware*) Wagner Mfg. Co.

Liquids or solids they keep hot or cold
(*vacuum bottle*) Cannon Oiler Co.

Makes that long haul to the curb seem shorter
(*Baggies trash bags*) Colgate–Palmolive Co.

New Hearth. Around great names, great kitchens are built.
(*kitchen equipment retailer*) New Hearth

No-stick cooking with no-scour clean-up
(*Teflon*) Du Pont

Nothing else stacks up to it
(*Microwave Cookware*) Rubbermaid Inc.

Now, more WEAR than EVER
(*Wear-Ever aluminum*) Wear-Ever Aluminum Inc.

Reflects good housekeeping
(*Mirro aluminum*) Aluminum Goods Mfg. Co.

The best cooks use aluminum
Aluminum Ware Association

The can opener people
Dazey Products Co.

The finest food preparer for the home
(*Kitchenaid mixer*) Hobart Corp.

The pressure cooker people
National Presto Industries Inc.

There's no better way to protect your investment
(*Ziplock storage bags*) Dow Chemical Co.

We lock in freshness
Tupperware

Worthy to become heirlooms
(*kitchenware*) Rome Mfg. Co.

KNITTING SUPPLIES
See SEWING AND KNITTING SUPPLIES

LAMPS
See LIGHTING PRODUCTS

LAUNDRY PRODUCTS
See CLEANING AND LAUNDRY PRODUCTS

LAWN AND GARDEN PRODUCTS
See also PEST CONTROL

A complete plant food, not just a stimulant
Olds & Whipple

A home is known by the lawn it keeps
Associated Seed Growers

A midget in size, a giant in power
Gravely Motor Plow & Cultivator Co.

Be wiser—buy Keiser
(*shears*) Keiser Mfg. Co.

Famous for power mowers for over 50 years
(*Toro*) Wheel Horse Products Co.

Father of tree surgery
Davey Tree Expert Co.

For everything green that grows
Loma Plant Food

Grow what you eat
(*seeds*) S. L. Allen & Co.

It's not a home until it's planted
Hillsdale Nurseries

Lawn and Garden Products

Kill lawn weeds without killing grass
    (*Weedone*) Union Carbide Agricultural Products Co.

Lets you take weekends easy the year around
    (*garden tractor*) Deere and Co.

Make every plot a garden spot
    Best Seed Co.

Next best to rain
    Double Rotary Sprinkler Co.

Nothing runs like a Deere
    John Deere Tractors

Quickly kills garden pests
    (*Snarol*) Antrol Laboratories

Reo Reliables ... the powerful performers
    Wheel Horse Products Co.

Seeds of satisfaction
    Associated Seed Growers

Spray "Jake" for safety sake
    (*insecticide*) Elkay Products Corp.

The lawn people
    O. M. Scott and Co.

The modern way to grow
    (*sprinkler*) National Rain Bird Sales and Engineering Corp.

The properly balanced organic plant food
    Olds & Whipple

There's simply nothing else quite like it under the sun
    (*Garden Way Sun Room/Solar Greenhouse*) Garden Way Research

The weed exterminator
    (*herbicide*) Reade Mfg. Co.

The year 'round insecticide
    McCormick & Co.

LIGHTING PRODUCTS
See also ELECTRICAL PRODUCTS AND SERVICE, HOME
APPLIANCES AND EQUIPMENT, INTERIOR DECORATION

After sunset, Lightoliers
  Lightolier Inc.

A full package of light
  Hygrade Sylvania Corp.

American dark chaser
  (*lamps and lanterns*) American Gas Machine Co.

A penny a night for the finest light
  Coleman Lamp Co.

Bores a 300-foot hole in the night
  Niagara Searchlight Co.

Brayco Light makes all things clear
  Bray Screen Products

Brightens the night
  Fullerton Electric Co.

Brite-Lite has a brilliant future
  Britelite Co.

Built for a palace, priced for a cottage
  Moe–Bridges Co.

Buy a How searchlight today, you may need it tonight
  How Lamp & Mfg. Co.

Daylight's only rival
  Silverglo Lamps Inc.

Eye-ease at the snap of the switch
  Silverglo Lamps Inc.

Give long-lasting light, bullet-fast
  (*Winchester flashlight*)

Guardian lighting
  Guardian Light Co.

Jewelry for the home
  Greene Bros. Inc.

Kind to the eyes
(*Emeralite desk lamp*) H. G. McFadden & Co.

Lamps for see-ability
Westinghouse Electric Corp.

Lamps of elegance
Frederick Cooper Lamps Inc.

Lighting from concealed sources
National X-Ray Reflector Co.

Lighting over a million homes tonight
Aladdin Mfg. Co.

Lights the home, lightens the works
Gray & Davis Inc.

Put your lighting up to Whiting
H. S. Whiting Co.

Safe as sunshine
(*lanterns*) R. E. Dietz Co.

The double duty searchlight
F. W. Wakefield Brass Co.

The lamp that chases gloom and glare
Silverglo Lamps Inc.

The lamp with the 1500-hour guarantee
Solex Co., Ltd.

The light that always shines welcome
Coleman Lamp Co.

The light that never fails
Rapid Mfg. Co.

The light to live with
Duplex Lighting Works of General Electric

The sunshine of the night
Coleman Lamp Co.

Turns night into day
Gleason Tiebout Glass

BORES A 300-FOOT HOLE IN THE NIGHT

LINENS
See BEDS AND BEDDING

LINGERIE
See UNDERWEAR

Liquors

LIQUORS
See also BEER AND ALE;   BEVERAGES, MISCELLANEOUS;   WINES

A blend of all straight whiskies
> (*Paul Jones whiskey*) Summit Sales Co.

Aged for 8
> (*Bell's Blended scotch*) Heublein Inc.

A gentleman's drink
> (*Cutty Sark Whiskey*) Berry Bros. & Co.

A glorious beginning
> (*Pinch scotch*) Renfield Importers Ltd.

America's most famous bouquet
> (*Four Roses whiskey*) Four Roses Distillers Co.

America's social-light whiskey
> Ben Burk Inc.

An American gentleman's whiskey since 1860
> (*Hunter whiskey*) Four Roses Distillers Co.

A new high in whiskey smoothness
> (*Ten High whiskey*) Hiram Walker Inc.

"An inch of Pinch, please."
> (*scotch*) Renfield Importers Ltd.

A noble Scotch
> Train & McIntyre Ltd.

A rainbow of distinctive flavors
> (*cordials*) Hiram Walker Inc.

Arrow means quality in any language
> Arrow Liquors Co.

A singular experience
> (*Tanqueray gin*) Somerset Importers Ltd.

A truly great name among America's great whiskies
    (*Old Crow*) National Distillers and Chemical Corp.

Baileys raises the art of the everyday
    (*Baileys Original Irish Cream Liqueur*) Paddington Corp.

Best buy in rye
    Kasko Distillers Corp.

Blended whiskey of character
    Carstairs Bros.

Born where a king of France was born
    (*Otard cognac*)

Break away from the ordinary
    (*Seagram's V.O.*) Seagram's Distillers

Charcoal mellowed drop by drop
    Jack Daniels Distillery

Cheerful as its name
    (*Old Sunny Brook whiskey*)

Clean clear through
    (*rye*) Continental Distilling Corp.

Clean, smooth and unmistakably refreshing
    (*C.J. Wray Dry Rum*) Carriage House Imports Ltd.

Clear heads call for Calvert
    (*Calvert blended whiskey*) J. E. Seagram & Sons Inc.

Don't be vague ... ask for Haig and Haig
    Renfield Importers Ltd.

Drink moderately, insist on quality
    James Clark Distilling Corp.

Dutch name, world fame
    (*Bols liqueurs*) Brown–Forman Distillers Corp.

Enjoyable always and *all* ways
    (*rum*) Bacardi Imports Inc.

Everything it touches turns delicious
    (*Kahlua*) Maidstone Wine & Spirits Inc.

Excitement you can taste
    (*Hazelnut Liquor*) Avon Liquors Company

Famous. Smooth. Mellow.
  (*Old Crow*) National Distillers and Chemical Corp.

Fine coffee liqueur ... from sunny Mexico
  (*Kahlua*) Jules Berman and Associates Inc.

Fine whiskey on the *mild* side
  (*Corby's*) Jas. Barclay and Co. Ltd.

Finlandia. Vodka from the top of the world.
  Alko Ltd.

Fond of things Italiano? Try a sip of Galiano.
  Liquor Division, McKesson & Robbins Inc.

For a man who plans beyond tomorrow
  J. E. Seagram & Sons Inc.

For men of distinction
  (*Calvert blended whiskey*) J. E. Seagram & Sons Inc.

For men who know fine whiskies
  (*Kentucky Tavern*) Glenmore Distilleries Co.

For the king of old-fashioneds
  (*King whiskey*)

For the man who cares
  (*White Seal whiskey*) Carstairs Bros.

Gentle as a lamb
  (*scotch whiskey*) Train & McIntyre Ltd.

Gets a hand in any land
  Arrow Liquors Co.

Give your guest what he wishes
  National Distilleries

Good taste is always an asset
  (*Johnnie Walker scotch*) Schiefflin & Somerset Co.

Have the genius to chill it
  (*Chartreuse*) Schiefflin and Co.

Head of the bourbon family
  (*Old Grand-Dad bourbon*) National Distillers and Chemical Corp.

Home is where you find it
(*Smirnoff vodka*) Heublein Inc.

If it isn't P. M., it isn't an evening
(*P. M. whiskey*)

If you can find a better bourbon ... buy it!
(*Ancient Age Bourbon*)

It leaves you breathless
(*Smirnoff vodka*) Heublein Inc.

It's the flavor
(*Teachers Scotch*) Bacardi Imports Inc.

It's "velveted"
(*Imperial whiskey*) Hiram Walker Inc.

Jamaica's legendary liqueur
(*Tia Maria*) W. A. Taylor and Co.

Just smooth, very smooth
(*Johnnie Walker Red Label scotch*) Somerset Importers Ltd.

Known by the company it keeps
(*Seagram's Canadian V.O.*) J. E. Seagram & Sons Inc.

La grande liqueur Française
(*DOM Benedictine*) Julius Wile Sons and Co. Inc.

Light or dry, in step with the times
(*Maraca rum*)

Mist Behavin'
(*Canadian Mist liqueur*) Brown–Forman Beverage Co.

Needs no chaser
(*Spot Bottle whiskey*) Ben Burk Inc.

No extravagant claims, just a real good product
(*Brown Friar whiskey*)

No Scotch improves the flavour of water like Teachers
(*Teachers Scotch*) Bacardi Imports Inc.

Not a drop is sold till it's seven years old
(*John Jameson whiskey*) John Jameson & Son

Nothing else quite measures up
(*Walker's DeLuxe bourbon*) Hiram Walker Inc.

Liquors

Red stands out. Tastefully.
>(*Johnnie Walker Red Label scotch*) Somerset Importers Ltd.

Remember Ronrico, best rum, bar none
>Ronrico Corp.

Same great whiskey today as before the war
>(*Four Roses whiskey*) Four Roses Distillers Co.

Savor the taste of time
>(*Pinch 15-year-old scotch* Schenley Imports Inc.

Say Galliano instead of goodnight
>(*Liquore Galliano*)

Say Seagram's and be sure
>(*whiskey*) J. E. Seagram & Sons Inc.

Signed, sealed, and delicious
>(*Old Taylor whiskey*) National Distillers and Chemical Corp.

Smooth as silk, but not high hat
>(*Kessler's blended whiskey*) The Seagram Co. Ltd.

Smooth sippin' Tennessee whiskey
>Jack Daniels Distillery

Taste the magic
>(*Bailey's Irish Cream liqueur*)

Taste the temptation
>Scoresby Scotch

The brandy of Napoleon
>(*Courvoisier cognac*) W. A. Taylor and Co.

The centaur ... your symbol of quality
>(*Remy–Martin cognac*) Renfield Importers Ltd.

The crown jewel of England
>(*Beefeater gin*) Kobrand Corp.

The crystal clear gin in the crystal clear bottle
>American Distilling Corp.

The first taste will tell you why!
>Fleischmann Distilling Corp.

The gold medal whiskey
>(*I. W. Harper bourbon*) Schenley Industries Inc.

The grand old drink of the South
    (*Southern Comfort whiskey*) Southern Comfort Corp.

The heart of a good cocktail
    (*Gordon's gin*) Schenley Industries Inc.

The imported one
    (*Beefeater gin*) Kobrand Corp.

The man who cares says: "Carstairs White Seal"
    (*whiskey*) Carstairs Bros.

The medal Scotch of the world
    (*Dewar's*) Schenley Industries Inc.

The possibilities are endless
    (*Gordon's gin*) Renfield Importers Ltd.

The responsibility of being the best
    (*Wild Turkey bourbon*) Austin, Nichols and Co. Inc.

The right spirit
    (*Teachers Scotch*) Bacardi Imports Inc.

The Scotch with character
    (*Black and White*) Fleischmann Distilling Corp.

The sportsman's whiskey
    W. A. Taylor & Co.

The true old-style Kentucky bourbon
    (*Early Times bourbon*) Brown–Forman Distillers Corp.

The whiskey with no regrets
    Oldetyme Distilling Co.

The whiskey you feel good about
    (*Golden Wedding*) J. S. Finch & Co.

The world knows no better Scotch
    (*Haig & Haig*) Renfield Importers Ltd.

The world's best climate makes the world's best rum
    (*Puerto Rican*) Schiefflin and Co.

Those in the know ask for Old Crow
    (*Old Crow*) National Distillers and Chemical Corp.

Time works wonders
    (*Seagram's whiskey*) J. E. Seagram & Sons Inc.

Ultimately, there's Black
    (*Johnnie Walker Black Label scotch*) Schiefflin & Somerset Co.
    Inc.

Wed in the wood
    (*Old Thompson whiskey*) Glenmore Distilleries Co.

Welcomed in the best homes
    (*Royal Banquet whiskey*) Glenmore Distilleries Co.

We'll wait. Grant's 8.
    (*scotch*) Austin, Nichols and Co. Inc.

When you would serve the best
    (*Johnnie Walker scotch*) Somerset Importers Ltd.

LOCKS
See HARDWARE

LUGGAGE
See also TRAVEL

America's best traveling companion
    (*trunks*) Mendel–Drucker

Built to fit the trip
    (*Miller luggage*)

Built to last through every trip
    (*Rennus luggage*

Created to carry your belongings in perfection throughout your
    lifetime
    (*Halliburton travel cases*)

For people who travel ... and expect to again and again
    (*Stafflight*) The Sardis Luggage Co.

For those who go first class
    Horn Luggage Co.

If you have an instinct for quality
    (*Amelia Earhart luggage*) Baltimore Luggage Co.

Luggage you will love to travel with
    Rauchbach–Goldsmith Co.

Our strengths are legendary
> Samsonite Corp.

So high in fashion ... so light in weight
> Ventura Travelward Inc.

Someone's always looking at your luggage
> Amelia Earhart Luggage Co.

Takes the ''lug'' out of luggage
> (*Karry-lite luggage*)

Take your travel lightly
> Horn Luggage Co.

The luggage that knows its way around the world
> Samsonite Corp.

The trunk with doors
> Winship & Sons

Travel begins with Everwear
> (*trunks, luggage*) Rauchbach–Goldsmith Co.

Travel light, travel right
> (*Val-A-Pak luggage*) Atlantic Products Corp.

Travel with Everwear; Everwear travels everywhere
> Rauchbach–Goldsmith Co.

LUMBER
See BUILDING SUPPLIES

MACHINERY
See also ELECTRICAL PRODUCTS AND SERVICE, FARMING SUPPLIES AND EQUIPMENT, TRUCKS AND TRUCKING INDUSTRY

All work and no play
> Timken Roller Bearing Co.

Always *right* on the job
> The Bowdil Co.

Blue brutes
> Worthington Pump & Machinery Corp.

Machinery

Dependable power, absolute safety
> Troy Engine & Machine Co.

Designed for your industry, engineered for you
> Coppers Engineering Corp.

First in automation
> The Cross Co.

For your pressing needs
> Hydraulic Press Mfg. Co.

Handle it mechanically
> Jeffrey Mfg. Co.

HEAD work always wins over HARD work on pay day
> Chicago Engineering Works

It's wise to conveyorize
> Rapids–Standard Co. Inc.

Known by the companies we keep
> (*industrial machinery*) Baker Bros. Inc.

Machines for total productivity
> Ghisholt Machine Co.

Machines that build for a growing America
> Caterpillar Tractor Co.

Miles ahead
> (*road machinery*) The Galion Iron Works and Mfg. Co.

Moves the earth
> Euclid Road Machinery Co.

Portable pony power
> (*Johnson Iron Horse gas engine*)

Powered by Howard
> (*motors*) Howard Industries Inc.

Progress begins with digging
> Marion Power Shovel Co.

Strong where strength is needed
> Athol Machine & Foundry Co.

The all-purpose one-man crane
> Byers Machine Co.

The performance line
HPM Division, Koehring Co.

The pump of compulsory accuracy
Milwaukee Tank Works

There should be a Lee in your future
Lee Machinery Corp.

The strong arm of industry
Electric Hoist Manufacturers' Association

Who changed it?
H. K. Porter Co. Inc.

MAGAZINES
See PERIODICALS AND NEWSPAPERS

MAINTENANCE
See CLEANING AND LAUNDRY PRODUCTS

MAKE-UP
See COSMETICS

MARKETING
See ADVERTISING

MEASURING DEVICES
See INSTRUMENTS AND GAUGES

MEATS
See also FOOD, MISCELLANEOUS

A Kansas product from Kansas farms
Butzer Packing Co.

All the taste without the waste
(*Council meats*) Indian Packing Corp.

America's first choice for flavor
Armour & Co.

A square meal from a square can
(*Broadcast Redi-Meat*)

Folks favor Fromm's flavor
(*sausage, meat products*) Fromm Bros.

Meats

For those who really like to eat
      Smithfield Ham & Products Co. Inc.

Fresh ideas in meat ... from Hormel
      Geo. A. Hormel and Co.

From the goodness of Louis Rich
      (*Louis Rich cold cuts*) Dykstra's Food Service

From the tall corn country
      (*Dubuque ham*) Dubuque Packing Co.

Hygrade in name. Hygrade in fact.
      Hygrade Food Products Co.

If this Gold Seal is on it—there's better meat in it
      Wilson and Co. Inc.

Meals without meat are meals incomplete
      Theobald Industries

Nobody knows chicken like the folks at Weaver
      (*Weaver Chicken Rondelets*) Weaver Inc.

Our wurst is the best
      (*Mickelberry's sausage*) Mickelberry Corp.

Pick the polka dot package
      Swift & Co.

Smoked with hickory
      (*ham*) Rath Packing Co.

Smoke that never varies from fires that never die
      Swift & Co.

Tastes too good to be good for you
      (*Deli-thin cold cuts*) Louis Rich Co.

The best and nothing but the best is labeled Armour
      Armour & Co.

The best-lookin' cookin' in town
      Armour & Co.

The ham what am
      (*Star ham*) Armour & Co.

The other white meat
      America's Pork Producers

The sandwich spread of the nation
    (*deviled ham*) Wm. Underwood Co.

The Wilson label protects your table
    Wilson and Co. Inc.

With that sweet smoke taste
    (*bacon*) Swift & Co.

You can trust the man who sells this brand
    (*Swift's Premium*) Swift & Co

MEDICATIONS
See DRUGS AND REMEDIES

METALS INDUSTRY
See also BUILDING SUPPLIES

A bronze as strong as nickel steel
    American Manganese Bronze Co.

America's pioneer manufacturer of prefinished metals
    American Nickeloid Co.

Change for the better with Alcoa Aluminum
    Aluminum Co. of America

Developers and producers of extraordinary materials
    The Beryllium Corp.

Die casting is the process ... zinc, the metal
    St. Joseph Lead Co.

For almost any product, aluminum makes it better and Kaiser
    aluminum makes aluminum work best
        Kaiser Aluminum and Chemical Corp.

For strength where the stress comes
    International Nickel Co.

From mine to market
    La Belle Iron Works

If you see rust, you'll know it's not aluminum
    Reynolds Metals Co.

Imagination in steel for the needs of today's architecture
Granco Steel Products Co.

In a word, confidence
The Carpenter Steel Co.

Look ahead with lead
Lead Industries Association

Metal, the fifth medium
Mathews Industries Inc.

Nickel ... its contribution is quality
International Nickel Co.

Nothing equals stainless steel
United States Steel Corp.

Service that never sleeps
Reynolds Aluminum Supply Co.

The house of experience
Mirro Aluminum Co.

The most progressive name in steel
Nippon Kokan

The *specialty* steel company
Latrobe Steel Co.

The steels with the Indian names
Ludlum Steel Co.

Think copper
(*Anaconda*) American Brass Co.

Value engineering favors zinc
American Zinc Institute

What next from Alcoa!
Aluminum Co. of America

Where big ideas turn into aluminum extrusions
Superior Industries Inc.

Where the big idea is innovation
United States Steel Corp.

MOTELS
See HOTELS AND MOTELS

MOTOR OIL
See PETROLEUM PRODUCTS

MOTORCYCLES
See also AUTOMOBILES, RECREATIONAL EQUIPMENT

Come ride with us
     American Honda Motor Co. Inc.

Follow the leader, he's on a Honda
     (*Honda*) American Honda Motor Co. Inc.

Kawasaki lets the good times roll
     Kawasaki Motors Corp.

Through and through
     Harley–Davidson Motor Cycles

Worth the obsession
     BMW

Yamaha—the way it should be
     Yamaha Motor Corp., U.S.A.

MOVIES AND ENTERTAINMENT
See also AUDIO EQUIPMENT, BROADCASTING,
PHOTOGRAPHIC EQUIPMENT, TELEVISIONS, VIDEO
EQUIPMENT

A King can have no more
     (*movies*) Paramount Pictures Corp.

Ars gratia artis
     Metro–Goldwyn–Mayer

Create happy hours
     Selznick Pictures Corp.

Gems of the screen
     Columbia Pictures Corp.

If it's a Paramount picture, it's the best show in town
     Paramount Pictures Corp.

Moral pictures most mothers approve
Hygienic Productions

More stars than there are in heaven
Metro–Goldwyn–Mayer

Movies make many merry moments
Royal Pictures

Only the best can cut it here
Ice Capades

Royal releases release your worries
Royal Pictures

The greatest show on earth
Ringling Brothers and Barnum & Bailey Circus

We are your movie star
(*cable television movie service*) Cinemax

MOVING AND STORAGE
See also TRUCKS AND TRUCKING INDUSTRY

America's most recommended mover
(*Mayflower*) Aero Mayflower Transit Co. Inc.

America's number 1 mover
Allied Van Lines Inc.

Dedicated to people on the move
U. S. Van Lines Inc.

Leave the *moving* to us
Greyhound Lines Inc.

Let Lyon guard your goods
Lyon Van Lines Inc.

Moving with care ... everywhere
United Van Lines Inc.

The *gentlemen* of the moving industry
North American Van Lines Inc.

The people who care about people who move
Fernstrom Storage and Van Co.

WE MOVE FAMILIES, NOT JUST FURNITURE

Moving and Storage

The professionals
>Bekins Van and Storage Co.

United Moves the people that move the world
>United Van Lines Inc.

We move families, not just furniture
>Allied Van Lines Inc.

Musical Instruments

MUSICAL INSTRUMENTS

A beautiful piano with a magnificent tone
>(*Betsy Ross spinet*)

Choice of the masters
>(*organ*) George Kilgen & Son

Choose your piano as the artists do
>Baldwin Piano & Organ Co.

Drum makers to the profession
>Ludwig Drum Co.

Easy to play, pay and carry
>Clark Harp Mfg. Co.

For the home that enjoys home life
>Conn Organ Corp.

Keyboard of the nation
>(*pianos*) Kimball International

Little piano with the big tune
>Miessner Piano Co.

Made by masters, played by artists
>Buescher Band Instrument Co.

Made by OUR family for YOURS
>(*pianos*) Sohmer & Co.

Made with the extra measure of care
>(*Cordova guitars*) David Wexler and Co.

Most famous name on drums
>Ludwig Drum Co.

Music's most glorious voice
>Hammond Organ Co.

No other instrument so richly rewards the efforts of the beginner
    Hammond Organ Co.

One chord is worth a thousand words
    (*pianos*) Sohmer & Co.

The instrument of the immortals
    (*pianos*) Steinway & Sons

The master's fingers on your piano
    Auto-Pneumatic Action Co.

The name to remember in flutes
    (*Armstrong flutes*) Chicago Musical Instrument Co.

The sound investment
    D. H. Baldwin Co.

The tone heard 'round the world
    Wm. S. Haynes Co.

The voice of the cathedrals
    Liberty Carillon

We challenge comparison
    Vose & Sons Piano Co.

With all the grace and beauty of its name
    (*Minute Model Gulbransen piano*) Gulbransen Industries Inc.

World's most respected accordion
    (*Nunziola accordion*)

Wurlitzer means music to millions
    Wurlitzer Co.

You can bank on a Frank
    (*trumpet*) Wm. Frank Co.

NAUTICAL SUPPLIES
See BOATS AND BOATING EQUIPMENT

NEWSPAPERS
See PERIODICALS AND NEWSPAPERS

NOTIONS
See SEWING AND KNITTING SUPPLIES

NUTS
See FRUITS AND NUTS

OFFICE EQUIPMENT AND SUPPLIES
See also COMPUTER EQUIPMENT, COPYING EQUIPMENT, PAPER PRODUCTS, WRITING INSTRUMENTS

A million yards of good will
    (*gummed paper moistener*) A. C. Hummel Co.

A real safe, not a pretense
    (*safes*) J & J Taylor

Built like a skyscraper
    (*steel filing cabinets*) Shaw–Walker Co.

Built to last a business lifetime
    Monroe Calculating Machine Co.

Correct mistakes in any language
    (*erasers*) Weldon Roberts Rubber Co.

Dictate to the Dictaphone
    Columbia Graphophone Co.

Distinguished furniture for distinguished offices
    Stow and Davis Furniture Co.

Don't write, Voice-O-Graph
    (*voice recorder*) International Mutoscope Corp.

End the day with a smile
    (*Royal typewriters*) Royal Typewriter Co. Inc.

Every business form for every form of business
    Baltimore Salesbook

Every year, more Royal typewriters are bought in America than any
    other brand
    (*Royal typewriters*) Royal Typewriter Co. Inc.

First and foremost in microfilming since 1928
    Recordak Corp.

First name in filing
    Oxford Filing Supply Co.

For those who must make best impressions
    (*typewriter supplies*) Shallcross Co.

Get your man, no waiting, no walking
    Dictograph Products Corp.

IBM ... Dedicated to the office: where it is now and where it will be
    IBM

It beats talking!
    (*Omninote printed messager*) Telautograph Corp.

Look and listen
    Fairchild–Wood Visaphone Corp.

Machines should work. People should think.
    IBM

Master of mathematics
    Marchant Calculating Machine Co.

Most modern of lightweight typewriters
    Royal Typewriter Co. Inc.

Precision typewriters
    Olympia Division, Inter-Continental Trading Corp.

Push the button and run
    Diebold Safe Co.

Put errors out of business
    Victor Computer Corp.

Puts its quality in writing
    Eberhard Faber

Puts you ahead in offset duplicating
    (*Kodak Ektalith*) Eastman Kodak Co.

Record systems that talk facts fast
    (*filing system*) Diebold Safe Co.

Speed. Simplicity. Versatility.
    (*business machines*) Dura Corp.

The company with the "know-how"
    Metropolitan Furniture Adjusters

The Document Company
    Xerox Corp.

The machine to count on
    (*Ohner adding machine*)

The machine you will eventually buy
(*Underwood typewriters*) Olivetti Corp.

The quick brown fox
SCM Corp.

The right business form for every form of business
Moore Business Forms Inc.

The safe investment
Gary Safe Co.

The trend to dictaphone swings on
Columbia Graphophone Co.

The world's safest safe
Safe–Cabinet Co.

They express success
Cutler Desk Co.

Think
IBM

We pave the way to save delay
(*office equipment*) Currier Mfg. Co.

Wherever money is handled or records are kept
National Cash Register Co.

World's largest manufacturer of staplers for home and office
Swingline Inc.

World-wide voice writing service
(*Ediphone*)

You can pay more, but you can't buy more
(*Royal typewriters*) Royal Typewriter Co. Inc.

You're better off with Bostitch
Bostitch Division, Textron Inc.

OUTBOARD MOTORS
See BOATS AND BOATING EQUIPMENT

OUTDOOR SUPPLIES
See RECREATIONAL EQUIPMENT, SPORTING GOODS

PAINT AND PAINTING SUPPLIES
See also INTERIOR DECORATION

A liquid finish that decorates as it preserves
    Colfanite Prods. Co.

A little varnish makes a lot of difference
    O'Brien Varnish Co.

All you need to know about paint
    Sherwin–Williams Co.

Beautifies before your eyes
    Hilo Varnish Corp.

Beauty by the brushful
    Brooklyn Varnish Co.

Beauty that protects
    Atlantic Drier & Varnish Co.

Between wood and weather
    Jewel Paint & Varnish Co.

Carter White Lead is concentrated paint
    Carter White Lead Co.

Challenges the elements
    (*paint*) S. Friedman & Sons

Cover the earth
    Sherwin–Williams Co.

Defies the elements
    Flint Paint & Varnish Ltd.

Don't put it off, put it on
    Kuehnle–Wilson

Dries before your eyes
    Hilo Varnish Corp.

Eats paint and bites varnish
    (*Bulldog paint remover*) W. M. Barr & Co.

First because it lasts
(*paint*) Felton, Sibley & Co.

First on the finish
(*Regatta yacht paints*) Baltimore Copper Paint

Good paint costs nothing
Bradley & Vrooman Co.

Heelproof, marproof and waterproof
(*varnish*) Pratt & Lambert

Hit it with a hammer
(*varnish*) Pratt & Lambert

Houses painted with Carter White Lead stay painted
Carter White Lead Co.

If you prize it ... Krylonize it
Krylon Department, Borden Chemical Co.

It's all in the finish
American Cyanamid Co.

Laughs at time
Du Pont

Light in the darkest corner
Gardco Paint Co.

More years to the gallon
(*Dutch Boy*) Pigments and Chemicals Division, National
Lead Co.

Neighbor tells neighbor
Foy Paint Co.

No one knows wood as good
(*Formby's wood finishing products*) Richardson–Merrell Inc.

No other paint stays brighter under the sun
Felton, Sibley & Co.

Paint saves the surface, zinc saves the paint
New Jersey Zinc Co.

Paints fast as man walks
Tennessee Tool Works

Paint with the two bears, it wears
   Baer Bros.

Right on the floor
   Jewel Paint & Varnish Co.

Shows only the reflection
   (*varnish*) Pratt & Lambert

Simply brush it on
   (*Kyanize*) Boston Varnish Co.

Start with the finish
   (*paint products*) I. F. Laucks Inc.

Stops rust!
   Rust-Oleum Corp.

Tested in the waters of the world
   (*Valspar paints*) Valspar Corp.

The coat with nine lives
   National Paint Co.

The disinfecting white paint
   Carbola Chemical Co.

The lead with the spread
   Carter White Lead Co.

The life of paint
   (*linseed oil*) Spencer, Kellogg & Sons

The skill is in the can
   (*paint*) Bradley & Vrooman Co.

The varnish invulnerable
   The Morgan Co.

The varnish that won't turn white
   Valentine & Co.

Tough as the hide of a rhinoceros
   (*Rhino enamel*)

Weather armour for homes
   (*Valspar paints*) Valspar Corp.

Weathers our weather
   Utley Paint Co.

Paint and Painting Supplies

We've been protecting the American dream for over half a century
(*Olympic Stain*)

You may dent the wood, but the varnish won't crack
Pratt & Lambert

You're money ahead when you paint with White Lead
Lead Industries Association

Paper Products

PAPER PRODUCTS
See also KITCHEN PRODUCTS AND UTENSILS, OFFICE EQUIPMENT AND SUPPLIES

A clean that's cleaner than bath tissue alone
(*Sofkins*) Scott Paper Co.

A good business letter is always better ... written on a Gilbert paper
Gilbert Paper Co.

Always correct
Eaton Paper Co.

Always makes good printing better
Northwest Paper Co.

America's cities are Bergstrom's forests
Bergstrom Paper Co.

Any mail for me?
Eaton Paper Co.

A world of paper products—from frozen food cartons to printing paper
International Paper Co.

Brain-built boxes
Milwaukee Paper Co.

Call the Fort
Fort Howard Paper Co.

Chillicothe papers make the best impressions
Chillicothe Paper Co.

Consider paper
Champion Papers Inc.

THE COAT WITH NINE LIVES

Paper Products

Fine letter papers
Eaton Paper Co.

First in carbonless papers
National Cash Register Co.

For every occasion of social correspondence
White & Wyckoff Mfg. Co.

For serving ... it's Erving
Erving Paper Mills

For those letters you owe
White & Wyckoff Mfg. Co.

Good papers for good business
W. C. Hamilton & Sons

H & D delivers the goods
(*shipping boxes*) Hinde & Dauch Paper Co.

If it's paper
Dillard Paper Co.

If you can't fight, you can write
Eaton Paper Co.

Invest in memory insurance
Standard Diary Co.

Lasting impressions begin with Oxford papers
Oxford Paper Co.

Made strong to work hard
(*tissues, paper towels*) Scott Paper Co.

No "peeping Tom" can decipher the contents
(*window envelopes*) Magill–Weinsheimer

Our word of honor to the public
Hammermill Paper Co.

Packed to attract
Hinde & Dauch Paper Co.

Paper engineering
Paper Center Inc.

Paper is part of the picture
Strathmore Paper Co.

Paper makers of America
 The Mead Corp.

Put it on paper
 Wahl Co.

ScotTissue is soft as old linen
 Scott Paper Co.

Send me a man who reads!
 International Paper Co.

Since 1976 ... The leader in quality recycled paper
 Conservatree Paper Co.

Softness is Northern
 (*toilet paper*) Marathon Division, American Can Co.

That reminds me
 Ever Ready Calendar Mfg. Co.

The envelope is the first impression
 Standard Envelope Mfg. Co.

The line with the carbon gripper
 Codo Mfg. Co.

The mark that is a message in itself
 (*Crane's papers*) Crane & Co. Inc.

The nation's business paper
 Howard Paper Co.

The paper people
 Brown Co.

The quicker picker upper
 (*Bounty paper towels*) Procter & Gamble Co.

To get a letter, write a letter
 Eaton Paper Co.

Transos envelope the world
 Transo Envelope Co.

Two layers of softness ... and one is purest white
 (*Aurora toilet paper*) Marathon Division, American Can Co.

We believe in the power of the printed word
 International Paper Co.

Paper Products

Whenever good impressions count, rely on carbonizing papers by Schweitzer
> Peter J. Schweitzer Division, Kimberly–Clark Corp.

Writing paper that welcomes the pen
> White & Wyckoff Mfg. Co.

Your letterhead is the voice of your business
> Rag Content Paper Mfrs.

Your printer's performance starts with fine papers
> Crocker Hamilton Papers Inc.

PENCILS
See WRITING INSTRUMENTS

PENS
See WRITING INSTRUMENTS

Perfumes and Fragrances

PERFUMES AND FRAGRANCES
See also BATH ACCESSORIES, COSMETICS, SHAVING SUPPLIES, TOILETRIES

A new talc with a new odor
> Pompeian Inc.

Anything can happen when you wear Fame
> Parfums Corday Inc.

As different from all other perfumes as you are from all other women
> (*Emir*) Dana Perfumes Corp.

Be swept away to another world
> (*Senchal perfume*) Charles of the Ritz Group Ltd.

Cherished as one of the world's seven great fragrances
> (*Intimate*) Revlon Inc.

Cie. For all the women you are.
> (*Cie*)

Deliberate witchery
> (*Menace perfume*) Evyan Ltd.

England's choicest lavender
> Potter & Moore

Every woman alive wants Chanel No. 5
        Chanel Inc.

Experience the power of femininity
        (*perfume and bath products*) Oscar De La Renta

Feel the power
        (*Drakkar Noir men's cologne*) Guy Laroche

For her. For him. Forever.
        (*Santa Fe men's and women's colognes*)

For men whose emotions run deep
        (*Fathom cologne for men*) MEM Cos. Inc.

For the woman who dares to be different
        (*Emeraude*) Coty Division, Chas. Pfizer and Co. Inc.

High fashion in fragrance from France
        Carven Parfums

It's all in fun
        (*Skylark fragrance*)

Languid splendour set to fragrance
        (*Lentheric*) Yardley of London Inc.

Perfumes of youth
        Cheramy Inc.

Potent essence of desire to touch
        (*White Shoulders perfume*) Evyan Ltd.

Prelude to adventure
        (*Gay Diversion perfume*) Evyan Ltd.

Promise her anything but give her Arpege
        Lanvin–Charles of the Ritz Inc.

Pump some iron
        (*Iron cologne for men*) Coty Inc.

Spirited new scent of the sixties
        (*Richard Hudnut Sportsman*) Warner–Lambert Pharmaceutical
        Co.

Surround your life with fragrance
        Mary Chess

The American symbol of feminine charm
House of Tre-Jur

The daytime fragrance
(*Lentheric*) Yardley of London Inc.

The "forbidden" fragrance
(*Tabu*) Dana Perfumes Corp.

The fragrance of youth
(*April Showers perfume*) Houbigant Inc.

The gay-hearted fragrance
Yardley of London Inc.

The line of least resistance
House of Tre-Jur

The most treasured name in perfume
Chanel Inc.

The perfume of romance
(*Chanel No. 22*) Chanel Inc.

Tussy really cares about the sorcery
Lehn and Fink Consumer Products

We dare you to wear it
(*Sand and Sable*) Coty Inc.

What sexy is
(*Jovan Musk*) Quintessence Inc.

PERIODICALS AND NEWSPAPERS
See also PUBLISHING

A brisk magazine of Parisian life
Paris Nights

A business journal of furnishing and decoration
Good Furniture Magazine

A business paper for the farm chemical industry
Crop Life

A Clean Home newspaper
Press-Telegram, Long Beach, California

A good newspaper
> *Chicago American*, Chicago, Illinois

A human interest newspaper
> *Evening Graphic*, New York, New York

A journal for all who write
> *Writer's Monthly*

A liberal church journal
> *The Churchman*

A live picture tabloid newspaper for all the family
> *Daily Mirror*, New York, New York

All the facts, no opinion
> *United States Daily*, Washington, D. C.

All the flexibility of a newspaper with the coverage of a national magazine
> *United States Daily*, Washington, D. C.

All the news that's fit to print
> *New York Times*, New York, New York

All the news while it is news
> *Automotive Daily News*

Always first, always fair
> *Indianapolis Star*, Indianapolis, Indiana

Always in the lead
> *Detroit News*, Detroit, Michigan

Always reaches home
> *Newark Evening News*, Newark, New Jersey

Always reliable
> *Philadelphia Record*, Philadelphia, Pennsylvania

A magazine for all Americans
> *American Legion Monthly*

A magazine for farm and home
> *Grain Growers Guide*, Winnipeg, Manitoba, Canada

A magazine for farm women
> *Farmer's Wife*

A magazine for southern merchants
Merchants Journal and Commerce

A magazine of better merchandising for home finishing merchants
Furniture Record

A magazine of good, clean humor
Laughter

A magazine only a homemaker could love
Family Circle

A magazine with a mission
Hearst's Magazine

America's best read weekly
Liberty Magazine

America's biggest home magazine
Better Homes & Gardens

America's biggest selling weekly magazine
TV Guide

America's biggest suburban home market
Better Homes & Gardens

America's family magazine
Look

America's investment weekly
Financial World

America's largest dairy magazine
The Dairy Farmer

America's largest Polish newspaper
Everybody's Daily, Buffalo, New York

America's leading power boat magazine
Power Boating

America's magazine for the outdoorsman
Field & Stream

America's most potent editorial force
Life

America's number one sportman's magazine
Field & Stream

America's quality magazine of discussion
Forum

A monthly business paper for chain store executives
Chain Store Age

A monthly magazine devoted to more profitable painting
American Painter and Decorator

An American institution
Saturday Evening Post

A national magazine for dry goods and department stores
Dry Goods Merchants Trade Journal

A national publication devoted to ship operation and shipbuilding
Marine Review

A national publication for the wholesale grocer
Groceries

A newspaper for everybody; it goes into the home
Boston Traveler, Boston, Massachusetts

A newspaper for the makers of newspapers
Fourth Estate

An illustrated weekly of current life
Outlook

An independent newspaper
Los Angeles Evening Herald, Los Angeles, California

An international daily newspaper
Christian Science Monitor, Boston, Massachusetts

A powerful constructive force in the development of Georgia
The Georgian and Sunday American, Atlanta, Georgia

A proud paper for a proud industry
Tavern Weekly

As national as agriculture
Farm Life

A story-telling pictorial of stage, art, screen, humor
American Beauties

Authority of industry, national and international
Iron Trade Review

A weekly for the whole family
Liberty

A weekly magazine of philately
Stamps

A weekly newspaper of insurance
National Underwriter

Baltimoreans don't say newspaper, they say SUNpaper
Baltimore Sun, Baltimore, Maryland

Best bet in Baltimore
News-Post, Baltimore, Maryland

Better your home, better your living
House Beautiful

Biggest, brightest, best magazine for boys in all the world
American Boy

Biggest in the country
Farm Journal

Canada's greatest newspaper
Montreal Daily Star, Montreal, Quebec, Canada

Canada's national farm journal
Family Herald and Weekly Star

Canada's national magazine
Maclean's Magazine

Canada's national newspaper
Toronto Globe, Toronto, Ontario, Canada

Capitalist tool
Forbes

Central Pennsylvania's greatest daily
Harrisburg Telegraph, Harrisburg, Pennsylvania

Chicago's best and cleanest paper
Evening Post, Chicago, Illinois

Chicago's only illustrated tabloid newspaper
Illustrated News, Chicago, Illinois

Chronicle of current Masonic events
Square and Compass

Class magazine in a class by itself
Harper's Bazaar

Covers Spokane and the Spokane country like the sunshine
Spokesman-Review, Spokane, Washington

Covers the country intensively
American Press Association

Dallas is the door to Texas
Dallas Morning News, Dallas, Texas

"Dedicated to serving the families of the West and Hawaii ... no
one else"
Sunset

Deep in the heart of Dixie
Commercial Appeal and *Evening Appeal*, Memphis, Tennessee

Detroit's home newspaper
Detroit News, Detroit, Michigan

Devoted to the best interests of South Florida
Palm Beach Times, Palm Beach, Florida

Dominate Philadelphia
The Bulletin, Philadelphia, Pennsylvania

Don't say "paper," say "Star"
St. Louis Star, St. Louis, Missouri

Don't watch TV in the dark
TV Guide

Each week the facts add up to success
Sports Illustrated

Edited by yachtsmen for yachtsmen
Yachting

Everything in Baltimore revolves around the Sun
Baltimore Sun, Baltimore, Maryland

Fileworthy
Post-Dispatch, St. Louis, Missouri

First, by merit
Milwaukee Journal, Milwaukee, Wisconsin

First for the South
Times–Picayune, New Orleans, Louisiana

First in Chicago
Daily News, Chicago, Illinois

First in Cleveland
Cleveland Press, Cleveland, Ohio

First in Dayton, third in Ohio
Daily News, Dayton, Ohio

First in film news
Film Daily

First in the farm field
Farm Journal

First in the field
Moving Picture World

First magazine for women
McCall's

First to last, the truth: news, editorials, advertisements
Herald–Tribune, New York, New York

Florida's great home daily
Tampa Daily Times, Tampa, Florida

Florida's most important newspaper
Miami Herald, Miami, Florida

Follow the journal and you follow the oil industry
Oil and Gas Journal

For business people who think for themselves
(*Inc. Magazine*) Inc. Publishing Co.

For busy business men
Forbes

For home lovers in cities, towns, and suburbs
Better Homes & Gardens

For oil marketing
National Petroleum News

For the men in charge
Fortune

For the smart young woman
Mademoiselle

Fortune means business
Fortune Magazine

For you and your town
Kansas City Kansan, Kansas City, Kansas

Founder of better homes in America
Delineator

Gateway to the Jewish market
Daily Forward, New York, New York

Give light and the people will find their own way
Scripps–Howard

Go as a travel adventurer
Travel Adventures

Goes home and stays home
Baltimore News–Post, Baltimore, Maryland

Good writing is good thinking
The New York Times Magazine, New York, New York

Greatest concentration in the world's richest farm region
Successful Farming

Great national shoes weekly
Boot and Shoe Recorder

Growing just like Atlanta
The Georgian and Sunday American, Atlanta, Georgia

If you love words, You'll love VERBATIM
(VERBATIM, *The Language Quarterly*) Laurence Urdang Inc.

If you're not in Cuisine, you're not in the kitchen
(*Cuisine*)

Important to important people
Advertising Age

Industry Spokesman to CPI management
Chemical Week

In Philadelphia nearly everybody reads the Bulletin
Philadelphia Evening Bulletin, Philadelphia, Pennsylvania

Iowa's greatest evening paper
Evening Tribune, Des Moines, Iowa

Is the Telegram on your list?
World–Telegram, New York, New York

It costs no more to reach the first million first
National Geographic Magazine

It is our business to help your business
Building Supply News

It's the life they lead, it's the book they read
Better Homes & Gardens

Largest daily circulation in Brooklyn of any Brooklyn newspaper
Brooklyn Standard Union, Brooklyn, New York

Largest evening circulation in America
Evening Journal, New York, New York

Leading clay journal of the world
Brick and Clay Record

Leads among the leaders of today ... and tomorrow
Legion Magazine

Made to order for America's business farmer and his wife
Successful Farming

Magazine of today and tomorrow
American

More than a magazine, a national institution
Maclean's Magazine, Toronto, Ontario, Canada

Much more of the world, much sooner
(*The New York Times* home delivery), New York, New York

National magazine for mothers of infants
American Baby

Never underestimate the power of a woman
Ladies Home Journal

New England's greatest Sunday newspaper
Sunday Advertiser, Boston, Massachusetts

News of consequence for people of consequence
U. S. News and World Report

New York's picture newspaper
    Daily News, New York, New York

No guts, no story
    (Forbes

Nothing to serve but the public interest
    Des Moines Capital, Des Moines, Iowa

Ohio's greatest home daily
    Columbus Dispatch, Columbus, Ohio

Oklahoma's greatest newspaper
    Tulsa World, Tulsa, Oklahoma

One hundred years young
    Youth's Companion

One of America's great weeklies
    Railway Age

One of the West's great newspapers
    Oakland Tribune, Oakland, California

Only one magazine edited for rural women exclusively
    Farmer's Wife

On rearing children from crib to college
    Parents

Our readers manage the country
    Successful Farming

People have faith in *Reader's Digest*
    Reader's Digest

Power farming is profit farming
    Power Farming

Practical poultry paper for practical poultry people
    American Poultry Advocate

Predominant with the 18 to 30 age group
    Photoplay Magazine

Profit by it
    (BusinessWeek)

Promoting Thrift as a viable alternative lifestyle
    (The Tightwad Gazette)

Prosperity follows the plow
   Agricultural Publishers Association

Published in the heart of America: most prosperous district of
   the world
      Kansas City Post, Kansas City, Missouri

Published to promote good farming and right living
   Nor'West Farmer, Winnipeg, Manitoba, Canada

Put your money where the market is
   Modern Machine Shop

Reaches the mother through her child
   Child Life

Reach her when home is on her mind
   American Home

Reaching influential America
   United States Daily, Washington, D. C.

Read and preferred by construction men
   Construction Methods and Equipment

Read *Time* and understand
   (*Time magazine*) Time–Life Inc.

Required reading for the business class
   (*Fortune*)

Salt of the earth, the subscribers to *Needlecraft*, over one million
   of them
      Needlecraft Magazine

San Francisco's leading evening newspaper
   San Francisco Call, San Francisco, California

Saskatchewan's only farm magazine
   Saskatchewan Farmer, Regina, Saskatchewan, Canada

Seattle's only morning newspaper
   Post Intelligencer, Seattle, Washington

Sell at the decision level
   BusinessWeek

Sells hard wherever hardware sells
   Hardware Age

So long as the rig is on the location
Drilling

South America's greatest newspaper
La Prensa

Southern Ohio's greatest newspaper
Cincinnati Post, Cincinnati, Ohio

Sports isn't just fun and games
Sports Illustrated

Start enjoying life
(*Life Magazine*) Time–Life Inc

Starts the day in Detroit
Free Press, Detroit, Michigan

Start with the "heart" where farmers are worth 2 for 1
Successful Farming

St. Louis' largest daily
Globe–Democrat, St. Louis, Missouri

Talk to the right people in the right places
Time

Tell it in the morning, tell it in the *Philadelphia Inquirer*
(*Philadelphia Inquirer*), Philadelphia, Pennsylvania

Texas' oldest newspaper
Galveston News, Galveston, Texas

The best comedy in America
College Humor

The best of the world's press
Woman's Digest

The best way to reach Maturity
(*Modern Maturity*)

The Boy Scouts' magazine
Boys' Life

The business management magazine
Dun's Review and Modern Industry

The business paper of the electrical industry since 1892
Electrical Record

The children's own magazine
Child Life

The dairy paper of the New York City milk shed
Dairymen's League News

The dime that covers the world
News Week

The dominant newspaper of the Great Northwest
Minneapolis Tribune, Minneapolis, Minnesota

The dominant newspaper of the rich Montreal and Quebec Province Market
La Presse, Quebec, Canada

The dry goods daily
Daily News Record

The engineering magazine
Industrial Management

The environmental magazine
(*E Magazine*)

The farm paper of service
Michigan Business Farmer

The farm paper with a mission
American Farming

The farm weekly of largest circulation and most influence
Progressive Farmer

The fastest-growing newspaper and fastest-growing city in Texas
Houston Post–Dispatch, Houston, Texas

The first really different magazine in a generation
Interlude

The gateway to the Chicago market
Herald and Examiner, Chicago, Illinois

The giant of the South
Southern Agriculturist, Nashville, Tennessee

The Globe sells Boston
Boston·Globe, Boston, Massachusetts

The great newspaper of the great southwest
  Los Angeles Examiner, Los Angeles, California

The happy medium
  Judge

The home craft magazine
  People's Popular Monthly

The home paper of the industrial worker and the farmer
  Industrial News

The Jewish market at its best
  Workmen's Circle Call

The Journal covers Dixie like the dew
  Atlanta Journal, Atlanta, Georgia

The journal of diagnosis and treatment
  Modern Medicine

The key to happiness and success in over a million farm homes
  Comfort Magazine

The largest Catholic magazine in the world
  Columbia

The leading journal of the Episcopal Church
  The Churchman

The livest lumber journal on earth
  Gulf Coast Lumberman

The Louisiana–Mississippi farm paper
  Modern Farming, New Orleans, Louisiana

The magazine farm families depend on
  Farm Journal

The magazine farm people believe in
  Capper's Farmer

The magazine for Milady
  Fashionable Dress

The magazine for parents
  Children

The magazine of a re-made world
  Red Book

The magazine of broadcast advertising
Sponsor

The magazine of business leaders around the world
Fortune

The magazine of opportunities
Money Making

The magazine of Romance
McClure's

The magazine of service
The Rotarian

The magazine of the American market
Look

The magazine of the fifth estate
Photoplay

The magazine of Western living
Sunset

The magazine that brings the outdoors in
Outdoor Recreation

The magazine women believe in
Ladies Home Journal

The man's magazine
Beau

The market with the "rainbow round its shoulder"
Pacific Rural Press and California Farmer, San Francisco, California

The massive men's market in print
True

The minister's trade journal since 1899
The Expositor

The modern farm paper
Country Gentleman

The most important magazine to the world's most important people
Time

WORLD'S LARGEST NEWSPAPER

The national guide to motion pictures
Photoplay Magazine

The national magazine of sports and recreation
Sportlife

The national magazine with local influence
American Weekly

The national newspaper of marketing
Advertising Age

The national weekly
Collier's

The national weekly of programs and personalities
Radio Guide

The necessary two million
True Story

The news of the day in the newsiest way
Daily Metal Trade

The newspaper of the buying population
Detroit Times, Detroit, Michigan

The news unbiased and unbossed
Ohio State Journal, Columbus, Ohio

The Newsweekly of Motoring
(*AutoWeek*)

The newsweekly that separates fact from opinion
Newsweek

The no. 1 men's service magazine
Argosy

The oldest farm paper in America
Southern Planter, Richmond, Virginia

The Pacific coast magazine of motoring
Motor Land

The paper that blazes trade trails
New York Commercial, New York, New York

The paper that IS England
Punch, London, England

The pioneer farm journal of Western Canada
Nor'West Farmer, Winnipeg, Manitoba, Canada

The quality magazine of the boating field
Yachting

The real magazine of the small towns
American Woman

The retailer's daily newspaper
Women's Wear

The South's greatest newspaper
Commercial Appeal, Memphis, Tennessee

The Star is Kansas City and Kansas City is the Star
Kansas City Star, Kansas City, Missouri

The state's greatest newspaper
Arizona Republican, Phoenix, Arizona

The taste that sets the trend
Harper's Bazaar

The three-cent quality medium of America's greatest market
World, New York, New York

The trade paper of the home
Modern Priscilla, Boston, Massachusetts

The traveler's world
Venture

The truth without courting favor or fearing condemnation
Kansas City Post, Kansas City, Missouri

The voice of authority
(*Business Week magazines*) McGraw–Hill Inc.

The weekly news magazine
Time

The West's great national magazine
Sunset

The West's great paper
Tribune, Salt Lake City, Utah

The world's greatest Catholic monthly
Extension Magazine

The world's greatest industrial paper
Iron Age

The world's greatest newspaper
Chicago Tribune, Chicago, Illinois

The world's greatest travel publication
Golfer's Magazine

The world's only tourists' magazine
Tourist

They almost talk to you
Pictorial Review

The young man's magazine
Varsity

Through pictures to inform
Life

Thundering power in the eye of the market
Metalworking News

To build a stronger nation
Physical Culture

True stories from real life
Smart Set

We make a difference in 100 million lives worldwide
(*Reader's Digest*)

What's happening. In business. To business.
Nation's Business

Where Anerican dreams still come true
(*Money*)

Where important people turn to say important things
American Magazine

While there is Life there is hope
Life

With youth, first impressions last
Scholastic Magazines

World's best seller
Reader's Digest

World's largest newspaper
        Times, Los Angeles, California

World's outstanding boxing magazine
        The Ring

Written so you can understand it
        Popular Mechanics

You ought to be in pictures
        Parade Magazine

PEST CONTROL
See also CHEMICAL INDUSTRY, LAWN AND GARDEN
PRODUCTS

Better products for man's best friend
        (*Sergeant's*) Polk Miller Products Co.

Dead moths eat no holes
        (*Moth-Tox*)

Doesn't stun 'em, kills 'em
        The Fly-Foon Co.

Don't get bit, get Flit
        (*insect spray*) Exxon Corp.

Double doom to flies and mosquitoes
        (*Fly-Ded insect spray*) Midway Chemical Co.

Guaranteed moth protection
        The Lane Co.

It's bug tested
        (*Black Flag insect spray*) A. S. Boyle Co.

Kills ants in the nest
        (*Antrol*) Antrol Laboratories

Kills bugs dead
        (*Raid*) S. C. Johnson & Son Inc.

Kills crawling bugs where they hide
        (*Raid*) S. C. Johnson & Son Inc.

Kills them off and keeps them off
        (*Pulvex flea powder*) William Cooper & Nephews Inc.

Pest Control

Roaches check in, but they don't check out
    (Raid Roach Motel)

The clean way to kill dirty rats
    (D-Con mouse and rat killer) D-Con Co. Inc.

Wipe 'em out, don't stir 'em up
    (Sergeant's flea powder) Miller–Morton Co.

Pet Food and Products

PET FOOD AND PRODUCTS
See also FOOD, MISCELLANEOUS; PEST CONTROL

A lopsided diet may ruin your canary's song
    The R. T. French Co.

A song in every seed
    (bird seed) The R. T. French Co.

Dog food of champions
    (Ken-L-Biskit) Ken-L-Products Division, Quaker Oats Co.

Dogs stay for Mainstay
    (Mainstay dog food)

From world leaders in nutrition
    (Friskies) Carnation Co.

Full of life, for a lifetime
    (Gaines Cycle dog food) Quaker Oats Co.

Generations of healthy, happy pets
    Alpo Petfoods Inc.

Helping pets live longer, healthier lives
    Ralston Purina Co.

Help make him all the dog he's meant to be
    (Ken-L-Biskit) Ken-L-Products Division, Quaker Oats Co.

Help you cat to Thrive!
    (Thrive! cat food)

Maker of America's number 1 cat food
    (Puss 'n Boots) Quaker Oats Co.

Makes its own gravy
    (Gravy Train dog food) General Foods Corp.

Nothing, but nothing will tear cats away
        (*Friskies Buffet cat food*) Carnation Co.

Nourishes every inch of your dog
        (*Gaines dog food*) General Foods Corp.

Our business is going to the dogs
        Champion Animal Food Co.

Pep for your pup
        Min-A-Gro Corp.

Recommended by top breeders
        Kal Kan Foods Inc.

Special pet foods found only at special places
        (*Iams*)

Taste that calls dogs to dinner
        (*Come 'n Get It dog food*)

The complete family of dog and cat foods from the world leader in
  nutrition
        (*Friskies*) Carnation Co.

Their choice every time
        (*dog food*) Perfection Foods Co.

The taste your dog's been fishing for
        (*Sea Dog dog food*)

When it comes to cooking for dogs—Rival has no rival
        Rival Pet Foods Division, Associated Products, Inc.

When it's time for a change ... Cat's Pride stays fresher longer
        (*Cat's Pride kitty litter*)

PETROLEUM PRODUCTS
See also AUTOMOTIVE SERVICE, HEATING AND COOKING
FUELS

A great name in oil
        Sinclair Oil Corp.

An extra quart of lubrication in every gallon
        (*motor oil*) Quaker State Oil Refining Corp.

Be *sure* with Pure
    The Pure Oil Co.

Blue Sunoco, the over-drive motor fuel
    Sun Oil Co.

Does four jobs at once
    (motor oil) Shell Oil Co.

Economy gasoline
    (Tydol) Tide Water Oil Co.

Engine life preserver
    (motor oil) Quaker State Oil Refining Corp.

Ever since America learned to drive
    Pennzoil Co.

Finest anti-knock non-premium gasoline ever offered at no extra cost
    Union Oil Co.

Fire up with Firebird
    The Pure Oil Co.

Flows fast, stays tough
    Pennzoil Co.

Food for speed
    British Petroleum Co., London, England

For a change, try Sohio
    Standard Oil Co. (Ohio)

For good advice ... and good products ... depend on your Mobil
    dealer
    Mobil Oil Corp.

Full powered
    (Pomiac gasoline) Winona Oil Co.

Gasoline, not cut price guessoline
    Sun Oil Co.

Gives your engine an extra margin of safety
    Pennzoil Co.

Go *first class* ... go Phillips 66
    Phillips Petroleum Co.

Gulf makes things run better
Gulf Oil Corp.

Happy motoring
Exxon Corp. (formerly Standard Oil Co., New Jersey)

It keeps your engine running like new
(*synthetic oil*) Mobil 1

It makes a difference
(*Havoline motor oil*) Indian Refining Co.

It pays to be particular about your oil
Wolf's Head Oil Refining Co. Inc.

It's a lucky day for your car when you change to Quaker State
Motor Oil
(*motor oil*) Quaker State Oil Refining Corp.

Keeps your motor clean as a whistle
(*motor oil*) Sinclair Consolidated Oil Corp.

Knock out that "knock"
Imperial Oil Co.

Makes a better motor, keeps your motor better
(*Hyvis motor oil*)

Making petroleum do more things for more people
Atlantic Richfield Refining Co.

Miles of smiles
Sherwood Bros.

More power to you
National Refining Co.

Oil that goes farther, faster, safer
Pennzoil Co.

Pour smoothness into your motor
O'Neil Oil Co.

Put a tiger in your tank
(*Enco*) Humble Oil and Refining Co.

Puts wings on your car
(*Tydol*) Tide Water Oil Co.

Rely on the Tiger
     Exxon Corp.

See what happens when you start using American ingenuity
     Standard Oil Division, American Oil Co.

STP is the racer's edge
     (*STP oil treatment*) STP Corp.

Superstar power for more car power
     (*Texaco Super unleaded gasoline*) Texaco Inc.

Take it slow, it's rarin' to go
     (*N-tane*) Conoco Inc.

The chevron—the sign of excellence
     Standard Oil Co. of California

The choice of champions
     (*motor oil*) Kendall Refining Co.

The energy to go further
     Texaco Inc.

The extra miles are free
     Lion Oil Refining Co.

The knock-out fuel, nox out nox
     Canfield Oil Co.

The one right oil for Ford cars
     (*Ivaline–Foralyn*) Winona Oil Co.

The pass word of the road
     Sun Oil Co.

There's power in every drop
     Odol Corp.

We are rich in resources
     Williams Pipe Line Co.

We take better care of your car
     Standard Oil Division, American Oil Co.

Wherever shafts move
     (*motor oil*) National Oil Co.

PUT A TIGER IN YOUR TANK

Petroleum Products

World's first—world's finest
>   (*motor oil*) Valvoline Oil Co., Division of Ashland Oil and Refining Co.

Worth changing brands to get
>   The Pure Oil Co.

You can be sure of Shell
>   Shell Oil Co.

You *expect* more from Standard and you *get* it
>   Standard Oil Division, American Oil Co.

You need an oil this good
>   (*Quaker State motor oil*) Quaker State Oil Refining Corp.

PHARMACEUTICAL PRODUCTS
See DRUGS AND REMEDIES

PHONOGRAPHIC EQUIPMENT
See AUDIO EQUIPMENT

PHONOGRAPHS
See AUDIO EQUIPMENT

Photographic Equipment

PHOTOGRAPHIC EQUIPMENT
See also MOVIES AND ENTERTAINMENT

Before it's a memory, it's a Polaroid
>   Polaroid Corp.

Bell and Howell brings out the expert in you (automatically!)
>   Bell and Howell Co.

Canon meets tomorrow's challenges today
>   Canon Inc.

Classics of optical precision
>   (*Schneider lenses*) Burleigh Brooks Inc.

... for a good look
>   (*print paper*) Eastman Kodak Co.

Forever yours
>   (*snapshots*) Eastman Kodak Co.

For superb personal movies
      (*film*) Bell & Howell Co.

If it isn't an Eastman, it isn't a Kodak
      (*cameras*) Eastman Kodak Co.

I'm gonna get you with the Kodak Disc
      (*Kodak Disc camera*) Eastman Kodak Co.

It deserves to be preserved
      Dura Pictures Corp.

Life is a movie; Cine-Kodak gets it all
      (*movie cameras*) Eastman Kodak Co.

One pictograph tells more than a thousand words
      Pictograph Corp.

Only from the mind of Minolta
      (*Minolta X100 camera*) Minolta Corp.

Photographs tell the story
      Photographer's Association of America

Say it with pictures
      Commercial Photo Service Co.

Show your true colors
      (*Kodak Gold film*) Eastman Kodak Co.

The more you learn about photography, the more you count
  on Kodak
      Eastman Kodak Co.

The name quality made famous
      (*Zoom 8*) Minolta Corp.

The negative for positive results
      (*Gevaert film*)

There are no game laws for those who hunt with a Kodak
      Eastman Kodak Co.

The 60-second excitement
      (*Polaroid Color Pack Camera*) Polaroid Corp.

The state of the art now
      (*Pentax cameras*) The Pentax Corporation

Photographic Equipment

We take the world's greatest pictures
(*Nikon cameras*) Nikon Inc.

With Graflex, the payoff is in the picture
Graflex Inc.

World's second largest manufacturer of cameras and films
Agfa–Gevaert Inc.

You press the button, we do the rest
Eastman Kodak Co.

PHYSICAL FITNESS
See HEALTH AND FITNESS

PIPES
See SMOKING ACCESSORIES

PLUMBING SUPPLIES
See HARDWARE

Political Issues

POLITICAL ISSUES
See also PRESIDENTIAL CAMPAIGNS

ERA Yes
National Organization for Women

Feed the poor. Eat the rich.
(*T-shirt*) Timeless Art

God didn't give His only begotten Son to be a spokesman for the
Moral Majority
St. Luke's Episcopal Church

Hell no, we won't go
Vietnam-era draft resisters

If you're not recycling you're throwing it all away
Environmental Defense Fund

Let's wage war on drugs, not on animals. It's time for animal
experimenters to kick the habit.
The American Anti-Vivisection Society

Liberté! Égalité! Fraternité!
rallying cry of the French Revolution

254

Never again
> Jewish exhortation forswearing a recurrence of the Nazi Holocaust

No taxation without representation
> U.S. rallying cry during Revolutionary War

Nuclear energy means cleaner air
> U.S. Council for Energy Awareness

Remember Pearl Harbor
> U.S. rallying cry during World War II

Remember the Alamo!
> rallying cry in the war for Texas independence

Remember the *Maine*
> U.S. rallying cry during Spanish–American War

Replace black on black crime with black on black love
> Black on Black Love Campaign Inc.

Take back the night
> in support of actions to prevent violent crimes against women

Tax the rich. They can afford it.
> (*T-shirt*) Spirit Mountain Press

We shall overcome
> in support of civil rights for black Americans

POTTERY
See GLASS AND CERAMICS

PRESIDENTIAL CAMPAIGNS
See also POLITICAL ISSUES

Abraham Lincoln/Honest Abe of the West
> Abraham Lincoln (*Republican*), 1860

A chicken in every pot, a car in every garage
> Herbert Hoover (*Republican*), 1928

A choice for a change
> Barry Goldwater (*Republican*), 1964

A choice—not an echo
Barry Goldwater (*Republican*), 1964

Adlai and Estes are the bestes
Adlai Stevenson (*Democrat*), 1956, with Estes Kefauver, the
vice-presidential candidate

Adlai likes *me*
Adlai Stevenson (*Democrat*), 1956

A halo shines as bright as day around the head of Henry Clay
Henry Clay (*Whig*), 1844

A house divided against itself cannot stand
Abraham Lincoln (*Republican*), 1860

All I have left is a vote for Willkie
Wendell Willkie (*Republican*), 1940

All the way with Adlai
Adlai Stevenson (*Democrat*), 1952

All the way with J. F. K.
John F. Kennedy (*Democrat*), 1960

All the way with LBJ
Lyndon B. Johnson (*Democrat*), 1964

Al Smith: up from the street
Alfred E. Smith (*Democrat*), 1928

A man of character
Calvin Coolidge (*Republican*), 1924

America always
Charles Evans Hughes (*Republican*), 1916

America calls another Roosevelt
Franklin Delano Roosevelt (*Democrat*), 1932

America cannot be bought
Alf Landon (*Republican*), 1936 (referring to heavy spending of
the New Deal)

America efficient
Charles Evans Hughes (*Republican*), 1916

America for Americans—no free trade
Benjamin Harrison (*Republican*), 1888

America needs Eisenhower—Draft Ike in '56
        Dwight D. Eisenhower (*Republican*), 1956

American Republicans! Beware of foreign influence! Our country first!
        (*American Republican Party*), 1844

Americans must rule America
        (*The American Party* ["Know-Nothings"]), 1856

American wages for American workingmen
        Benjamin Harrison (*Republican*), 1888

A public office is a public trust
        Grover Cleveland (*Democrat*), 1884

A republic can have no colonies
        William Jennings Bryan (*Democrat*), 1900

Ask yourself, are you better off now than you were four years ago?
        Ronald Reagan (*Republican*) 1980

A solid man in a sensitive job
        Jimmy Carter (*Democrat*) 1980

A square deal all around
        Theodore Roosevelt (*Progressive* or *Bull Moose Party*), 1912

A superb soldier—a model president
        Gen. Winfield S. Hancock (*Democrat*), 1880

A uniform & sound currency: the Sub Treasury
        Martin Van Buren (*Democrat*), 1840 (referring to Democratic
        support of the Independent Treasury System)

Avoid rebel rule
        Rutherford B. Hayes (*Republican*), 1876

A vote for Coolidge is a vote for chaos
        John W. Davis (*Democrat*), 1924

A vote for Roosevelt is a vote against Hoover
        Franklin Delano Roosevelt (*Democrat*), 1932

Away with the New Deal and its inefficiency
        Wendell Willkie (*Republican*), 1940

Back to Independence
        Thomas E. Dewey (*Republican*), 1948 (Independence, Missouri, was the home of his opponent, Harry Truman)

Back to normalcy
>   Warren G. Harding (*Republican*), 1920

Better a part-time president than a full-time phony
>   Dwight D. Eisenhower (*Republican*), 1956 (in answer to concerns raised about Eisenhower's health following a heart attack he suffered during his first administration)

Betty's husband for president in '76
>   Gerald R. Ford (*Republican*), 1976 (Ford's wife, Betty, enjoyed a high level of public support)

Be vigilant and watchful that internal dissensions destroy not your prosperity
>   Millard Fillmore (*Whig*), 1856

Bring back prosperity with a Republican vote
>   Herbert Hoover (*Republican*), 1932

Bring us together
>   Richard M. Nixon (*Republican*), 1968

Clean house with Dewey
>   Thomas E. Dewey (*Republican*), 1948

Cleveland runs well in England
>   Benjamin Harrison (*Republican*), 1888 (implying that Grover Cleveland's tariff policies would benefit England while injuring the United States)

Come home, America
>   George McGovern (*Democrat*), 1972

Congress has no more power to make a SLAVE than to make a KING
>   Martin Van Buren (*Free Soil Party*), 1848 (in opposition to the expansion of slavery into additional states or territories)

Constitution and Union
>   James Buchanan (*Democrat*), 1856
>   John Bell (*Constitutional Union party*), 1860

Coolidge and Dawes—Full dinner pail
>   Calvin Coolidge (*Republican*), 1924

Coolidge and prosperity
>   Calvin Coolidge (*Republican*), 1924

Coolidge of course
Calvin Coolidge (*Republican*), 1924

Coolidge or chaos
Calvin Coolidge (*Republican*), 1924 (referring to the possibility that lack of a decisive win by one of the three candidates would force a settlement of the election by the House of Representatives)

Courage, confidence, and Coolidge
Calvin Coolidge (*Republican*), 1924

Crime, corruption, Communism, and Korea
Dwight D. Eisenhower (*Republican*), 1952

Cuba must be ours
John C. Breckinridge (*Southern Democrat*), 1860 (acquisition of Cuba was seen as a means of expanding slave territory and thus the political power of the slave states)

Deeds—not words
Calvin Coolidge (*Republican*), 1924

Defeat the New Deal and its reckless spending
Alf Landon (*Republican*), 1936

Dem-Ike-Crats for Eisenhower
Dwight D. Eisenhower (*Republican*), 1952

Democracy is good enough for all
John C. Breckinridge (*Southern Democrat*), 1860

Democracy prevails throughout the union
Andrew Jackson (*Democrat-Republican*), 1828

Democracy, reform, and one presidential term
William Henry Harrison (*Whig*), 1840 (expressing opposition to re-election of Martin Van Buren for a second term)

Democracy stands for bimetallism not monometallism, people not trusts, republic not empire
William Jennings Bryan (*Democrat*), 1900

Dewey is due in '48
Thomas E. Dewey (*Republican*), 1948

Dewey or don't we?
Thomas E. Dewey (*Republican*), 1944

Dewey the racket buster—New Deal buster
  Thomas E. Dewey (*Republican*), 1948

Don't bump a good man out of the White House
  Dwight D. Eisenhower (*Republican*), 1956

Don't let them take it away
  Harry S Truman (*Democrat*), 1948

Don't swap horses in the middle of the stream
  Abraham Lincoln (*National Unionist*), 1864 (the election took place in the midst of the Civil War)

Don't swap horses—stand by Hoover
  Herbert Hoover (*Republican*), 1932

Don't tear down the Statue of Liberty! Refuse dictatorship!
  Wendell Willkie (*Republican*), 1940 (referring to the issue of Franklin D. Roosevelt's candidacy for a third presidential term)

Down with free trade
  James G. Blaine (*Republican*), 1884

Drop LeMay on Hanoi
  expressing opposition to George C. Wallace and Gen. Curtis C. LeMay, (*American Independent Party*), 1968 (LeMay had taken a very aggressive position on the bombing of North Vietnam's capital)

Dump the Hump
  expressing opposition to Hubert H. Humphrey (*Democrat*)), 1968

Elect me president—freedom and the reunion of states shall be permanently established
  John C. Frémont (*Radical Republican*), 1864

Elect none but natives to office
  (*American Republican Party*), 1844

Equal & full protection to American industry
  Henry Clay (*Whig*), 1836

Equal rights to all, special privileges to none
  William Jennings Bryan (*Democrat*), 1900

Experience counts: vote Nixon–Lodge for a better America
>   Richard M. Nixon, with Henry Cabot Lodge as the vice-presidential candidate (*Republican*), 1960

Fear God and take your own part
>   Charles Evans Hughes (*Republican*), 1916

54° 40' or Fight
>   James K. Polk (*Democrat*), 1844

First in the hearts of his soldiers
>   George McClellan, who was commander of Union forces until his removal by Lincoln (*Democrat*), 1864
>   Ulysses S. Grant (*National Republican*), 1868

For freedom—Four Freedoms
>   Franklin Delano Roosevelt (*Democrat*), 1944 (referring to his enunciation of ideals for international order)

For God for home and native land—the saloon must go
>   Clinton B. Fisk (*Prohibition party*), 1888

For the love of Ike vote Republican
>   Dwight D. Eisenhower (*Republican*), 1952

Forward together
>   Richard M. Nixon (*Republican*), 1968

4–H Club—help hustle Harry home
>   Thomas E. Dewey (*Republican*), 1948

Four more Roosevelt lucky years
>   Franklin Delano Roosevelt (*Democrat*), 1936

Four More Years
>   Richard M. Nixon (*Republican*), 1972

Freedom to all
>   Abraham Lincoln (*Republican*), 1860

Freedom to all men—war for the Union
>   Abraham Lincoln (*National Unionist*), 1864

Free homes for the homeless
>   Abraham Lincoln (*Republican*), 1860 (referring to Republican support for land grants from the public lands)

Free Kansas—and the Union
>   John C. Frémont (*Republican*), 1856 (opposing the issue of the extension of slavery into Kansas)

Free land, free speech and free men
  Abraham Lincoln (*Republican*), 1860

Free soil, free men, free speech, and Frémont
  John C. Frémont (*Republican*), 1856 (referring to Republican opposition to the expansion of slavery)

Free soil, free speech, free labor, and free men
  Martin Van Buren (*Free Soil Party*), 1848 (expressing the Free Soil Party's opposition to expansion of slavery into additional states or territories)

Free soil to a free people
  Martin Van Buren (*Free Soil Party*), 1848

Free speech. Free press. Frémont.
  John C. Frémont (*Radical Republican*), 1864

Free territory for a free people
  Abraham Lincoln (*Republican*), 1860

From the Tow Path to the White House
  James Garfield (*Republican*), 1880 (referring to Garfield's work as a mule driver on the tow paths of the Ohio Canal in his youth)

General amnesty—uniform currency—equal taxes and equal rights
  Horatio Seymour (*Democrat*), 1868

General Taylor never surrenders
  Gen. Zachary Taylor (*Whig*), 1848

Gen. Frank Pierce the statesman & soldier
  Franklin Pierce (*Democrat*), 1852

Gen. Winfield Scott—first in war, first in peace
  Gen. Winfield Scott (*Whig*), 1852

George Bush: an authentic American hero
  George Bush (*Republican*), 1988

George Bush—a president we won't have to train
  George Bush (*Republican*), 1988

Give-'em-Hell Harry
  Harry S Truman (*Democrat*), 1948

Give 'em Jessie
  John C. Frémont (*Republican*), 1856 (referring to the candidate's wife, Jessie Benton Frémont)

Give the presidency back to the people
  Pre-nomination campaign of Eugene McCarthy (*Democrat*), 1968

God would not permit a Roman Catholic to be president of the United States
  Anti-Smith slogan, 1928 (referring to candidate Alfred E. Smith, Democrat, a Catholic)

Goldwater for president—victory over Communism
  Barry Goldwater (*Republican*), 1964

Goldwater in 1864
  Lyndon B. Johnson (*Democrat*), 1964 (referring to his opponent, Barry Goldwater, who was often labeled a reactionary)

Good Republicans don't bolt the party ticket
  William Howard Taft (*Republican*), 1912 (referring to Theodore Roosevelt's break from the Republican party to run as a Progressive)

Go 4th to win the war
  Franklin Delano Roosevelt (*Democrat*), 1944 (Roosevelt was seeking a fourth term in an election which took place during World War II)

Governments derive their just powers from the consent of the governed
  William Jennings Bryan (*Democrat*), 1900

Grandfather's hat
  Benjamin Harrison (*Republican*), 1888 (referring to Harrison's grandfather, former president William Henry Harrison)

Grand old party, good as gold
  William McKinley (*Republican*), 1896

Grandpa's pants won't fit Benny
  Grover Cleveland (*Democrat*), 1888 (the grandfather of Cleveland's opponent, Benjamin Harrison, was former president William Henry Harrison)

Grantism means poor people made poorer
  Samuel J. Tilden (*Democrat*), 1876

Grant us another term
  Ulysses S. Grant (*Republican*), 1872

Greeley—Brown & reconciliation
> Horace Greeley (*Liberal Republican*), 1872 (the Liberal Republicans favored ending reconstruction in the South)

Grover, Grover, all is over
> Benjamin Harrison (*Republican*), 1892

Had enough?
> Dwight D. Eisenhower (*Republican*), 1952

Harding and prosperity
> Warren G. Harding (*Republican*), 1920

Hari-kari with Barry
> Lyndon B. Johnson (*Democrat*), 1964 (referring to his Republican opponent, Barry Goldwater)

Hayes, hard money and hard times
> Samuel J. Tilden (*Democrat*), 1876

He kept us out of suffrage
> Anti-Wilson slogan, 1916 (referring to Woodrow Wilson's opposition to women's suffrage)

He kept us out of war
> Woodrow Wilson (*Democrat*), 1916 (referring to Wilson's success in avoiding direct U.S. involvement in the European war that began in 1914, later known as World War I)

He leaves the plough to save his country
> William Henry Harrison (*Whig*), 1840

Hello Central, give us Teddy
> Theodore Roosevelt (*Republican*), 1904 (borrowing a phrase from customers of telephone service, then a new and novel feature of American life)

Help Barry stamp out peace
> Lyndon B. Johnson (*Democrat*), 1964 (referring to his Republican opponent, Barry Goldwater)

Help Hoover help business
> Herbert Hoover (*Republican*), 1928

Henry Clay for his country feels, but Polk would stop our water wheels
> Henry Clay (*Whig*), 1844 (Clay was portrayed as a friend of industry because of his support for a protective tariff)

Henry Clay, the champion of a protective tariff
    Henry Clay (*Whig*), 1844

He proved the pen mightier than the sword
    Woodrow Wilson (*Democrat*), 1916 (referring to Wilson's successful efforts to maintain American neutrality in the European war that began in 1914, later known as World War I)

He's all right
    John P. St. John (*Prohibition party*), 1884

He saved America
    Franklin Delano Roosevelt (*Democrat*), 1936

Hold on to Hoover
    Herbert Hoover (*Republican*), 1932

Honest days with Davis
    John W. Davis (*Democrat*), 1924 (alluding to scandals uncovered in the Harding administration)

Honest money, honest government
    Rutherford B. Hayes (*Republican*), 1876

Honesty at home—honor abroad
    John W. Davis (*Democrat*), 1924

Honor where honor's due to the hero of Tippecanoe
    William Henry Harrison (*Whig*), 1840 (referring to Harrison's military victory in 1811, over allied Native American forces led by Tecumseh's brother, at the Battle of Tippecanoe; Harrison's victory successfully broke treaties concerning the Indiana Territory)

Hoover and happiness
    Herbert Hoover (*Republican*), 1932

Hoover and happiness or Smith and soup houses: which shall it be?
    Herbert Hoover (*Republican*), 1928

Horrors of war—blessings of peace
    George McClellan (*Democrat*), 1864 (the Democratic platform supported a negotiated end to the Civil War)

I ask no favors & I shrink from no responsibility
    Gen. Zachary Taylor (*Whig*), 1848

If I am re-elected president slavery must be abolished with the reunion of states
> Abraham Lincoln (*National Unionist*), 1864

If you liked Hitler, you'll love Wallace
> expressing opposition to the American Independent candidate, George C. Wallace, 1968

If you want a change to better times, vote for Grover Cleveland
> Grover Cleveland (*Democrat*), 1884

I intend to fight it out on this line if it takes all summer
> Ulysses S. Grant (*Nat. Republican*), 1868 (quoting one of Grant's wartime statements)

I like Ike
> Dwight D. Eisenhower (*Republican*), 1952

I like Ike but I am going to vote for Stevenson
> Adlai Stevenson (*Democrat*), 1952

I'm extremely fond of Barry
> Barry Goldwater (*Republican*), 1964

I'm on the water wagon now
> in support of continuing Prohibition, 1932

I'm safe with Ike
> Dwight D. Eisenhower (*Republican*), 1956

In Hoover we trusted, now we are busted
> Franklin Delano Roosevelt (*Democrat*), 1932

In your guts you know he's nuts
> Lyndon B. Johnson (*Democrat*), 1964 (referring to his Republican opponent, Barry Goldwater)

In your heart you know he's right
> Barry Goldwater (*Republican*), 1964

I propose to move immediately on your works
> Ulysses S. Grant (*Nat. Republican*), 1868 (quoting a statement made by Grant at Fort Donelson during the Civil War)

It might have been worse
> Herbert Hoover (*Republican*), 1932 (referring to economic depression that began under Hoover, later known as The Great Depression of the 1930s)

It's McKinley we trust to keep our machines free of rust
  William McKinley (*Republican*), 1896

James Buchanan—no sectionalism
  James Buchanan (*Democrat*), 1856

John and Jessie forever! Hurrah!
  John C. Frémont (*Republican*), 1856 (Jessie Benton Frémont
  was the candidate's wife)

Keep cool with Coolidge
  Calvin Coolidge (*Republican*), 1924

Keep faith with our sons—bring America into the League of
Nations—Vote for Cox and Roosevelt
  James M. Cox (*Democrat*), 1920 (his running mate was
  Franklin Delano Roosevelt)

Labor is king
  James G. Blaine (*Republican*), 1884

Land for the landless
  Abraham Lincoln (*Republican*), 1860 (referring to Republican
  support for land grants from the public lands)

LBJ for the USA
  Lyndon B. Johnson (*Democrat*), 1964

Leadership for a change
  Jimmy Carter (*Democrat*), 1976

Leadership for the '50's
  expressing opposition to Richard M. Nixon (*Republican*), 1968

Leadership for the '60's
  John F. Kennedy (*Democrat*), 1960

Let liberty be national & slavery sectional
  Abraham Lincoln (*Republican*), 1860

Let's be done with wiggle and wobble
  Warren G. Harding (*Republican*), 1920

Let's clean house with Ike and Dick
  Dwight D. Eisenhower (*Republican*), 1952 (Eisenhower's
  running mate was Richard M. Nixon)

Let's get another deck
  Alf Landon (*Republican*), 1936

Let's keep what we've got: prosperity didn't just happen
> Herbert Hoover (*Republican*), 1928

Let the people rule
> William Jennings Bryan (*Democrat*), 1908

Let the people speak
> George C. Wallace (*American Independent*), 1968

Let us continue
> Lyndon B. Johnson (*Democrat*), 1964

Let us encourage our own manufactures
> Henry Clay (*Whig*), 1844 (referring to his support of a protective tariff)

Let us have a clean sweep
> Samuel J. Tilden (*Democrat*), 1876 (advocating civil service reform in the wake of the scandals under the Grant administration)

Let us have peace
> Ulysses S. Grant (*Nat. Republican*), 1868 (urging resolution of issues remaining from the Civil War)

Let well enough alone
> Calvin Coolidge (*Republican*), 1924

Liberty, equality, and fraternity
> Horace Greeley (*Liberal Republican*), 1872

Liberty, equality and no king
> Pro-Jefferson forces, 1796 (referring to allegedly monarchical tendencies of George Washington and, by implication, the Federalist Party)

Liberty, equality & fraternity, the cardinal principles of true democracy
> Gen. Lewis Cass (*Democrat*), 1848

Liberty, justice and humanity
> William Jennings Bryan (*Democrat*), 1900

Liberty, union, and victory
> Abraham Lincoln (*National Unionist*), 1864

Lincoln and liberty—good for another heat
> Abraham Lincoln (*National Unionist*), 1864

Loyalty shall govern what loyalty has preserved
 Ulysses S. Grant (*Nat. Republican*), 1868

Make America happen again
 George McGovern (*Democrat*), 1972

Make the White House the Dwight House
 Dwight D. Eisenhower (*Republican*), 1952

Match him
 Ulysses S. Grant (*Nat. Republican*), 1868

McCarthy and peace in '68
 Pre-nomination campaign of Eugene McCarthy (*Democrat*), 1968

McKinley and the full dinner pail
 William McKinley (*Republican*), 1896

Millard Fillmore for the whole country
 Millard Fillmore (*Whig*), 1856

Millions for freedom—not one cent for slavery
 Abraham Lincoln (*Republican*), 1860

Mr. Nixon: how long will this new pose last?
 Anti-Nixon slogan expressing suspicion about the sincerity of Richard M. Nixon (*Republican*), 1968

My brand's LBJ
 Lyndon B. Johnson (*Democrat*), 1964

My favorite son is Stevenson
 Adlai Stevenson (*Democrat*), 1952

My pick is Dick
 Richard M. Nixon (*Republican*), 1960

New leadership—Kennedy and Johnson
 John F. Kennedy (*Democrat*), 1960 (Lyndon B. Johnson was Kennedy's running mate)

Nixon + Spiro = zero
 Hubert H. Humphrey (*Democrat*), 1968 (referring to the Republican candidates, Richard M. Nixon and Spiro Agnew)

Nix on Ike
 Adlai Stevenson (*Democrat*), 1952 (Richard M. Nixon was the running mate of Eisenhower, "Ike")

Nix on Nixon
> John F. Kennedy (*Democrat*), 1960 (running against Richard M. Nixon)

Nixon now more than ever
> Richard M. Nixon (*Republican*), 1972

Nixon's the one
> Richard M. Nixon (*Republican*), 1968

No beer, no work
> Anti-Prohibition, 1932

No British pauper wages for Americans
> James G. Blaine (*Republican*), 1884 (referring to the Republican credo that a protective tariff helped to elevate the wages of laborers)

No compromise with armed rebels—may the Union flourish
> Abraham Lincoln (*National Unionist*), 1864

No compromise with traitors
> Abraham Lincoln (*National Unionist*), 1864

No crown for Roosevelt
> Wendell Willkie (*Republican*), 1940 (reflecting concern about Franklin D. Roosevelt's power, as he was seeking an unprecedented third presidential term)

No crown of thorns, no cross of gold
> William Jennings Bryan (*Democrat*), 1896 and 1900 (quoting a speech given by Bryan)

No emancipation, no miscegenation, no confiscation, no subjugation
> George McClellan (*Democrat*), 1864

No fourth term either
> Wendell Willkie (*Republican*), 1940 (referring to Franklin D. Roosevelt's candidacy for a third presidential term)

No Franklin the First
> Wendell Willkie (*Republican*), 1940 (reflecting fears of the power Franklin D. Roosevelt would gain from a third term as president)

No man is good three times
> Wendell Willkie (*Republican*), 1940 (referring to Franklin D. Roosevelt's candidacy for a third presidential term)

No more fireside chats
> Wendell Willkie (*Republican*), 1940 (referring to Franklin D. Roosevelt's frequent radio messages broadcast to the American public)

No more slave states and no more slave territory
> Martin Van Buren (*Free Soil Party*), 1848

No more slave teritory
> Abraham Lincoln (*Republican*), 1860

No North, no South, but the whole country
> Millard Fillmore (*Whig*), 1856

No North, no South, no East, no West, nothing but the Union
> John Bell (*Constitutional Unionist*), 1860

No North—no South—the Union inseperable
> Horatio Seymour (*Democrat*), 1868

No submission to the North
> John C. Breckinridge (*Southern Democrat*), 1860

No substitute for experience
> Richard M. Nixon (*Republican*), 1960

Off the rocks with Landon and Knox
> Alf Landon (*Republican*), 1936 (William Franklin Knox was Landon's running mate)

Old Abe removed McClellan—we'll now remove Old Abe
> George McClellan (*Democrat*), 1864 (President Abraham Lincoln had previously removed McClellan from command of the Union army)

One country, one flag
> William McKinley (*Republican*), 1900

One flag and one Union now and forever
> George McClellan (*Democrat*), 1864

One man rule
> Thomas E. Dewey (*Republican*), 1944 (referring to the issue of Franklin D. Roosevelt's fourth-term candidacy)

On the right track with Jack
> John F. Kennedy (*Democrat*), 1960

Our centennial president
> Rutherford B. Hayes (*Republican*), 1876

Our country and our rights
John C. Breckinridge (*Southern Democrat*), 1860

Our country needs Roosevelt for another term
Theodore Roosevelt (*Progressive* or *Bull Moose party*), 1912

Our Dewey Special is due
Thomas E. Dewey (*Republican*), 1948

Out of the red with Roosevelt
Franklin Delano Roosevelt (*Democrat*), 1932

Pass prosperity around
Theodore Roosevelt (*Progressive* or *Bull Moose Party*), 1912

Patient of toil/Serene amidst alarms/Inflexible in faith/Invincible in
arms
Ulysses S. Grant (*Nat. Republican*), 1868

Peace and power with Eisenhower
Dwight D. Eisenhower (*Republican*), 1952

Peace at any price. Peace and Union.
Millard Fillmore (*Whig*), 1856

Peace, freedom, abundance
Henry A. Wallace (*Progressive*), 1948

Peace, jobs, and McGovern
George McGovern (*Democrat*), 1972

Peace with dishonor
Abraham Lincoln (*National Unionist*), 1864 (mocking the
Democratic platform)

Perhaps Roosevelt is all you deserve
Wendell Willkie (*Republican*), 1940

Phooey on Dewey
Harry S Truman (*Democrat*), 1948

Play safe with Hoover
Herbert Hoover (*Republican*), 1932

Polk and Texas; Clay and no Texas
James K. Polk (*Democrat*), 1844 (referring to the question of
expansion into Texas)

Polk and the Democratic Tariff of 1842
>James K. Polk (*Democrat*), 1844 (supporting the low-protection tariff law of 1842)

Polk, Dallas, Texas, Oregon, and the Tariff of '42
>James K. Polk (*Democrat*), 1844 (expressing support for territorial expansion into Texas and Oregon; George Mifflin Dallas was Polk's running mate)

Preserve home industries
>James G. Blaine (*Republican*), 1884 (referring to Republican support of a high protective tariff)

Press onward—enlarge the boundaries of freedom—Young Hickory
>James K. Polk (*Democrat*), 1844 (referring to his support for territorial expansion, and the fact that he was portrayed as the successor to Andrew Jackson, "Old Hickory")

Principles, not men
>Gen. Lewis Cass (*Democrat*), 1848

Proclaim liberty throughout the land
>Abraham Lincoln (*National Unionist*), 1864 (the Emancipation Proclamation had defined the abolition of slavery as a goal of the ongoing Civil War)

Prosperity at home, prestige abroad
>William McKinley (*Republican*), 1900

Prosperity is just around the corner
>Herbert Hoover (*Republican*), 1932

Protection and prosperity
>Benjamin Harrison (*Republican*), 1888

Protection for home industries
>Benjamin Harrison (*Republican*), 1888 (Republicans supported a high protective tariff)

Protection to all at home and abroad
>Abraham Lincoln (*Republican*), 1860 (the Republican platform included support for a higher tariff)

Protection to American industry—and no extension of slave power
>John C. Frémont (*Republican*), 1856

Protection to honest industry
>Abraham Lincoln (*Republican*), 1860 (alluding to Republican support for a higher tariff)

Protection to the working class is an assurance of success
  Henry Clay (*Whig*), 1844 (referring to benefits of a protective tariff for the working man)

Read my lips: no new taxes
  George Bush (*Republican*), 1988

Reduce taxation before taxation reduces us
  Horatio Seymour (*Democrat*), 1868

Re-elect Roosevelt: his heart's with the people
  Franklin Delano Roosevelt (*Democrat*), 1936

Reform is necessary in the civil service
  Samuel J. Tilden (*Democrat*), 1876

Reform is necessary to establish a sound currency
  Samuel J. Tilden (*Democrat*), 1876

Remember: Governor Reagan couldn't start a war; President Reagan could
  Gerald Ford (*Republican*), 1976

Remember Hoover?
  Franklin Delano Roosevelt (*Democrat*), 1936

Remember Teapot Dome
  John W. Davis (*Democrat*), 1924 (referring to a major scandal of the Harding administration)

Repeal and prosperity
  Anti-Prohibition, campaign of 1932

Repeat with Roosevelt or repent with Willkie
  Franklin Delano Roosevelt (*Democrat*), 1940

Repudiate the repudiators
  Ulysses S. Grant (*Nat. Republican*), 1868 (referring to a plan accepted by the Democratic platform to pay off certain war debts with greenbacks rather than gold coin)

Return the country to the people
  Franklin Delano Roosevelt (*Democrat*), 1932

Roosevelt and protection
  Theodore Roosevelt (*Republican*), 1904

Roosevelt and recovery
  Franklin Delano Roosevelt (*Democrat*), 1932

Roosevelt and repeal
>Franklin Delano Roosevelt (*Democrat*), 1932, advocating an end to Prohibition

Roosevelt for ex-president
>Wendell Willkie (*Republican*), 1940

Roosevelt—friend of the people
>Franklin Delano Roosevelt (*Democrat*), 1932

Roosevelt is robust
>Franklin Delano Roosevelt (*Democrat*), 1932 (affirming Roosevelt's good health and vigor in spite of his crippling as a result of polio)

Roosevelt? No! No! 1000 times NO!
>Wendell Willkie (*Republican*), 1940

Roosevelt or ruin
>Franklin Delano Roosevelt (*Democrat*), 1932

Roosevelt's way is the American way, America needs Roosevelt
>Franklin Delano Roosevelt (*Democrat*), 1940

Rough and Ready: the hero of Monterrey
>Gen. Zachary Taylor (*Whig*), 1848 (referring to his leadership in the Mexican War; Taylor's informal mode of dress earned him the nickname "Old Rough and Ready")

Rum, Romanism, and Rebellion
>Grover Cleveland (*Democrat*), 1884 (the opposing candidate was James G. Blaine, whose silence at a speech in which the Democratic party was associated with "rum, Romanism and rebellion" seemed to contribute to his eventual loss)

Safe and sane
>William Howard Taft (*Republican*), 1908

Safe and sane Cool-idge
>Calvin Coolidge (*Republican*), 1924

Safe on third
>Franklin Delano Roosevelt (*Democrat*), 1940 (using a phrase borrowed from baseball to refer to Roosevelt's candidacy for a third term)

Save America—don't save beer and wine
>In support of continuing Prohibition, campaign of 1932

Save the Constitution—Thurmond for president
>J. Strom Thurmond (*Dixiecrat Party*), 1948

Save what's left
>Thomas E. Dewey (*Republican*), 1948

Scott & Graham, union & constitution
>Gen. Winfield Scott (*Whig*), 1852 (William Alexander Graham was the vice-presidential candidate)

Scratch a Democrat and you'll find a Rebel under his skin
>Ulysses S. Grant (*Nat. Republican*), 1868

Segregation now, segregation tomorrow, and segregation forever
>George C. Wallace (*American Independent*), 1968

Shall the people rule?
>William Jennings Bryan (*Democrat*), 1908

Sieg Heil ya'll
>expressing opposition to George C. Wallace, (*American Independent*), 1968 (Wallace, a Southerner, was sometimes labeled a fascist)

Sixteen to one
>William Jennings Bryan (*Democrat*), 1896 (the Democratic platform supported unlimited coinage of silver and gold at the ratio of 16 to 1)

60 million people working—why change?
>Harry S Truman (*Democrat*), 1948

Slavery is a moral, social, and political wrong
>Abraham Lincoln (*Republican*), 1860

Soap! Soap! Blaine's only hope!
>Grover Cleveland (*Democrat*), 1884 (*Soap* referred to campaign donations)

Son of his grandfather
>Benjamin Harrison (*Republican*), 1888 (grandson of former president William Henry Harrison)

Sound money, expansion, protection, prosperity
>Theodore Roosevelt (*Republican*), 1904

Sound money—good markets
>William McKinley (*Republican*), 1900

Speed recovery—re-elect Hoover
>Herbert Hoover (*Republican*), 1932

Stand pat
>Theodore Roosevelt (*Republican*), 1904

Stand Pat with Nixon
>Richard M. Nixon (*Republican*), 1972 (Pat Nixon was the candidate's wife)

Stand up for America—Wallace–LeMay
>George C. Wallace (*American Independent*), 1968 (Curtis C. LeMay was the vice-presidential candidate)

Steady America
>Warren G. Harding (*Republican*), 1920

Stick with Roosevelt
>Franklin Delano Roosevelt (*Democrat*), 1940

Stop all unnecessary taxation
>Grover Cleveland (*Democrat*), 1888

Strike three F. D. you're out
>Wendell Willkie (*Republican*), 1940 (using phrases borrowed from baseball to refer to Franklin D. Roosevelt's candidacy for a third presidential term)

Support "the Little Giant' who has proved himself the greatest statesman of the age
>Stephen A. Douglas (*Democrat*), 1860

The advocate of the American System
>Andrew Jackson (*Democrat-Republican*), 1828 (referring to the "American System" of protective tariffs financing internal improvements, proposed by Henry Clay)

The American way with Willkie
>Wendell Willkie (*Republican*), 1940

The Bank must perish
>Andrew Jackson (*Democrat*), 1832 (referring to the Bank of the United States, opposed by Jackson as unconstitutional and undemocratic)

The Big Stick
>Theodore Roosevelt (*Republican*), 1904 (from Roosevelt's admonition "Speak softly and carry a big stick")

The boys in blue will see it through
> Rutherford B. Hayes (*Republican*), 1876 (associating the Republican party with the Northern cause in the Civil War)

The champion of internal improvements
> Henry Clay (*Whig*), 1844 (Clay supported a high protective tariff to finance internal improvements)

The champion of popular sovereignty
> Stephen A. Douglas (*Democrat*), 1860 (Douglas advocated popular sovereignty as the means to resolve the issue of slavery in the territories)

The champion of Republicanism and the American System
> Henry Clay (*Nat. Republican*), 1832 (the "American System" proposed a protective tariff to help finance internal improvements)

The Constitution and the flag, one and inseparable, now and forever
> William Jennings Bryan (*Democrat*), 1900

The Constitution and the freedom of the seas
> Gen. Lewis Cass (*Democrat*), 1848 (in opposition to Britain's attempts to stop slave ships flying the American flag)

The Constitution as it is, the Union as it was
> George McClellan (*Democrat*), 1864

The Constitution & Union forever
> Abraham Lincoln (*Republican*), 1860

The country demands his re-election
> Martin Van Buren (*Democrat*), 1840

The firm and fearless advocate of democracy
> Martin Van Buren (*Democrat*), 1840

The flag of a republic forever, of an empire never
> William Jennings Bryan (*Democrat*), 1900

The gallant & successful defender of New Orleans
> Andrew Jackson (*Democrat–Republican*), 1828 (referring to Jackson's heroism in the War of 1812)

The great railsplitter of the West must & shall be our next president
> Abraham Lincoln (*Republican*), 1860

The Happy Warrior
> Alfred E. Smith (*Democrat*), 1928

The hero of Buena Vista
> Gen. Zachary Taylor (*Whig*), 1848 (referring to a major battle of the Mexican War)

The honest old farmer of Chappaqua
> Horace Greeley (*Liberal Republican*), 1872 (Greeley owned a farm in Chappaqua, New York)

The "I" in Nixon stands for integrity
> Richard M. Nixon (*Republican*), 1968

The log cabin candidate, the people's choice
> William Henry Harrison (*Whig*), 1840 (portrayed as a humble man of the soil though actually descended from an elite Virginia family)

The man of the hour
> William Howard Taft (*Republican*), 1908

The man of the hour is Eisenhower
> Dwight D. Eisenhower (*Republican*), 1952

The man of the hour—Woodrow Wilson
> Woodrow Wilson (*Democrat*), 1916

The man that can split rails can guide the ship of state
> Abraham Lincoln (*Republican*), 1860

The men will need their horses to plow with
> Ulysses S. Grant (*Nat. Republican*), 1868 (from a statement made by Union General Grant to Confederate General Robert E. Lee at Appomatox, at the end of the Civil War)

The mighty tower—Eisenhower
> Dwight D. Eisenhower (*Republican*), 1956

The Natick cobbler—the Galena tanner—there's nothing like leather
> Ulysses S. Grant (*Republican*), 1872 (Grant and his running mate, Henry Wilson, had both been involved in leatherwork earlier in their lives, the former in Galena, Ohio, the latter in Natick, Massachusetts)

The nation needs fixin' with Nixon
> Richard M. Nixon (*Republican*), 1972

The nation needs Richard M. Nixon
> Richard M. Nixon (*Republican*), 1960

The new Nixon
>Richard M. Nixon (*Republican*), 1968 (Nixon was portrayed as a man who had undergone drastic and positive change since his defeat in the presidential election of 1960)

The old red bandanna
>Grover Cleveland (*Democrat*), 1888 (referring to the vice-presidential candidate, Allen G. Thurman, and his ever-present red bandanna)

The party that saved the Union must rule it
>Ulysses S. Grant (*Nat. Republican*), 1868

The pen is mightier than the sword
>Horace Greeley (Liberal Republican), 1872 (Greeley was editor of the New York *Tribune*)

The people against the bosses
>William McKinley (*Republican*), 1896

The principles & prudence of our forefathers
>Martin Van Buren (*Democrat*), 1836

There's no indispensable man
>Wendell Willkie (*Republican*), 1940 (referring to his opponent, Franklin Delano Roosevelt, who was seeking an unprecedented third term as president)

The Rocky Mountains echo back Frémont
>John C. Frémont (*Republican*), 1856 (referring to Frémont's exploits as an explorer)

The same curency for the bondholder and the plowholder
>Horatio Seymour (*Democrat*), 1868 (supporting the "Ohio idea" of paying certain war debts in greenbacks rather than gold coin)

The star of the West
>Henry Clay (*Whig*), 1844

The Territories must be free to the people
>Abraham Lincoln (*Republican*), 1860

The Union must and shall be preserved
>Andrew Jackson (*Democrat*), 1832 (referring to the nullification controversy, which tested the limits of state vs. national power)
>John Bell (*Constitutional Unionist*), 1860
>Stephen A. Douglas (*Democrat*), 1860
>Abraham Lincoln (*National Unionist*), 1864

The Union now, the Union forever
>Millard Fillmore (*Whig*), 1856

The union of Whigs for the sake of the Union
>William Henry Harrison (*Whig*), 1840

The Union one and indivisable *sic*—the crisis demands his election
>James Buchanan (*Democrat*), 1856

The United States is rich enough to give us all a farm
>Abraham Lincoln (*Republican*), 1860 (the Republican platform supported land grants from public lands

The White House—no place for an old bachelor
>John C. Frémont (*Republican*), 1856 (his opponent, James Buchanan, was a bachelor)

The won't do Congress won't do
>Harry S Truman (*Democrat*), 1948

The worst is past
>Herbert Hoover (*Republican*), 1932 (referring to the economic depression that began under Hoover, later known as The Great Depression of the 1930s)

They understand what peace demands
>Richard M. Nixon (*Republican*), 1960

Think of America first
>Warren G. Harding (*Republican*), 1920 (expessing reaction against Wilson's peace objectives)

Three good terms deserve another
>Franklin Delano Roosevelt (*Democrat*), 1944 (seeking a fourth presidential term)

$329
>Gen. Winfield S. Hancock (*Democrat*), 1880 (referring to profit allegedly made by the Republican candidate, James Garfield, in the Crédit Mobilier scandal)

Throw the spenders out
>   Franklin Delano Roosevelt (*Democrat*), 1932

Time for a change
>   Thomas E. Dewey (*Republican*), 1944

Time to swap horses—November 8th
>   George McClellan (*Democrat*), 1864

Tippecanoe and Morton too
>   Benjamin Harrison (*Republican*), 1888 (Harrison was the grandson of former president William Henry Harrison, hero of Tippecanoe; Levi Parsons Morton was B. Harrison's running mate)

Tippecanoe and tariff, too
>   Benjamin Harrison (*Republican*), 1888 (referring to his grandfather, William Henry Harrison, and to support for a high protective tariff)

Tippecanoe and Tyler too
>   William Henry Harrison (*Whig*), 1840 (referring to Harrison's military victory in 1811, over allied Native American forces led by Tecumseh's brother, at the Battle of Tippecanoe; Harrison's victory successfully broke treaties concerning the Indiana Territory; John Tyler was Harrison's running mate)

Together—A new beginning
>   Ronald Reagan (*Republican*), 1980

Tried and true Truman
>   Harry S Truman (*Democrat*), 1948

Truman fights for human rights
>   Harry S Truman (*Democrat*), 1948

Truman was screwy to build a porch for Dewey
>   Thomas E. Dewey (*Republican*), 1948 (referring to improvements made on the White House during Truman's administration)

Truth, justice and the Constitution
>   slogan of the Democratic National Convention of 1860, which was so divided it adjourned without agreeing on a presidential candidate

Twenty years of treason
> Dwight D. Eisenhower (*Republican*), 1952 (reflecting the viewpoint of right-wing Republicans who believed the U. S. government was under the influence of Communist sympathizers)

Two good terms deserve another
> Franklin Delano Roosevelt (*Democrat*), 1940 (referring to Roosevelt's candidacy for an unprecedented third term)

Union and Constitution—preservation of the rights of the people
> Horatio Seymour (*Democrat*), 1868

Union of States
> John Bell (*Constitutional Unionist*), 1860

Universal amnesty and impartial suffrage
> Horace Greeley (*Liberal Republican*), 1872 (referring to issues dealing with reconstruction in the South)

Unnecessary taxation is unjust taxation
> Grover Cleveland (*Democrat*), 1884 (Democrats supported lowering tariffs to reduce the surplus in the U. S. Treasury)

Untrammelled with party obligations
> Gen. Zachary Taylor (*Whig*), 1848

Up with Alf, down with the alphabet
> Alf Landon (*Republican*), 1936 (expressing opposition to numerous New Deal agencies and programs referred to by acronyms)

Vote as you shot
> Abraham Lincoln (*National Unionist*), 1864 (the National Union Party was a coalition of Republicans and War Democrats)
> Ulysses S. Grant (*Nat. Republican*), 1868 (calling for loyalty to the leader of Union forces during the Civil War)

Vote as you shot, boys
> Rutherford B. Hayes (*Republican*), 1876 (calling for continued loyalty to the party that prosecuted the Civil War)

Vote early and often
> appeared in 1848, attributed to John Van Buren, son of Free Soil candidate Martin Van Buren (used repeatedly in following elections to encourage the illegal practice of casting multiple ballots)

Vote for champions of the 8 hour law
   Woodrow Wilson (*Democrat*), 1916 (Wilson had supported legislation providing an eight-hour work day for certain railroad workers)

Vote gladly for Adlai
   Adlai Stevenson (*Democrat*), 1952

Vote Kennedy for peace
   Pre-nomination campaign of Robert F. Kennedy (*Democrat*), 1968 (campaign ended with his assassination)

Vote like your whole life depended on it
   Richard M. Nixon (*Republican*), 1968

Vote Republican—the party of Lincoln
   Richard M. Nixon (*Republican*), 1960

Vote right with Dwight
   Dwight D. Eisenhower (*Republican*), 1952

Vote straight Democratic: protect America
   Franklin Delano Roosevelt (*Democrat*), 1944

Vote yourself a farm
   Abraham Lincoln (*Republican*), 1860 (referring to Republican support of land grants to settlers through a homestead bill)

Wall Street wears a Willkie button, America wears a Roosevelt button
   Franklin Delano Roosevelt (*Democrat*), 1940

War in the East! Peace in the West! Thank God for Wilson
   Woodrow Wilson (*Democrat*), 1916 (referring to Wilson's success in keeping America out of World War I)

Washington wouldn't! Grant couldn't! Roosevelt shan't! No third term!
   William Howard Taft (*Republican*), 1912 (Theodore Roosevelt had served most of McKinley's term as president after the latter's assassination and had then been elected to another term of his own; in 1912 he ran again)

Washington wouldn't, Grant couldn't, Roosevelt shouldn't
   Wendell Willkie (*Republican*), 1940 (referring to Franklin D. Roosevelt's candidacy for an unprecedented third term as president)

We are going to win the war and the peace that follows
   Franklin Delano Roosevelt (*Democrat*), 1944

We are not going to vote away our wages
> Benjamin Harrison (*Republican*), 1888 (Republicans portrayed Democrats as free-traders whose policies would endanger American industry and labor)

We demand a rigorous frugality in every department of the government
> Samuel J. Tilden (*Democrat*), 1876 (responding to the corruption uncovered in the Ulysses S. Grant administration)

We demand that our customhouse taxation shall be for revenue only
> Samuel J. Tilden (*Democrat*), 1876 (expressing opposition to excessive protective tariff)

We demand the *Habeas Corpus*
> George McClellan (*Democrat*), 1864 (President Abraham Lincoln had suspended the writ of *habeas corpus* in some instances during the Civil War)

We don't want Eleanor either
> Wendell Willkie (*Republican*), 1940 (referring to Franklin D. Roosevelt's wife, Eleanor)

We'll vote for the Buckeye boy
> Rutherford B. Hayes (*Republican*), 1876 (Hayes was from Ohio, the "Buckeye State")

We love him for the enemies he has made
> Grover Cleveland (*Democrat*), 1884

We millionaires want Willkie
> Franklin Delano Roosevelt (*Democrat*), 1940

We Polked 'em in '44; we'll Pierce 'em in '52
> Franklin Pierce (*Democrat*), 1852

We're madly for Adlai
> Adlai Stevenson (*Democrat*), 1952

We shall be redeemed from the rule of Nigger drivers
> John C. Frémont (*Republican*), 1856 (expressing the anti-slavery conviction of the Republican Party)

We still like Ike
> Dwight D. Eisenhower (*Republican*), 1956

We want none but white men at the helm
> John C. Breckinridge (*Southern Democrat*), 1860

We want Willkie—third term means dictatorship
>   Wendell Willkie (*Republican*), 1940 (Franklin D. Roosevelt, the Democratic candidate, was seeking a third term as president)

We will follow where the White Plume waves
>   James G. Blaine (*Republican*), 1884 (Blaine was nicknamed "The Plumed Knight")

What's wrong with being right?
>   Barry Goldwater (*Republican*), 1964 (referring to Goldwater's right-wing stance)

Where were you in '32?
>   Franklin Delano Roosevelt (*Democrat*), 1936

While I am able to move I will do my duty
>   Gen. Lewis Cass (*Democrat*), 1848

White men to govern the restoration of constitutional liberty
>   Horatio Seymour (*Democrat*), 1868

Who but Hoover
>   Herbert Hoover (*Republican*), 1928

Who but Hubert?
>   Hubert H. Humphrey (*Democrat*), 1968

Willkie for president—of Commonwealth and Southern
>   Franklin Delano Roosevelt (*Democrat*), 1940 (referring to the utilities company of which Wendell Willkie had been chief executive)

Willkie for the millionaires—Roosevelt for the millions
>   Franklin Delano Roosevelt (*Democrat*), 1940

Willkie or bust
>   Wendell Willkie (*Republican*), 1940

Win with Willkie
>   Wendell Willkie (*Republican*), 1940

Win with Wilson
>   Woodrow Wilson (*Democrat*), 1912

Workingmen, don't be fooled
>   Grover Cleveland (*Democrat*), 1884 (questioning Republican claims of the benefits of a high protective tariff)

Workingmen's friend
>   Benjamin Butler (*Greenback party*), 1884

Work with Wallace for peace
Henry A. Wallace (*Progressive*), 1948

Would you buy a used car from this man?
1972 (expressing suspicion of the trustworthiness of the
Republican candidate, Richard M. Nixon)

Would you let your sister marry this man?
1968 (expressing suspicion of the trustworthiness of the
Republican candidate, Richard M. Nixon)

You never had it so good
Herbert Hoover (*Republican*), 1928

PUBLIC SERVICE
See also GOVERNMENT SERVICE

A mind is a terrible thing to waste
United Negro College Fund

Children. They're the only future we've got.
(*advocacy group*) Children NOW

College is America's best friend
Council for Financial Aid to Education

Conservation through private action
The Nature Conservancy

Don't take the chance. Take the test.
(*AIDS prevention/detection*) Michigan Department of Public
Health

Give so more will live
Heart Fund

Give them life and make it worth living
United Jewish Appeal

Give to conquer cancer
American Cancer Society

Give yourself the chance of a lifetime
American Cancer Society

Help others help themselves
Salvation Army

Public Service

It brings out the best in all of us
United Way

It's a matter of life and breath
American Cancer Society

It's the right thing to do
Foster Parents Plan

It takes a man to help a boy
Big Brother

Please! Only *you* can prevent forest fires
The Advertising Council

To make every community as clean as its cleanest home
National Clean Up Campaign Bureau

Support the club that beats the streets
Boys & Girls Club

Together, we can change things
American Red Cross

We're fighting for your life
American Heart Association

We're not asking you to save the world. Just the life of one child.
Christian Children's Fund

Public Utilities

PUBLIC UTILITIES

A citizen, wherever we serve
Georgia Railway & Power Co.

Ask the man from Northern Plains
Northern Natural Gas Co.

At your service
New York Edison

Better light brings better living
Consumers Public Power District

Electricity gives you matchless cooking
Los Angeles Bureau of Power and Light

Electricity ... it's still hard to find a better value
Northeast Utilities

288

People-Powered
>Pacific Gas and Electric Co.

People you can depend on to power America's progress
>Investor-Owned Electric Light and Power Cos.

Power for progress
>Consolidated Edison Co.

Putting more warmth in your life
>(*gas*) Michcon

Taxpaying servant of a great state
>New Jersey Public Service Electric and Gas Co.

The power that lights and moves Alabama
>Alabama Power Co.

The power to please!
>Florida Power Corp.

This is the center of industrial America
>Ohio Edison–Pennsylvania Power

PUBLISHING
See also PERIODICALS AND NEWSPAPERS

A good society is good business
>McGraw–Hill Inc.

Balanced reading for discriminating people
>(*Circle 12 books*)

Built through generations
>(*Encyclopedia Americana*)

For the climate of excellence
>Cahners Publishing Co. Inc.

For the best in paperbacks, look for the Penguin
>Penguin Books

Kind to your pocket and pocket book
>Pocket Books Inc.

Like sending your family to college
>(*Webster's International Dictionary*) G. & C. Merriam Co.

Publishing

Reading that's worlds apart
    Science Fiction Book Club

Serving America's schools, homes, commerce and industry
    Rand McNally and Co.

Serving man's need for knowledge ... in many ways
    McGraw–Hill Inc.

The accepted educational standard
    (*Compton's Encyclopaedia*)

The leading name in dictionaries since 1847
    (*Merriam–Webster*) G. & C. Merriam Co.

The live ones!
    Cahners Publishing Co. Inc.

The Supreme Authority
    (*Merriam–Webster*) G. & C. Merriam Co.

The world is yours with the World Book
    W. F. Quarrie & Co.

To be sure you're right ... insist on Merriam–Webster
    G. & C. Merriam Co.

With Time/Life Books, you've got it made
    (*Home Repair & Improvements*) Time–Life Inc.

World's largest specialized publisher
    Gulf Publishing Co.

Radio Equipment

RADIO EQUIPMENT
See also AUDIO EQUIPMENT, TELECOMMUNICATIONS

A famous name in radio since 1921
    DeWald

Air unlox to Magnavox
    Magnavox Co.

Alone in tone
    (*receiving sets*) Magnavox Co.

Always a year ahead
    Zenith Radio Corp.

PIONEERS IN THE RADIO INDUSTRY

Radio Equipment

Always good company
    Radio Industries Corp.

America's smart set
    Admiral Corp.

A musical instrument of quality
    Philco Corp.

A radio that you can play
    Eckhardt Corp.

Beautiful beyond belief in tone and styling
    Bendix Radio Division

Behind the panels of better built sets
    General Radio Corp.

Believe your own ears
    General Electric Co.

Built like a fine watch
    Lombardi Radio Mfg. Co.

Built like a violin
    (*Teletone radio speakers*)

Clear to the ear
    Magnavox Co.

Every one a good one
    Davidson Radio Corp.

Everything for the radio man
    Midwest Radio Co.

Famous for quality the world over
    Philco Corp.

Fits and matches the car you're driving
    (*car radios*) Motorola Inc.

FM at its finest
    Bendix Radio Division

For the man who believes his own ears
    A-C Electrical Mfg. Co.

Grand piano of the radio world
    Fada Radio, Ltd.

Great thrill in radio by the pioneers of short-wave radio
    Stewart–Warner Corp.

In harmony with home and air
    Magnavox Co.

Install it, forget it
    Kodel Radio Corp.

Just as if you were there
    Borkman Radio Corp.

Just plug in, then tune in
    (*batteryless radio sets*) Standard Radio Corp. Ltd.

Known for tone
    (*Stradivara*) Pacific Phonograph Mfg. Co.

Listen, and you'll buy Westinghouse
    Westinghouse Electric Corp.

Listening luxury beyond your highest hopes
    Bendix Radio Division

Mighty monarch of the air
    Majestic

More pleasure per mile
    (*car radios*) American Bosch Corp.

Pioneers in the radio industry
    All-American Radio Corp.

Rivaled only by reality
    Federal Radio Corp.

Royalty of radio since 1920
    Air King

Sensation of radio
    Thermodyne Radio Corp.

The blue tube with the life-like tone
    Arcturus Radio Tube Co.

The choice of noted music critics
    All-American Radio Corp.

The greatest name in aircraft radio
    Bendix Radio Division

Radio Equipment

The heart of reliable radio power
Raytheon Mfg. Co.

The heart of your radio
RCA Radiotron Co.

The original self-contained radio
Operadio Corp.

The pick of the portables
RCA Victor

The proof is in the listening
Motorola Inc.

The radiant name in radio
Magnavox Co.

The radio used by the broadcasting stations
Day-Fan Electric Co.

The radio with the big plus value
General Electric Co.

The real voice of radio
Bendix Radio Division

The sine of merit
Daven Radio Corp.

The tube to buy to satisfy
Magnavox Co.

Wake up to music
General Electric Co

Rail Travel and Cargo

RAIL TRAVEL AND CARGO
See also TRAVEL

A dependable railway
Great Northern Railway

All Aboard Amtrak
(*Amtrak*) National Railroad Passenger Corp.

America's sleepheart
Chesapeake & Ohio Railroad

Be specific, say Union Pacific
    Union Pacific Railroad

Chessie knows the territory
    Chesapeake & Ohio Railroad

Everywhere west
    Chicago, Burlington & Quincy Railroad Co.

First of the Northern Transcontinentals
    Northern Pacific Railway

Four great routes for transcontinental travel
    Southern Pacific Railroad

Freight Railroads are on the move
    American Association of Railroads

Gateway to and from the booming west
    Union Pacific Railroad

Grow, grow by the rail way
    Association of American Railroads

Hauls more freight and handles more passengers than any other
    railroad in the world
        Pennsylvania Railroad

Holiday all the way with …
    Canadian Pacific Railway

In partnership with all America
    Association of American Railroads

Largest railway system in America
    Canadian National Railroad Co.

Linking 13 great states with the nation
    Baltimore & Ohio Railroad

Look ahead. Look South.
    Southern Railway Co.

Miles of travel comfort
    Missouri–Kansas–Texas Railroad Co.

Most popular route to the Rockies
    Burlington Route

Rail Travel and Cargo

Motor coach to train side, the New York idea of travel convenience
Baltimore & Ohio Railroad

On time every day is the Burlington way
Chicago, Burlington & Quincy Railroad Co.

Retire in our sleepers instead of retiring your car
Baltimore & Ohio Railroad

Ride the big red cars
Pacific Electric Railway, Los Angeles

Road of the daily streamliners
Union Pacific Railroad

Road to the future
New York Central System

Route of the incomparable empire builder
Great Northern Railway

Santa Fe all the way
Santa Fe Railroad

Saves a business day
(*DeLuxe Golden State Limited*) Southern Pacific Railroad

Scenic line of the world
Rio Grande Railroad

See America first
Great Northern Railway

See it all by train
Associated British Railways

Serves all the West
Union Pacific Railroad

Serving the Golden Empire
Southern Pacific Railroad

Serving the heart of industrial America
Erie Railroad

Sleep like a kitten, arrive fresh as a daisy
Chesapeake & Ohio Railroad

Southern's accent is on you
Southern Railway Co.

Spans the world
>Canadian Pacific Railway

The aristocrat of winter trains
>Atlantic Coast Line Railroad

The B & O is the way to go
>Baltimore & Ohio Railroad

The Honeymoon Line
>International Railway Co.

The nation's BASIC transportation
>Association of American Railroads

The nation's going-est railroad
>Norfolk and Western Railway

The outstanding scenic way west
>Missouri Pacific Railroad Co.

The railroad of planned progress ... geared to the nation's future
>Rock Island Lines

The railroad that runs by the customer's clock
>Nickel Plate Railroad

The road of a thousand wonders
>Southern Pacific Railroad

The road of planned progress
>Rock Island Lines

The safest, most comfortable way of going places fast
>Pullman Co.

The scenic route
>New York Central Railroad

The seasoned traveler goes by train
>Union Pacific Railroad

The service railroad of America
>Chicago & Eastern Illinois Railway

The summer route you'll brag about
>Burlington Route

The wheels of transportation help turn the wheels of industry
>Union Pacific Railroad

Rail Travel and Cargo

The world's most romantic adventure
    Orient Express

This is the way to run a railroad
    Northern Pacific Railway

To promote the American way of life, depend on the railroad
    Baltimore & Ohio Railroad

Water level route, you can sleep
    New York Central Railroad

RANGES
See HOME APPLIANCES AND EQUIPMENT

Recordings

RECORDINGS
See also AUDIO EQUIPMENT

Angels of the highest order
    (*Seraphim records*) Capitol Records Inc.

"Capitol" of the world
    Capitol Records Inc.

Listen to America
    (*Decca records*)

Pioneers in recording achievement
    Recordisc Corp.

Recordings for the connoisseur
    Vanguard Recording Society Inc.

The best films you never saw
    (*videotape library*) Home Film Festival

The better sex video series
    Chapel Hill Institute for Sexual Enrichment

The music you want when you want it
    RCA Corp.

The stars who make the hits are on RCA Victor records
    RCA Victor

World leader in recorded sound
    (*Command*) ABC Records Inc.

World's largest selection of audio books
        Books on Tape

RECORD PLAYERS
See AUDIO EQUIPMENT

RECORDS
See RECORDINGS

RECREATIONAL EQUIPMENT
See also BOATS AND BOATING EQUIPMENT,   FIREARMS,
FISHING SUPPLIES,   HEALTH AND FITNESS,   MOTORCYCLES,
SPORTING GOODS,   SWIMWEAR,   TOYS AND GAMES

America's finest campers
        Highway Cruisers Inc.

America's largest builder of camping trailers
        Nimrod Ward Mfg. Co.

America's most popular camp stove
        American Gas Machine Co.

Cook stove and gas plant all in one
        Coleman Lamp Co.

Fits the sport
        (*outdoor equipment*) Red Head Brand Co.

Foremost brand in outdoor living
        American Thermos Products Co.

Get out while you can
        Jansport travel packs

Greatest name in the great outdoors. Foremost name in indoor
    comfort.
        Coleman Co. Inc.

Light, heat and cook the Coleman way
        Coleman Lamp Co.

Made like a gun
        (*Royal Enfield bicycle*)

Quality requires no apology
        (*outdoor clothing*) Red Head Brand Co.

Recreational Equipment

The bike you'll like
> (*Yale bicycles*) Davis Sewing Machine Co.

The smooth way to rough it
> (*camp stoves*) Coleman Lamp Co.

REFRIGERATORS
See HOME APPLIANCES AND EQUIPMENT

RELISHES
See CONDIMENTS AND SPICES

REMEDIES
See DRUGS AND REMEDIES

Restaurants

RESTAURANTS
See also FOOD, MISCELLANEOUS

Are you ready for some real food?
> Hardee's

Good food is good health
> National Restaurant Association

Have it your way
> Burger King

Host of the highways
> Howard Johnson Co.

It's a good time for the great taste of McDonald's
> McDonald Corp.

It's worth the trip
> Dunkin' Donuts of America Inc.

Landmark for hungry Americans
> Howard Johnson Co.

Makin' it great
> Pizza Hut

McDonald's and you
> McDonald's Corp.

The nation's host from coast to coast
> Child's Restaurants

UNTOUCHED BY HUMAN HANDS

Restaurants

Untouched by human hands
    Chock Full O' Nuts Restaurants

What foods these morsels be
    J. N. Adams Tea Room, Buffalo, New York

Where's the beef?
    Wendy's

You deserve a break today
    (*McDonald's*) McDonald's Corp.

You want something better, you're Wendy's kind of people
    Wendy's International Inc.

Retail Stores

RETAIL STORES

Always first quality
    J. C. Penney & Co. Inc.

Always the low price. Always.
    Wal-Mart Corp.

America's most beautiful store
    Russek's, New York

A place to discover
    Pier 1 Imports

Cleveland's better food markets
    Kroger Co.

For good eating at sensible cost
    (*A & P Stores*) Great Atlantic & Pacific Tea Co. Inc.

For important clothes, it's Kerman Stores
    Kerman Stores

For that certain kind of woman
    Peck and Peck

It's always a pleasure
    B. Altman & Co.

King of them all
    Rexall Stores

Known for values
    W. T. Grant Co.

Largest in the world because we serve the people best
    United Cigar Stores

Meet me at the fountain
    Greenhut–Siegel–Cooper

Meet me at the Music Box
    Economy Drug Co., Cleveland

No one is in debt to Macy's
    Macy's

On the Square
    Klein's, New York

Pittsburgh's greatest store
    Kaufmann & Baer Co.

Shop at Sears and save
    Sears, Roebuck & Co.

Shop with people of taste
    B. Altman & Co.

Specialty shop of Originations
    Bonwit Teller & Co.

Store of individual shops
    Franklin Simon & Co.

The difference between dressed, and well dressed
    Bally of Switzerland

The Friendly Store
    Oliver A. Olson Co. Inc.

The Heart of Milwaukee
    Boston Store

The maxx for the minimum
    T.J. Maxx

The meeting place of the thrifty
    Hunter's Variety Store, Memphis, Tennessee

The oldest mail order house is today the most progressive
    Montgomery Ward

The quality you need, the price you want
    Kmart Corp

303

There is one near you
>> Rexall Drug Co.

There's always a new reason to shop Bradlees
>> The Stop & Shop Companies

There's more for your life at Sears
>> Sears, Roebuck & Co.

There's one near you to serve you
>> Singer Sewing Center

The saving place
>> Kmart Corp.

We've got it good
>> Kmart Corp.

You can count on us
>> Sears, Roebuck & Co.

You can't do better than Sears
>> Sears, Roebuck & Co.

You never pay more at Best's
>> Best & Co.

SCALES
See INSTRUMENTS AND GAUGES

SCHOOLS

America's foremost school of commercial art
>> Federal Schools

A real education for the real world
>> Marine Military Academy

Be wise, protect your future
>> Cal-Aero Technical Institute, Glendale, California

Broadcasts as she bakes
>> Radio Cooking School of America

Earn while you learn
>> International Correspondence Schools, Scranton, Pennsylvania

Go to high school in bedroom slippers
        International Correspondence Schools, Scranton, Pennsylvan-
        ia

Originators of radio home-study training
        National Radio Institute

SyberVision. For the way life can be.
        (*Video courses*) SyberVision Systems Inc.

The business leaders of today are the I. C. S. students of yesterday
        International Correspondence Schools, Scranton, Pennsylvan-
        ia

The foreign language experts
        Berlitz Publishing Co.

The West Point of Christian service
        Moody Bible Institute of Chicago

The world's largest business training institute
        LaSalle Extension University

University of the night
        International Correspondence Schools, Scranton, Pennsylvan-
        ia

We can free the writer in you
        (*NRI School of Writing*) McGraw–Hill Continuing Education
        Center

We teach wherever the mails reach
        International Correspondence Schools, Scranton, Pennsylvan-
        ia

Your future is closer than you think
        Wayne State University, Detroit, Michigan

SEA TRAVEL AND CARGO
See also BOATS AND BOATING EQUIPMENT, TRAVEL

Across the Atlantic
        United American Lines

African business is our business
        Farrell Lines Inc.

Allow us to exceed your expectations
  Celebrity Cruises

A thousand miles of travel, a thousand thrills of pleasure
  Canadian Steamship Lines Ltd.

Cruising everywhere under the sun
  American President Lines

Don't miss a thing
  American Hawaii Cruises and Land Vacations

It's more than a cruise, it's the Love Boat
  Princess Cruises

… Just for the sun of it
  T. S. Hanseatic German Atlantic Line

Knows the Pacific
  Matson Lines

Life at sea is like nothing on earth
  P and O Lines

Luxury and comfort with utmost safety
  United States Lines Inc.

More fun per ton than any other line
  Italian Line

Niagara to the sea
  Canada Steamship Lines Ltd.

Pleasure pirate pilgrimage
  United American Lines

Run away to sea with P and O
  P and O Lines

Sail a happy ship
  Holland–American Line

Sail with the British tradition wherever you go
  Cunard Lines

Sunlane cruises to Europe
  American Export Isbrandtsen Lines Inc.

Sunshine belt to the Orient
  Dollar Steamship Lines

The "Champagne Touch"
    Moore–McCormack Lines Inc.

The experience cruise line
    Furness, Withy and Co. Ltd.

The Grand Resorts of the Seven Seas
    (*cruise line*) Royal Caribbean

The lucky ones go Anchor Line
    The Anchor Line

The most popular cruise line in the world!
    Carnival Cruise Lines

The Official Cruise Line of Walt Disney World
    Premier's Big Red Boat

The people who invented a nicer way to cruise
    Holland–American Line

The ships that serve Hawaii, South Seas and Australia
    Matson Navigation Co.

The splendor has begun
    Majesty Cruise Line

The voyage of your dreams
    United American Lines

The white Viking fleet
    Swedish American Line

The world's supreme travel experience
    American President Lines

Unwind your way to Europe
    Italian Line

We're not the best because we're the oldest. We're the oldest because
    we're the best.
        (*cruise lines*) Cunard

SEEDS
See FARMING SUPPLIES AND EQUIPMENT

SEWING AND KNITTING SUPPLIES
See also TEXTILES

An extra collar for a dollar
  (*League collars*) Goodman Collar Co.

Buttons that are MORE than buttons
  (*Costumakers*) Lidz Brothers Inc.

Dispels dressing discords
  (*Harmony Brand*) Federal Snap Fastener Corp.

Every color in the rainbow
  (*yarns*) S. W. & B. W. Fleisher Inc.

Extra strength that never fails you
  (*Bell thread*)

Guaranteed without an IF
  (*blanket binding*) Warren Weatherbone Co.

It's the yarn that counts
  American Yarn & Process Co.

It takes needles to make shirts
  L. Needles–Brooker Co.

Join the knit parade
  (*knitting needles*) C. J. Bates & Son

Snap with the turtle back
  (*So E-Z snap fastener*) A. L. Clarke & Co.

The favorite home-sewing notion of the nation
  Slide Fasteners Inc.

The laundry proof snap fastener that ends button-bother
  (*Gripper fasteners*) Scovill Manufacturing Co.

The major zipper
  (*Conmar zippers*)

The third dimension pattern
  Advance Pattern Co.

The yarn you love to use
  (*Bear Brand yarn*) Bernhard Ulman Co.

Turn a circle without a wrinkle
  (*bias fold tapes*) Friedberger–Aaron Mfg. Co.

You call it a "zipper"; its real name is Prentice, the dependable slide
    fastener
        G. E. Prentice Mfg. Co.

SHAMPOO
See HAIR CARE

SHAVING SUPPLIES
See also BATH ACCESSORIES, PERFUMES AND FRAGRANCES,
SOAP, TOILETRIES

Avoid 5 o'clock shadow
        Gem Safety Razor Corp.

Below skin level shave
        (*Packard electric shaver*) Lektro Products Inc.

Cools and soothes as you shave
        F. F. Ingram Co.

Easy does it
        (*Enders shaver*)

For a cooling shave
        F. F. Ingram Co.

For a royal shave
        King Razor Co.

For shaving without brush or lather
        Pryde–Wynn Co.

For smooth shaves
        Twinplex Sales Co.

For the one man in 7 who shaves every day
        (*Glider brushless shave*)

Get ready for the extraordinary
        (*Edge Extra shaving gel*) Johnson & Johnson

Get the Atra advantage
        (*Atra razors*) The Gillette Co.

Good for its face value
        (*shaving cream*) Vantine & Co.

Has the "edge" five ways
Pal Blade Co.

How to get further with father
(*Seaforth shaving set*) Seaforth Corp.

It lulls the skin
(*shaving cream*) Coty Inc.

It's quick-wetting
(*Williams shaving cream*) J. B. Williams Co. Inc.

Just a darn good shaving cream
Commercial Laboratories

Look sharp! Feel sharp! Be sharp!
(*Gillette blades*) The Gillette Co.

Makes electric shaving easier
(*Lectric shave lotion*) J. B. Williams Co. Inc.

Must make good or we will
(*Genco razors*) Geneva Cutlery Corp.

No pull, no pain, no sting
(*Barbasol shaving cream*) Leeming/Pacquin

Nothing too good for men in service
The Mennen Co.

Saves shaving seconds and second shavings
(*Durex razor blades*) Perma-Sharp Manufacturing Corp.

Shave with a smile
Durham–Duplex Razor Co.

Softens the beard at the base
Colgate & Co.

The ball-bearing shave
E. R. Squibb & Sons

The blades men swear by, not at
Durham–Duplex Razor Co.

The brushless wonder
(*Benex brushless shave*)

The civilized way of shaving
(*Schick dry razor*) Warner–Lambert Pharmaceutical Co.

The close electric shave
> (*Norelco*) North American Philips Corp.

The comfort shave
> (*Norelco*) North American Philips Corp.

The gift that endears and endures
> (*Lektro shaver*)

The little barber in a box
> American Safety Razor Corp.

The only new idea in shaving since the safety razor
> (*Vaniva shaving cream*)

There's something about an Aqua Velva man
> (*Aqua Velva After Shave Lotion*) J. B. Williams Co. Inc.

The shave is better when the lather stays wetter
> (*Lifebuoy shaving cream*) Lever Bros. Co.

The woman's razor
> Curvfit Products Co.

The world's coolest shave
> (*shaving cream*) F. F. Ingram Co.

Where face fitness starts
> (*Williams shaving cream*) J. B. Williams Co. Inc.

Wilts whiskers
> (*shaving cream*) The Mennen Co.

You can shave in a foxhole with X-Ray
> Hamilton Preparations

You can't get any closer
> (*Norelco*) North American Philips Corp.

You pay less for Gem Blades because you need so few
> Gem Safety Razor Corp.

SHIPPING
See AEROSPACE, RAIL TRAVEL AND CARGO, SEA TRAVEL AND CARGO, TRUCKS AND TRUCKING INDUSTRY

SHOES
See FOOTWEAR

SILVER
See JEWELRY AND SILVER

SKIN CARE
See COSMETICS, TOILETRIES

SMOKING ACCESSORIES
See also TOBACCO PRODUCTS

A classic in wood
    (*pipes*) Kaywoodie Co.

America's most distinguished cigarette holder
    Kirsten Pipe Co.

Automatically better
    (*cigarette lighters*) Ronson Corp.

Cooler on the draw
    (*Royal Duke pipes*) Grabow Pre-Smoked Pipes Inc.

Dignifying the pipe
    (*One-Up tobacco case*) Smokers Products Inc.

Filters the smoke from bowl to tip
    (*Forecaster pipe*) National Briar Pipe Co.

Graduate to Kaywoodie
    (*pipes*) Kaywoodie Co.

"Heart of the root" briar
    (*Rembrandt pipes*) National Briar Pipe Co.

It filters the smoke
    (*De Nicotea cigarette holder*)

Look through and see
    (*cigarette holders*) Kirsten Pipe Co.

No breaking-in with Yello-Bole
    (*pipe*) Kaufman Bros. & Bondy

Pathfinders in pipedom
    M. Linkman & Co.

Press, it's lit; release, it's out
    (*lighters*) Ronson Corp.

THE WORLD'S COOLEST SHAVE

Smoking Accessories

Ripe 'n ready for smokin' steady
    Grabow Pre-Smoked Pipes Inc.

Smoke all you like, like all you smoke
    (*cigarette holders*) L. & H. Stern Co.

Sweeter as the years go by
    (*pipes*) Kaywoodie Co.

The insured pipe
    Wm. Demuth & Co.

The lighter that made the world lighter-conscious
    Zippo Mfg. Co.

The lighter that works
    Zippo Mfg. Co.

The people who keep improving flame
    (*lighters*) Ronson Corp.

The pipe of distinction
    L. & H. Stern Co.

The pipe that's broken in
    M. Linkman & Co.

The sweetest pipe in the world
    Wm. Demuth & Co.

The up-draft lighter
    (*Lord Oxford lighters*)

Try Hollycourt. Why? The bowl stays dry.
    (*pipes*) M. Linkman & Co.

Soap

SOAP
See also BABY PRODUCTS, BATH ACCESSORIES, CLEANING
AND LAUNDRY PRODUCTS, SHAVING SUPPLIES, TOILETRIES

Adorns your skin with the fragrance men love
    (*Cashmere Bouquet*) Colgate–Palmolive Co.

A lovelier skin with just one cake
    (*Camay soap*) Procter & Gamble Co.

Aren't you glad *you* use Dial? Don't you wish *everybody* did?
    Armour and Co.

Before you dress, Caress
Lever Brothers Co.

Best for you and baby, too
Albert Soaps Co.

Beware of B. O.
(*Lifebuoy*) Lever Bros. Co.

Cleans with a caress
(*Castile soap*) Conti Products

Doctors prove Palmolive's beauty results
(*Palmolive soap*) Colgate–Palmolive Co.

Don't face another day without Dial
Armour & Co.

Dove creams your skin while you wash
Personal Products Division, Lever Bros. Co.

Dove is 1/4 cleansing cream
(*Dove*) Lever Bros. Co.

Good morning! Have you used Pears' Soap?
A. & F. Pears Ltd.

It floats
(*Ivory soap*) Procter & Gamble Co.

It won't dry your face like soap
(*Dove*) Lever Brothers Co.

Ivory is kind to everything it touches
(*Ivory*) Procter & Gamble Co.

Keep that schoolgirl complexion
(*Palmolive soap*) Colgate–Palmolive Co.

Lux every day keeps old hands away
(*Lux soap*) Lever Bros. Co.

99 44/100% pure
(*Ivory soap*) Procter & Gamble Co.

Pussycat-smooth hands
(*soap*) Newell–Gutradt Co.

Removes the grime in half the time
(*powdered hand soap*) The Hanzo Co.

Soap

Soap without the "soupy" mess
(*Softsoap Liquid Soap*)

The cream of olive oil soaps
Peet Bros. Mfg. Co.

The deoderant soap that's better for your skin and all your 2,000 parts
(*Lever 2000*) Lever Bros. Co.

The eye-opener
(*Coast Deodorant Soap*) Procter & Gamble Co.

The health soap
(*Lifebuoy*) Lever Bros. Co.

The lovelier soap with the costlier perfume
(*Cashmere Bouquet*) Colgate–Palmolive Co.

The skin you love to touch
(*Woodbury's facial soap*) Andrew Jergens Co.

The soap of beautiful women
Procter & Gamble Co.

The soap that agrees with your skin
(*Sweetheart*) Manhattan Soap Co.

World's worst beauty soap. World's *best* hand soap.
(*Lava*) Procter & Gamble Co.

You're not fully clean unless you're Zest fully clean
(*Zest*)

SOCIAL ISSUES
See POLITICAL ISSUES

SOCKS
See HOSIERY

SODA
See SOFT DRINKS

America Dry for dry America
    (*ginger ale*) V. & E. Kohnstamm Inc.

America's most modern cola
    (*Diet-Rite*) Royal Crown Cola Co.

America's No. 1 low-calorie cola
    (*Diet-Rite*) Royal Crown Cola Co.

Best by taste test
    (*Royal Crown Cola*) Nehi Corp.

Buy a rack of Rooties
    Krueger Beverage Co.

Canada Dry Ginger Ale. For when your tastes grow up.
    Canada Dry Corp.

Caffeine free. Never had it. Never will.
    (*7-Up*) The Seven-Up Co.

Coke is it
    (*Coca-Cola*) Coca-Cola Co.

Come alive!
    (*Pepsi-Cola*) Pepsico Inc.

Delicious and refreshing
    Coca-Cola Co.

Drink Coca-Cola
    (*Coca-Cola*) Coca-Cola Co.

Drink RC for quick, fresh energy
    Royal Crown Cola Co.

First aid for thirst
    Lime Cola Co.

Flavor sealed in the brown bottle
    (*Orange Crush*) Crush International Inc.

For those who think young
    (*Pepsi-Cola*) Pepsico Inc.

Fresh-up with Seven-up
    The Seven-Up Co.

Good vibrations
    (*Sunkist Orange Soda*) Sunkist Growers Inc.

Gotta have it
    (*Pepsi*) Pepsicola Co.

Hires to you for a better tomorrow
    (*Hires rootbeer*) Crush International Inc.

Hits the spot
    (*Pepsi-Cola*) Pepsico Inc.

How can just 1 calorie taste so good!
    (*Tab*) Coca-Cola Co.

It's the real thing
    (*Coca-Cola*) Coca-Cola Co.

Join the Pepsi generation
    (*Pepsi-Cola*) Pepsico Inc.

Just for the taste of it
    (*Diet Coke*) Coca-Cola Co.

Kids love Kool-Aid
    (*Kool-Aid*) General Foods Corp.

Mellow as the greeting of old friends
    (*Canada Dry ginger ale*) Canada Dry Corp.

Refresh yourself
    Coca-Cola Co.

Taste champ of the colas
    (*Royal Crown Cola*) Nehi Corp.

Taste that beats the others cold
    (*Pepsi-Cola*) Pepsico Inc.

The drink you remember
    (*O'Keefe's ginger ale*)

The global high-sign
    Coca-Cola Co.

The pause that refreshes
    Coca-Cola Co.

The toast to good taste
    (*Hires rootbeer*) Crush International Inc.

The Uncola
	The Seven-Up Co.

Things go better with Coke
	Coca-Cola Co.

Thirst come, thirst served
	(*Goody Root Beer*) Bottlers Supply & Manufacturing Co.

With real root juices
	(*Hires rootbeer*) Crush International Inc.

You like it, it likes you
	The Seven-Up Co.

You're beautiful to me
	(*Tab*) Coca-Cola Co.

You're the Pepsi generation
	Pepsico Inc.

SOFTWARE
See COMPUTER EQUIPMENT

SPICES
See CONDIMENTS AND SPICES

SPORTING GOODS
See also BOATS AND BOATING EQUIPMENT, FIREARMS, FISHING SUPPLIES, FOOTWEAR, HEALTH AND FITNESS, RECREATIONAL EQUIPMENT, SWIMWEAR, TOYS AND GAMES

A national rider never changes his mount
	(*National bicycles*) Davis Sewing Machine Co.

And who makes great skis? Head, of course.
	Head Ski Co.

Ball that made baseball
	A. G. Spalding & Bros.

Bowl where you see the Magic Triangle
	(*AMF bowling equipment*) American Machine and Foundry Co.

Course tested golf clubs
	Crawford, McGregor & Canby Co.

From the Heart of the Mountains. Aspen, Colorado.
(*ski wear*) Obermeyer

Golfcraft for the finest
Golfcraft Inc.

Hand made to fit you
(*golf clubs*) Kenneth Smith

Hottest name in golf
Kroydon Golf Corp.

If the boot fits comfortably ... it's Dolomite
(*ski boots*) Dolomite America Inc.

King of all tees
(*Rex tees*) Jack Shipman

Leadership. By Example.
(*ski boots*) Tecnica USA

Make the mountain bleed
(*Monocoque slalom skis*) Salomon North America Inc.

Named for the original American professionals
Indian Archery Corp.

No. 1 name in bowling
Brunswick Corp.

Play ball with Pennsylvania
(*rubber balls*) Pennsylvania Tire Co.

Play safe with Wilco
(*float coat*) Willer & Son

Play to *win* with Wilson
Wilson Sporting Goods Co.

Remember: no one is paid to play Titleist
(*golf balls*) Acushnet Co.

Taking technology to the peak
(*ski gloves*) Gates Mills Inc.

The best with the *most* on the ball
Adirondack Bats Inc.

The greatest name in golf
(*golfing equipment*) MacGregor Co.

The nation's big name in archery
>Ben Pearson Inc.

The no. 1 name in billiards
>Brunswick Corp.

There's Wilson equipment for every sport
>Thos. E. Wilson Co.

The Swiss art in ski boots
>Raichle Molitor USA

They take every trick
>(*Grand Slam golf clubs*) Hillerich & Bradsby Co. Inc.

Vision Perfect
>(*Matrix AER ski goggles*) Smith Sport Optics Inc.

Wings of steel
>(*ice skates*) Nestor Johnson Mfg. Co.

World's most experienced ski maker
>Northland Ski Mfg. Co.

You don't have to be a millionaire to play like one
>Walter Hagen Golf Epuipment Co.

STATIONERY SUPPLIES
See OFFICE EQUIPMENT AND SUPPLIES, PAPER PRODUCTS, WRITING INSTRUMENTS

STEREOS
See AUDIO EQUIPMENT

STOCKINGS
See HOSIERY

STORAGE
See MOVING AND STORAGE

STOVES
See HOME APPLIANCES AND EQUIPMENT

SUNGLASSES
See EYEGLASSES

SWEETS
See CANDY AND GUM

Swimwear

SWIMWEAR
See also CLOTHING, MISCELLANEOUS;   RECREATIONAL
EQUIPMENT;   SPORTING GOODS

Come on, you sunners
       (*Jantzen swimsuit*) Jantzen Inc.

Delightfully see-worthy
       (*Jordan swimsuits*)

Shows good form in the stretch
       (*Lastex swimsuit*) Uniroyal Inc.

The season belongs to Jantzen
       Jantzen

TABLEWARE
See CHINA,   JEWELRY AND SILVER

TAPE DECKS
See AUDIO EQUIPMENT

TAPES
See RECORDINGS

Tea

TEA
See also BEVERAGES, MISCELLANEOUS;   COFFEE;   SOFT DRINKS

All natural. No caffeine.
       (*herb teas*) Celestial Seasonings

A personal blend
       (*Mother Parker's*)

Brighten up with Instant Tender Leaf Tea
       Standard Brands Inc.

Fresh from the gardens
       Salada Tea Co.

Makes good tea a certainty
       (*Tetley*) Joseph Tetley & Co. Inc.

Safe-Tea First
       Ridgeways Inc.

Soothing teas for a nervous world
  (*herb teas*) Celestial Seasonings

Tea doesn't have to be boring
  (*herb teas*) Celestial Seasonings

The brisk tea
  Thomas J. Lipton Inc.

The empire's best
  (*Lyon's*)

The most expensive tea grown
  Ming Inc.

There's more to it
  India Tea Bureau

"T" stands for Tetley's—Tetley stands for finest TEA
  Joseph Tetley & Co. Inc.

TELECOMMUNICATIONS
See also BROADCASTING, RADIO EQUIPMENT

All around the world
  Western Union

AT&T. The right choice.
  AT&T

Building better communications
  Mitel Corp.

Call Sprint. Find out about it.
  (*Sprint long distance system*) GTE

Communications for the next 100 years
  MCI Communications Corp.

Don't write, telegraph
  Western Union

Don't write, telephone
  Bell Telephone Co.

Everything you expect from a leader
  (*cellular communications*) MobileComm

For a better bottom line
     NEC Telephones Inc.

Gee! No, GTE
     GTE

In the twinkling of an eye
     (*telephone system*) Trans-Canada System

Let us show you
     MCI

Long distance is the next best thing to being there
     (*Bell System*) AT&T

One policy, one system, universal service
     AT&T

Our ambition: ideal telephone service for Michigan
     Michigan Bell Telephone Co.

Out of town not out of touch
     (*Sky Pager*) National Satellite Paging

Profit ability through telecommunications
     Continental Telephone Corp.

Reach out and touch someone
     (*long distance calling*) AT&T

Sharing greatly in America's growth
     General Telephone and Electronics Corp.

So many times a telegram means so much
     Western Union

Sprint is smart
     U.S. Sprint Communications Corp.

Talk things over, get things done ... by long distance!
     (*Bell System*) AT&T

Technology the world calls on
     Nothern Telecom

The global computer and communications company
     (*pocket cellular phone*) Fujitsu Network Transmission
     Systems Inc.

The knowledge business
    Bell Telephone Co.

The more you hear, the better we sound
    AT&T

The nation's long distance phone company
    MCI

The phone companies' phone company
    American Telecommunications Corporation

The voice with the smile
    Bell Telephone Co.

We bring the world closer
    AT&T

We're more than just talk
    Bell Atlantic Telecommunications

We're reaching out in new directions
    AT&T

Worldwide electronics telecommunications
    International Telephone and Telegraph Co.

You'll be hearing from us
    Mura

Your anywhere, anything, anytime network
    AT&T

Your best business connection
    CellularOne

TELEVISIONS
See also ELECTRONICS INDUSTRY, HOME APPLIANCES AND
EQUIPMENT, MOVIES AND ENTERTAINMENT, VIDEO
EQUIPMENT

A flair for elegance
    Sylvania Electric Products Inc.

A world leader in technology
    Hitachi Sales Corporation

Televisions

Built better because it's handcrafted
   Zenith Radio Corp.

Mark of quality throughout the world
   Admiral Corp.

The international one
   Toshiba America Inc.

The magnificent
   Magnavox Co.

The most expensive television set in America ... and darn well worth
   it
   (*Curtis–Mathes*) Curtis–Mathes Sales Co.

The most trusted name in television
   RCA Corp.

The quality goes in before the name goes on
   Zenith Radio Corp.

The theatre in your home
   U. S. Television Mfg. Corp.

We'll open your eyes
   (*RCA*) RCA Corp.

Window to the world
   U. S. Television Mfg. Corp.

Textiles

TEXTILES
See also INTERIOR DECORATION, SEWING AND KNITTING
SUPPLIES

Add a fiber from Celanese and good things get better
   Celanese Corp.

A man you can lean on, that's Klopman
   Klopman Mills Inc.

America lives in Dacron
   Du Pont

Be suspicious!
   (*Sanforized*) Cluett, Peabody & Co. Inc.

Comfortable, carefree cotton
Cotton Producers Institute

Contemporary fibers
Celanese Corp.

Cotton, you can feel how good it looks
National Cotton Council

Fine fabrics made in America since 1813
J. P. Stevens and Co. Inc.

If it's Darbrook, it's durable
(*silks*) Schwarzenbach Huber & Co.

It's better because it's made of Koroseal
Comprehensive Fabrics Inc.

Keeps the shape
Pellon Corp.

Linen damask, impressively correct
Irish & Scottish Linen Damask Guild

Luxury acrylic fiber
(*Creslan*) American Cyanamid Co.

Nothing but nylon makes you feel so female
Textiles Division, Monsanto Co.

Nothing but Spandex makes you look so female
Textiles Division, Monsanto Co.

One of the oldest names in textiles ... for the newest development in
synthetics
Conmark Plastics Division, Cohn–Hall–Marx Co.

Rhymes with increase
(*Cantrece*) Du Pont

The climate control fabric
(*Polartec*) Malden Mills

The fabric with reflex action
(*Expandra*) Burlington Industries Inc.

The home furnishings fiber
(*Herculon*) Hercules Inc.

Textiles

The luxury of velvet with the worry left out
(*Islon*) Textiles Division, Monsanto Co.

The more colorful nylon
(*Caprolan*) Allied Chemical Corp.

There are imitations, of course
Viyella International Inc.

The shrinkage control that lets the wool breathe
American Cyanamid Co.

"Well dressed/wool dressed"
American Wool Council

Woven where the wool is grown
Oregon City Woolen Mills

TIMEPIECES
See WATCHES AND CLOCKS

Tires

TIRES
See also AUTOMOTIVE PARTS AND PRODUCTS

A bear for wear
Gillette Rubber Co.

A good deal on a great tire
(*Kelly Tires*) Kelly–Springfield Tire Co.

Around the world on Dunlops
Dunlop Tire & Rubber Corp.

Because so much is riding on your tires
Michelin

Broad, black, and a brute for wear
Cupples Co.

Built from the road up
(*Biltwell tires*)

Built layer on layer
(*Miller tires*) B. F. Goodrich Co.

High-performance tirepower
Firestone Tire and Rubber Co.

Lots of Flatt tires running around
    R. A. Flatt Tire Co.

Makers of the safety stripe tread
    (*Fisk*) Uniroyal Tire Co.

Makes a blow-out harmless
    (*safety tubes*) Goodyear Tire and Rubber Co.

Means more mileage
    Mason Tire & Rubber Co.

More people ride on Goodyear tires than on any other brand
    Goodyear Tire and Rubber Co.

Most miles per dollar
    Firestone Tire and Rubber Co.

New dimensions in driving on the *safer* Kelly road
    The Kelly–Springfield Tire Co.

Outcleans, outpulls, outlasts
    Firestone Tire and Rubber Co.

Remember the horse-shoe tread
    (*Racine tires*)

Ride the road of satisfaction
    (*Atlas tires*) Atlas Supply Co.

Skip the rest and drive the best
    (*Federal tires*)

Smile at miles
    (*Lee balloon tires*)

Sooner or later, you'll own Generals
    General Tire and Rubber Co.

The best tires in the world have Goodyear written all over them
    Goodyear Tire and Rubber Co.

The greatest tire name in racing
    Firestone Tire and Rubber Co.

The most beautiful tire in America
    Hydro-United Tire Co.

The name that's known is Firestone—all over the world
    Firestone Tire and Rubber Co.

Tires

The round tire that rolls 3,000 miles further
>(*Atlas Plycron*) General Tire and Rubber Co.

The straight-talk tire people
>B. F. Goodrich Co.

Time to retire?
>Fisk Tire

You're miles ahead with General Tire
>General Tire and Rubber Co.

Tobacco Products

TOBACCO PRODUCTS
See also SMOKING ACCESSORIES

A fistful of flavor for small change
>(*Bull Durham cigarettes*)

After all, if smoking isn't a pleasure, why bother?
>(*Newport*) Lorilard Inc.

A honey of a tobacco
>(*Cookie Jar tobacco*) United States Tobacco Co.

Alive with pleasure
>(*Newport*) Lorilard Inc.

All out tobacco taste that satisfies without inhaling
>(*Tiparillo*)

Always better, better all ways
>(*Philip Morris*) Philip Morris Inc.

America's best tasting little cigar
>(*Between the Acts*) Lorillard Corp.

America's smoothest tobacco
>(*Velvet*) Liggett & Myers Inc.

A pinch is all it takes
>(*Skoal Bandits chewing tobacco*) United States Tobacco Co.

A pipe's best friend is fragrant Heine's blend
>Sutliff Tobacco Co.

A *real* cigarette
>(*Camel*) R. J. Reynolds Tobacco Co.

Aromatic in the pack, aromatic in the pipe
   (*Holiday tobacco*)

A sensible cigarette
   (*Fatima*) Liggett & Myers Inc.

A shilling in London, a quarter here
   (*Pall Mall*) American Tobacco Co.

Ask Dad, he knows
   (*Sweet Caporal*) American Tobacco Co.

Ask him why he smokes a Webster
   Webster Cigar Co.

Barking Dog never bites
   Continental Tobacco Co.

Be nonchalant, light a Deity
   (*Egyptian Deities*)

Buy word of millions
   (*King Edward cigars*)

Camels agree with me
   R. J. Reynolds Tobacco Co.

Camels suit your T-zone to a T
   R. J. Reynolds Tobacco Co.

Carlton is lowest
   (*cigarettes*) The American Tobacco Co.

Champion of blends
   (*Sportsman pipe mixture*)

Change to Bond Street for fragrant smoking
   (*Bond Street pipe tobacco*) Philip Morris Inc.

Chesterfield King tastes great ... tastes mild
   Liggett & Myers Inc.

Chew Mail Pouch
   (*Mail Pouch chewing tobacco*) Whitehall Products Inc.

Come to Marlboro Country
   (*Marlboro*) Philip Morris Inc.

Come to where the flavor is ... come to Marlboro country
   Philip Morris Inc.

Come up to the Kool taste
Brown & Williamson Tobacco Corp.

Discover extra coolness
(*Kool*) Brown & Williamson Tobacco Corp.

Every El Dueno cigar is smooth sailing
El Dueno Cigar Co.

Every puff a pleasure
(*cigars*) Gonzalez & Sanchez Co.

Executive America's top cigar
(*Webster*) Webster Cigar Co.

Experience is the best teacher
(*Camel*) R. J. Reynolds Tobacco Co.

Filters the smoke on the way to your throat—filters it and makes it
mild
(*Pall Mall*) American Tobacco Co.

Fine tobacco is what counts in a cigarette
(*Lucky Strike*) American Tobacco Co.

First in the social register
(*cigars*) Webster–Eisenlohr Inc.

For a taste that's *Springtime fresh*
(*Salem*) R. J. Reynolds Tobacco Co.

For deep-down smoking enjoyment smoke that smoke of fine
tobacco—Lucky Strike
(*Lucky Strike*) American Tobacco Co.

For digestion's sake, smoke Camels
R. J. Reynolds Tobacco Co.

For real enjoyment
(*El Producto cigars*) Consolidated Cigar Corp.

For real smoking pleasure
(*Chesterfield*) Liggett Group

For those who want *every* puff to taste as fresh as the *first* puff!
(*Montclair*) American Brands Inc.

For those with time for quality
(*Benson & Hedges*) Philip Morris Inc.

For young men and men with young ideas
General Cigar Co.

Four inches of a 25-cent cigar
The In-B-Tween Co.

Good people make good things
Philip Morris Inc.

Guard against throat-scratch
(*Pall Mall*) American Tobacco Co.

Have you tried a Lucky lately?
(*Lucky Strike*) American Tobacco Co.

I'd rather fight than switch
(*Tareyton*) American Tobacco Co.

I'd walk a mile for a Camel
R. J. Reynolds Tobacco Co.

I envy men the pleasant puffing of their pipes
(*Tuxedo tobacco*) American Tobacco Co.

If every smoker knew what Philip Morris smokers know, they'd all
change to Philip Morris
Philip Morris Inc.

If you want a treat instead of a treatment, smoke Old Golds
Lorillard Corp.

I'm particular
(*Pall Mall*) American Tobacco Co.

It's a pippin
(*cigars*) H. Traiser & Co. Inc.

Its blend is our secret, its fragrance your delight
(*Old Briar tobacco*) United Cigar Stores

It's good because it's fresh
(*Tuxedo tobacco*) American Tobacco Co.

It's mild and mellow
(*Revelation pipe tobacco*) Philip Morris Inc.

It's moisturized
(*Raleigh*) Brown & Williamson Tobacco Corp.

It's More you
> (*More cigarettes*) R. J. Reynolds Tobacco Co.

It started me smoking cigars
> (*Robert Burns cigars*) General Cigar Co.

It's toasted
> (*Lucky Strike*) American Tobacco Co.

Ivory tips protect your lips
> (*Marlboro*) Philip Morris Inc.

Join the first team. Reach for Winston.
> (*Winston cigarettes*) R. J. Reynolds Tobacco Co.

Judged best by the just
> (*Barister cigars*) Celestino Costello Co.

Just enough Turkish
> (*Fatima*) Liggett & Myers Inc.

Leaf tobaccos that satisfy
> (*Louis Greenwald*)

Lightest smoke of all
> (*Carlton*) American Brands Inc.

LS/MFT ... Lucky Strike means fine tobacco
> (*Lucky Strike*) American Tobacco Co.

Luckies are gentle on my throat
> (*Lucky Strike*) American Tobacco Co.

Lucky Strike green has gone to war
> (*Lucky Strike*) American Tobacco Co.

Make a date with Muriel
> (*Muriel cigars*) Consolidated Cigar Corp.

Making smoking "safe" for smokers
> Bonded Tobacco Co.

Man alive! Two for five
> Standard Cigar Co.

Man to man, Roi-Tan, a cigar you'll like
> (*Roi-Tan cigars*) American Cigar Co.

Measure yourself for a Kelly
> (*Kelly cigar*) American Cigar Co.

Menthol-cooled
(*Spuds*)

Mild as May
(*Marlboro*) Philip Morris Inc.

Mildness plus character
Congress Cigar Co.

Millions are saying "Tasting better than ever"
General Cigar Co.

More people are smoking Camels than ever before
R. J. Reynolds Co.

Never gets on your nerves
(*Girard cigar*) Antonio, Roag & Langsdorg

Newport smokes fresher—and tastes better than any other menthol
cigarette
Lorillard Corp.

New taste, *new* smoking convenience ... anywhere, anytime
(*Roi-Tan Little Cigars*) American Brands Inc.

No finer-tasting cigar at any price
(*Seidenberg cigars*) S. Frieder & Sons Co.

No other tobacco is like it
(*Prince Albert tobacco*) R. J. Reynolds Co.

Not a cough in a carload
(*Old Gold*) Lorillard Corp.

Now every man can enjoy his pipe
Sutliff Tobacco Co.

Once tried, always satisfied
(*Golden Virginia tobacco*)

Only Viceroy has this exclusive filter
Brown & Williamson Tobacco Corp.

Our continuing commitment to community service
Brown & Williamson Tobacco Corp.

Outstanding—and they are mild!
(*Pall Mall*) American Tobacco Co.

Pall Mall's grater length travels the smoke further ... gets rid of heat and bite on the way
 (*Pall Mall*) American Tobacco Co.

P. A. means Pipe Appeal
 (*Prince Albert tobacco*) R. J. Reynolds Co.

Players go places
 (*Players cigarettes*) Philip Morris Inc.

Product of Cuban soil and Cuban sun
 (*La Primadora cigars*) Universal Cigar Corp.

Reach for a Lucky instead of a sweet
 (*Lucky Strike*) American Tobacco Co.

Salem softness freshens your taste
 R. J. Reynolds Tobacco Co.

Satisfies *best*
 (*Kent*) Lorillard Corp.

She likes the fragrance
 Sutliff Tobacco Co.

Smart smokers smoke Seidenberg
 (*Seidenberg cigars*) S. Frieder & Sons Co.

Smells better in the pouch; smokes better in the pipe
 (*Model pipe tobacco*) United States Tobacco Co.

Smoke Omar for aroma
 American Tobacco Co.

Sooner or later, your favorite tobacco
 (*Sir Walter Raleigh*) Brown & Williamson Tobacco Corp.

So round, so firm, so fully packed—so free and easy on the draw
 (*Lucky Strike*) American Tobacco Co.

Take a pouch instead of a puff
 (*Skoal Bandits*) United States Tobacco Co.

Tastes great ... yet it smokes so mild
 (*Chesterfield*) Liggett Group

That's putting it MILDLY
 (*Country Doctor pipe mixture*) Philip Morris Inc.

The best in the Union, in pocket tins
   (*Union smoking tobacco*) Lorillard Corp.

The biteless blend
   (*Briggs pipe mixture*) United States Tobacco Co.

The brand with the grand aroma
   Mail Pouch Tobacco Co.

The choice of successful men
   (*Blackstone cigars*) Parodi Cigar Corp.

The cigar made with good judgment
   (*Tom Keene*) General Cigar Co.

The cigar that breathes
   (*Roi-Tan cigars*) American Cigar Co.

The first new no-filter cigarette in years
   (*York*) Lorillard Corp.

The flavor's all yours
   (*Philip Morris*) Philip Morris Inc.

The friendly smoke
   (*Royalist cigars*) Grabowsky Bros. Inc.

The makings of a nation
   (*Bull Durham tobacco*) American Tobacco Co.

The national joy smoke
   (*Prince Albert tobacco*) R. J. Reynolds Co.

The *one* cigarette for everyone who smokes!
   (*Kent*) Lorillard Corp.

The perfect cigarette
   (*Marlboro*) Philip Morris Inc.

The perfect recess
   (*Parliament Lights*)

The pleasure is back
   (*Barclay cigarettes*) Brown & Williamson Tobacco Corp.

There's many a castle built out of cigarette smoke
   Bonded Tobacco Co.

There's something about them you'll like
   (*Herbert Tareyton*) American Tobacco Co.

The sum-total of smoking pleasure
  (*Chesterfield*) Liggett Group

The tunnel at the end of our light
  (*Parliament Lights 100s*)

They respect your throat
  (*Alligator*)

They satisfy and yet they're mild
  (*Chesterfield*) Liggett Group

Watch his smoke
  (*Santa Fe cigars*) A. Sensenbrenner Sons

When a feller needs a friend
  (*Briggs pipe mixture*) United States Tobacco Co.

Where a man belongs
  (*Camel*) R. J. Reynolds Tobacco Co.

Wherever particular people congregate
  (*Pall Mall*) American Tobacco Co.

Why be irritated? Light an Old Gold
  (*Old Gold*) Lorillard Corp.

Why not smoke the finest?
  (*Dunhill*) Alfred Dunhill Co. London

Winston tastes good ... like a cigarette should
  R. J. Reynolds Tobacco Co.

With men who know tobacco best, it's Luckies 2 to 1
  (*Lucky Strike*) American Tobacco Co.

With pleasure, sir!
  General Cigar Co.

With the aroma of the rose
  (*Rosa Aroma cigars*) C. A. Nolan

Your nose quickly knows
  (*Tuxedo pipe tobacco*) American Tobacco Co.

Your smoke comes clean
  (*Viceroy*) Brown & Williamson Tobacco Corp.

You've come a long way, Baby
  (*Virginia Slims Lights*) Philip Morris Inc.

TOILETRIES
See also BATH ACCESSORIES, COSMETICS, DENTAL CARE, HAIR CARE, PERFUMES AND FRAGRANCES, SHAVING SUPPLIES, SOAP

Absorbs your worries about accidents and odor
(*Stayfree maxipads*) Personal Products Co.

As masculine as the trade mark
(*Royal Flush toiletries*) B. Ansehl Co.

A swab by any other name is not the same
(*Q-tips cotton swabs*) Chesebrough–Pond's Inc.

A winner with women
(*Quest deodorant*) Vicks Health Care

Because ...
(*Modess sanitary pads*) Personal Products Co.

Because a better fit means better protection
(*Depend Fitted Briefs*) Kimberly–Clark Co.

Cleaner, drier, better
(*Always maxi- and minipads*) Procter & Gamble Co.

Designed to stop accidents before they start
(*Stayfree Ultra Plus sanitary pads*) Personal Products Co.

Don't be half-safe. Be completely safe. Use Arrid—to be sure.
(*Arrid deodorant*) Carter-Wallace Inc.

For your special cleansing needs
(*Summer's Eve disposable douche*) Personal Laboratories

From intensive research comes intensive care
(*Vaseline Intensive Care lotion*) Chesebrough–Ponds

HUSH takes the odor out of perspiration
Hush Co.

Invented by a doctor—now used by millions of women
(*Tampax tampons*) Tampax Inc.

Keeps you sweet as an angel
(*Neet deodorant*) Whitehall Laboratories

MUM is the word
(*deodorant*) George B. Evans

Never let them see you sweat
  (*Dry Idea*) Gillette Co.

Not a shadow of a doubt
  (*Kotex sanitary pads*) Kimberly–Clark Corp.

Protects you like a man, but still treats you like a woman
  (*Lady Speed Stick deodorant*) The Mennen Co.

Psst ... it's not your mother's tampon
  (*Playtex Ultimates*) Playtex Family Products Corp.

Raise your hand if you're sure
  (*Sure deodorant*) Procter & Gamble Co.

Reduces the signs of aging
  (*L'Oreal Plenitude*) Cosmair Inc.

She's sure—are you?
  (*Odorono deodorant*) Chesebrough–Pond's Inc.

Simple solutions to hygiene problems
  Kimberly–Clark Ltd.

Skin things that do things
  (*Buf-Puf*) 3M Corp.

Stay shower-fresh all day long
  (*Seaforth deodorant for men*) Seaforth Corp.

Strong enough for a man, but PH balanced for a woman
  (*Secret wide solid deoderant*) Procter & Gamble Co.

The finishing touch you can't afford to forget
  (*Seaforth deodorant for men*) Seaforth Corp.

The gentler cream deodorant
  (*Yodora*) Norcliff Thayer Inc.

The perfect under-arm protective
  (*Perstik*) Feminine Products Inc.

The safe-and-sure deodorant
  (*Etiquet*)

The simple solution to saving face
  Old Spice Postshave Conditioner

The sensual moisturizer
  Neutrogena Body Oil

The thin one from day one
(*Sure & Natural sanitary pads*) Personal Products Co.

Tussy really cares about people who care
(*deodorant*) Lehn and Fink Consumer Products

We give you the edge
Gillette Co.

What Scandinavian men have
(*Teak*) Shulton Inc.

When your nose needs the softest
(*Softique tissues*) Kimberly–Clark Corp.

You feel so cool, so clean, so fresh ...
Tampax Inc.

You work hard, you need Right Guard
(*Right Guard deodorant*) The Gillette Co.

TOOLS
See also HARDWARE

Bonded for life ... because they're built that way
Ingersoll–Rand Co.

Choice of better mechanics
Snap-On Tools Corp.

Doggone good tools
Duro Metal Products Co.

Fingers of steel
(*Red Devil pliers*) Smith & Hemenway Co.

For industry, shop, farm and home
(*electric tools*) Black & Decker Mfg. Co.

It pays to use good tools
Vaughan & Bushnell Mfg. Co.

It's all in the wheel
(*glass cutter*) Landon P. Smith Inc.

Jack of all trades and master of plenty
(*Hand-ee tool*) Chicago Wheel & Mfg. Co.

Keep mechanics good tempered
  Velchek Tool Co.

Make an heirloom
  (*woodworker's tools*) Woodcraft Supply Co.

Make hard jobs easy
  K-D Manufacturing Co.

Maker of the world's first cordless electric tools
  Black & Decker Mfg. Co.

Matched tools for *unmatched* performance
  Baash–Ross Division, Joy Mfg. Co.

Relieves the daily grind
  Keystone Emery Mills

Right to the point
  (*Yankee tools*) North Bros. Mfg. Co.

Sands levels tell the truth
  (*levels*) Sands Level & Tool Co.

Service-backed shop equipment
  Snap-On Tools Corp.

Skil makes it easy
  Skil Corp.

The hammer with a backbone
  American Hammer Corp.

The jack that saves your back
  (*Rees jack*) Iron City Products Co.

The key to better grinding
  Black & Decker Mfg. Co.

The right tool for the right job
  True Temper Corp.

The saw most carpenters use
  Henry Disston & Sons

The small lathe for the big job
  Dalton Mfg. Co.

The third hand with a mighty grip
  Prentiss Vise Co.

The tool box of the world
        The Stanley Works

Yankee tools make better mechanics
        North Bros. Mfg. Co

TOOTHPASTE
See DENTAL CARE

TOURISM
See TRAVEL

TOYS AND GAMES
See also BABY PRODUCTS, RECREATIONAL EQUIPMENT,
SPORTING GOODS

A minute to learn. A lifetime to master.
        (*Othello board game*) Ideal Toy Corp.

BICYCLE is the card player's choice
        (*playing cards*) United States Playing Card Co.

Dad played marbles, too
        Akro Agate Co.

Engineering for boys
        (*Meccano*) Designatronics Inc.

For your children's sake
        (*slides, merri-go-rounds*) Merremaker Corp.

Gotta Getta Gund
        (*stuffed animals*) Gund Inc.

Have you had your fun today?
        (*Gameboy electronic game*) Nintendo

It is what it eats
        (*Infocom computer games*) Infocom Inc.

It must be good to be a Gund
        (*stuffed animals*) Gund Inc.

Ives Toys make happy boys
        Ives Mfg. Co.

Made by the tiny Arcadians
Arcade Mfg. Co.

Make men of boys
Structo Mfg. Co.

Our work is child's play
Fisher–Price Toys Inc.

Playtime Pals for the nation's kiddies
Coronet Toy Mfg. Co.

Quality toys with a purpose
(*Tinkertoys*) Toy Tinkers Division, A. G. Spalding and Bros.,
Inc.

Roller skate with three lives
Chicago Roller Skate Co.

Sane toys for healthy kids
Lionel Toy Corp.

The heart's desire for every youngster
(*Reliable dolls*)

The home of toys
F. A. O. Schwartz

The name for quality hobby kits
Monogram Models Inc.

The skate with a backbone
Winchester Repeating Arms Co.

The trains that railroad men buy for their boys
(*Lionel*) Fundimensions

The world of little people
Fisher–Price Toys Inc.

Toys that are genuine
The A. C. Gilbert Co.

Twice as much fun
(*Loco-Builder electric trains*) Dorfan Co.

World's largest creator of preschool toys
Fisher–Price Toys Inc.

TRACTORS
See FARMING SUPPLIES AND EQUIPMENT

TRANSPORTATION
See AIR TRAVEL AND CARGO, BUS LINES, RAIL TRAVEL AND
CARGO, SEA TRAVEL AND CARGO, TRUCKS AND TRUCKING
INDUSTRY

TRAVEL
See also AIR TRAVEL AND CARGO, AUTOMOBILE RENTAL
SERVICES, BUS LINES, ECONOMIC DEVELOPMENT, HOTELS
AND MOTELS, LUGGAGE, MOVING AND STORAGE, RAIL
TRAVEL AND CARGO, SEA TRAVEL AND CARGO

Abroad without crossing the seas
     Montreal Tourist & Convention Bureau, Montreal, Quebec,
     Canada

America borders on the magnificent
     Canadian Ministry of Tourism

America's dairyland
     Wisconsin

America's lake country
     The Thousand Lakes Association, St. Paul, Minnesota

America's most interesting state
     Tennessee Department of Conservation

A short trip to a perfect holiday
     Bermuda

A tradition of excellence
     Holland America Westours

A world in itself
     New Zealand

A world in one country
     South Africa

Birth state of the nation
     Pennsylvania

Center of scenic America
     Salt Lake City, Utah

Come and say G'day
  Australia

Come to Israel. Come stay with friends
  Israeli Government Tourist Office

Come to Jamaica and feel alright
  Jamaica Tourist Board

Come to life in Hawaii
  Hawaii Visitors Bureau

Cool off in Colorado
  Colorado

Crossroads of the Pacific
  Hawaii

Don't leave home without it
  (*American Express card*) American Express Co.

Embrace the Mexican fable
  Puerto Vallarta Tourism Fund, Puerto Vallarta, Mexico

Find your place in the sun
  San Francisco Peninsula

Friendly, familiar, foreign and near
  Ontario, Canada, Department of Tourism and Information

Friendly land of infinite variety
  South Dakota Department of Highways

Give yourself an altitude adjustment
  Idaho

Hub of the Americas
  New Orleans, Louisiana

I Love New York
  New York State Tourist Commission, New York, New York

Inside the rim of adventure
  Manitoba, Canada

It's better in the Bahamas
  Bahamas

Keystone of your vacation
  Pennsylvania

Land of scenic splendor
    New Hampshire

Mexico's Caribbean treasure
    Cozumel Island, Mexico

Nature's paradise, man's opportunity
    State of Washington

One management, ship and shore
    Canadian Pacific Steamship & Railroad Co.

Orlando's premier attraction
    Universal Studios Florida, Orlanda, Florida

See America best by car
    American Petroleum Institute

See this world before the next
    Canadian Pacific Steamship & Railroad Co.

So much to si
    Spain

State of excitement
    Oregon Highway Department

Stay an extra day
    Hong Kong

The ancient birthplace of good times
    Ireland

The big sky country
    Montana Highway Commission

The city with a rhythm all its own
    Miami, Florida

The company for people who travel
    American Express Co.

The difference is night and day
    Acapulco, Mexico

The great surprise
    Alabama

The happiest place on earth
    Disneyland, Anaheim, California

Travel

The heart of America
  Missouri

The hospitality state
  Mississippi

The land of enchantment is calling you
  Vancouver, British Columbia, Canada

The land of ten thousand lakes
  St. Paul, Minnesota

The land that was *made* for vacations
  Wisconsin Vacation and Travel Service

The magic never leaves you
  Mexico

The name that means smart travel
  Fodor's travel guides

The place to go
  Spanish National Tourist Office

The shining star of the Caribbean
  Puerto Rico Tourism Co.

The summer wonderland
  Mackinac Island, Michigan

The Sunshine State
  Florida

The surprising state
  State of Washington

The Turkey specialist
  Pacha Tours

The winter playground of America
  San Antonio, Texas

The world's most beautiful island
  Jamaica

The world's playground
  Atlantic City, New Jersey

Those who know us, love us
  Cayman Islands

Travel strengthens America
U. S. Travel Bureau

Vacationing in San Antonio is a family affair
San Antonio Municipal Information Bureau, San Antonio, Texas

Virginia is for lovers
Virginia

We've got your world
Collette Tours

Where summer spends the winter
West Palm Beach, Florida

Where summer stays and the nation plays
Sarasota, Florida

Winter fun under a "summer sun"
Sun Valley, Idaho

Within reach yet beyond belief
Canada's Northwest Territories

World's greatest travel system
Canadian Pacific Steamship & Railroad Co.

You can't get the whole picture in just a day or two
San Francisco Convention and Visitors Bureau, San Francisco, California

You haven't seen your country if you haven't seen Alaska
Alaska Travel Division, Department of Economic Development and Planning

TRAVELERS CHECKS
See FINANCIAL INSTITUTIONS AND SERVICES,   TRAVEL

TRUCKS AND TRUCKING INDUSTRY
See also FARMING AND SUPPLIES AND EQUIPMENT, MACHINERY, MOVING AND STORAGE

Because at ACL, we deliver
Atlantic Container Line

Brockway, the right way
    Brockway Motor Trucks

Build a truck to do a job—change it only to do better
    International Harvester Co.

Builder of trucks you can trust
    Studebaker Corp.

Built for business
    (*Duplex Truck*) Warner & Swasey Co.

Built to last longer
    (*Econoline vans*) Ford Motor Co.

Buy today's best truck. Own tomorrow's best trade.
    Hyster Co.

Chevrolet is more truck ... day in, day out
    Chevrolet Division, General Motors Corp.

Dodge builds tough trucks
    (*Dodge trucks*) Chrysler Corp.

More than a truck line—a transportation system
    Interstate Motor Freight System

No. 1 heavy-duty sales leader
    International Harvester Co.

Ram Tough
    (*Dodge trucks*) Chrysler Corp.

Since 1900, America's hardest working truck
    Mack Trucks Inc.

Speed with economy
    Yale Express System Inc.

Super service
    T. I. M. E. Freight Inc.

The big brother to the railroads
    (*Kelly-Springfield Motor Truck*)

The motor carrier with more Go-How
    Eastern Express System Inc.

The only truck bodies built like a trailer
    Fruehauf Corp.

The truck of continuous service
        Maccar Truck Co.

The wheels that go everywhere
        American Trucking Associations Inc.

They cost more because they're worth more
        (*Autocar*) White Motor Corp.

Total transportation
        Fruehauf Corp.

Uncommon carriers
        (*Oneida Motor Truck*)

Users know
        (*Garford Motor Truck*) Consolidated Motors Corp.

Vital link in America's supply line
        Transamerican Freight Lines Inc.

Wilson, that's haul
        (*Wilson trucks*)

World leader in heavy-duty trucks
        White Motor Corp.

You need our company
        Leaseway Transportation

Your best bet over the long haul
        D. C. Trucking Co. Inc

TYPEWRITERS
See OFFICE EQUIPMENT AND SUPPLIES

UMBRELLAS
See WARDROBE ACCESSORIES

UNDERWEAR
See also CLOTHING, MISCELLANEOUS; HOSIERY

A "fitting" tribute to the feminine figure
        (*Primrose foundations*)

All is vanity ... all is Vanity Fair
        Vanity Fair Mills Inc.

Beautiful corset worn by beautiful women to make them more beautiful
>> Lily of France Corset Co.

Behind every Olga there really is an Olga
>> Olga Co.

Checks your figure but not your freedom
>> Marvelette Inc.

Covers the subject
>> (*foundations*) Sid Levy & Sons

Don't say underwear, say Munsingwear
>> Munsingwear Inc.

Every Bali has a bow
>> Bali Brassiere Co.

Everything is under control
>> Vogue Foundations Inc.

Flatters where it matters
>> (*Adola brassiere*) Lovable Co.

For the lift of your lifetime
>> (*Life brassiere*) Formfit Rogers

For youthful figures of all ages
>> (*Lasticraft foundations*)

Glamour for teen-age and queen age
>> (*Kabo brassiere*)

Hanes makes you feel good all under
>> Hanes Corp.

Hips are fashionable, fat isn't
>> (*girdles*) Sidley Co.

Hold the bustline and you hold youth
>> (*La Resista corset*)

It's smart to conform with Reo-Form
>> Reo-Form Lingerie Co.

Keep your eye on Maidenform
>> Maidenform Inc.

Let Munsingwear cover you with satisfaction
      Munsingwear Inc.

Light as sea-foam, strong as the tide
      Paris–Hecker Co.

Never comes up anytime
      (*foundations*) Sid Levy & Sons

Next to nothing at all
      (*Du-ons*) Duofold Inc.

Nicest next to you
      H. W. Gossard Co.

No hips, no hips, hooray
      (*girdles*) Sid Levy & Sons

Nothing else feels so right
      Hanes Corp.

No woman is too stout to be stylish
      Weingarten Bros.

Puts your best figure forward
      (*Francette corsets*) Graceform–Camlin Corset Co.

So comfortable
      Jockey International Inc.

Step thru, button two
      The Sealpax Co.

The anti-freeze underwear for men and boys
      P. H. Hanes Knitting Co.

The foundation of American beauty
      (*Best Form corset*) Best Form Brassiere Co. Ltd.

The inner secret of outer beauty
      (*Charm underlift brassiere*)

The lift that never lets you down
      (*Perma-Lift brassiere*) Kayser–Roth Intimate Apparel Co.

There is only one Jockey
      Jockey International Inc.

The two-piece unionsuit
      Henderson & Erwin

Underwear

The uplift that stays up
  (*Surprise brassiere*) Carnival Creations Inc.

This is the dream you can be ... with Maidenform
  Maidenform Inc.

Two buttons on the shoulder, none down the front
  The Sealpax Co.

Unaware of underwear
  P. H. Hanes Knitting Co.

Underneath it all
  (*corsets and girdles*) Warner Bros.

Without the shadow of a stout
  (*corsets*) Stylish Stout

Your closest friend
  (*Cupid foundations*)

UTENSILS
See KITCHEN PRODUCTS AND UTENSILS

VARNISH
See PAINT AND PAINTING SUPPLIES

Video Equipment

VIDEO EQUIPMENT
See also MOVIES AND ENTERTAINMENT, TELEVISIONS

It's worth it
  (*video tape*) Maxell Corp.

Let RCA turn your television into Selectavision
  (*video cassette recorders*) RCA Corp.

More games. More fun.
  (*video games*) Atari

Nobody gives you better performance
  (*Fuji video tape*) Fuji Photo Film USA

The video with a future
  (*video cassette recorders*) Kenwood Electronics Inc.

We know what it takes to make great video
  (*Canovision 8*) Canon USA Inc.

WARDROBE ACCESSORIES
See also EYEGLASSES, FOOTWEAR, HOSIERY, JEWELRY AND SILVER

A "hank" for a Yank
      Bond Handkerchief Co.

A hat for every face
      Sam Bonnart Inc.

A lady to her gloved finger tips
      (*gloves*) Bacno Postman Corp.

A love of a glove
      (*gloves*) Acme Glove Corp.

All-weather leather
      (*handbags*) Dooney & Bourke Inc.

An American legacy
      Coach Leather

A new frame if the wind breaks it
      (*umbrellas*) Storm Hero Umbrella Co.

A shade better than the rest
      (*straw hats*) Superior Hat Co.

A thorobred air in every pair
      (*gloves*) Grewen Fabric Co.

Coolest hat under the sun
      Cardine Hat Co.

Distinctive designs in leather accessories
      Prince Gardner Co.

Every man should wear at least three straw hats
      National Association of Straw Hat Mfrs.

For men who care what they wear
      Pioneer Suspender Co.

Gloves that "go places"
      (*gloves*) Belle Glove Co.

Hand in hand with fashion
    (*mesh bags*) Whiting & Davis Co.

Like old friends they wear well
    (*gloves*) Louis Meyers & Son Inc.

Meyers make gloves for every father's son and mother's daughter
    (*Meyers gloves*) Meyers Manufacturing Co.

Nationally recognized as the "straw pioneer"
    (*handbags*) Simon Bros.

Overhead economy
    (*hats*) John B. Stetson Co.

Postman's, the gloves Milady loves
    (*gloves*) Bacno Postman Corp.

Ride like a feather in your pocket
    (*Rumpp wallets*) Aristocrat Leather Products

Right for Sunday morning
    (*hats*) John B. Stetson Co.

Soft as a kitten's ear
    (*belts*) Hews & Potter

The difference between dressed, and well dressed
    Bally of Switzerland

The "hanks" are coming
    (*handkerchiefs*) Bond Handkerchief Co.

The hat corner of the world
    Knox the Hatter

The hat of silent smartness
    Lamson & Hubbard Co.

The mark of the world's most famous hat
    John B. Stetson Co.

The perfect brace that stays in place
    (*suspenders*) Sidley Co.

The right hat for real men
    Langenberg Hat Co.

The royalty of leatherware
    (*Prince Gardner wallet*) Swank Inc.

They reign in the rain
    (*umbrellas*) Follmer, Clogg & Co.

Tropical masterpieces
    (*handbags*) Simon Bros.

Very individually yours
    (*Hickok buckles*)

We shelter the world from sun and rain
    (*umbrellas*) Follmer, Clogg & Co.

Why carry a cold in your pocket
    (*handkerchiefs*) Pervel Corp.

Your shoulders will thank you
    Pioneer Suspender Co

WATCHES AND CLOCKS

Accurate beyond comparison
    Warren Telechron Co.

A different world
    Rado Watch Co.

America appreciates good time
    (*Ribaux watches*)

America runs on Bulova time
    (*Bulova watches*) Bulova Watch Co. Inc.

America's "wake-up" voice
    Westclox Division, General Time Corp.

A unique breed of watch
    (*Noblia*) Citizen

Bulova Watch time, the gift of a lifetime
    (*Bulova watches*) Bulova Watch Co. Inc.

Casio. Where the miracles never cease.
    (*Casio watches*) Casio Inc.

Engineered for accuracy
    (*Rensie watches*)

First he whispers, then he shouts
    (*Big Ben*) Westclox Division, General Time Corp.

For a lifetime of proud possession
Omega Watch Co.

Get time from a timepiece, but if you want a watch get a Hamilton
Hamilton Watch Co.

In rhyme with time
Kingston Watch Co.

It remembers so YOU can forget
(*automatic clock*) James Clock Mfg. Co.

It S-T-R-E-T-C-H-E-S and springs back
(*watch bands*) Speidel Corp.

Keeps America on time
(*Big Ben*) Westclox Division, General Time Corp.

Laughs at time
(*Big Ben*) Westclox Division, General Time Corp.

Made in America by American craftsmen
Elgin National Watch Co.

Makes night time plain as day
(*radium dial clocks*) W. L. Gilbert Clock Co.

Modern masters of time
Seiko Time Corp.

One great face deserves another
(*Bulova watches*) Bulova Watch Co. Inc.

One of the great watches of our time
Waltham Watch Co.

People trust Seiko more than any other watch
(*Seiko Gold*) Seiko Time Corp.

Progress in the world of time
Westclox Division, General Time Corp.

Runs accurately without winding
(*Croton watch*) Croton Time Corp.

Sign of the right time
Zodiac Watch Co.

Takes a licking but keeps on ticking
Timex Corp.

Tells time in the dark
>   (*Radiolite*) Robt. H. Ingersoll & Bro.

The peak of Swiss watchmaking perfection
>   Rado Watch Co.

The precision watch, America's choice
>   (*Gruen watches*) The Gruen Watch Co.

The railroad timekeeper of America
>   Hamilton Watch Co.

There's no better time
>   (*Big Ben*) Westclox Division, General Time Corp.

The right choice for the right time
>   Harvel Watch Co.

The watch that times the airways
>   Benrus Watch Co.

The watch word of elegance and efficiency
>   Elgin National Watch Co.

The world's most honored watch
>   Longines–Wittnauer Watch Co.

The world's oldest watch manufacturer. Geneva since 1755.
>   Vacheron Constantin

The world's watch over time
>   Waltham Watch Co.

Time for a lifetime
>   (*Gotham watches*) Winton Nicolet Watch Co.

Watchful of the time
>   Hawkeye Clock Co.

We make technology beautiful
>   Timex Corp.

When something happy happens, it's Bulova time
>   Bulova Watch Co. Inc.

World's most "carefree" watch
>   (*Croton Aquamat*) Croton Time Corp.

WHISKEY
See LIQUORS

Wines

WINES
See also BEER AND ALE; BEVERAGES, MISCELLANEOUS;
LIQUORS

As good as gold and good for you
    Cercle d'Or Inc.

Be considerate, serve wine
    Wine Advisory Board, San Francisco, California

Blueprint of a perfect cocktail
    (*G & D vermouth*) United Vintners Inc.

California's premier wines
    Almaden Vineyards Inc.

Don't stir without Noilly Prat
    Browne Vintners Co.

Enjoy a sip of California sunshine
    Alta Vineyards Co.

From the largest cellars in the world
    (*Moët champagne*) Schiefflin and Co.

Here's to your health and happiness
    Cercle d'Or Inc.

Imported from Spain, of course. True sherry is.
    (*Duff Gordon*) National Distillers and Chemical Corp.

Italian wines. The quality of life—Vino.
    Italian Institute for Foreign Trade

It's time for a change to Gallo
    Ernest & Julio Gallo Winery

Made in California for enjoyment throughout the world
    (*Roma wines*) Guild Wineries & Distilleries

Made in the "champagne district of America"
    (*Gold Seal wines*) Gold Seal Vineyards Inc.

Make every meal a bouquet
    Bisceglia Bros. Corp.

Mountain grown
> Almaden Vineyards Inc.

Mumm's the word for champagne
> (*Mumm champagne*) G. H. Mumm and Co.

Orchard flavor in every sip
> (*Greystone fruit wines*) Bisceglia Bros. Corp.

Pop goes the Piper
> (*Piper–Heidsieck champagne*) Renfield Importers Ltd.

The finest wines of France
> Barton and Guestier

The flavor secret of the finest cocktails
> (*Martini & Rossi vermouth*) Renfield Importers Ltd.

The nobility of Italian wines
> Marchesi L and P Antinori

The wine that celebrates food
> (*Inglenook*) International Vintage Wines

The wine that tastes as good as it looks
> (*Cresta Blanca*) Guild Wineries & Distilleries

The wine with the champagne taste
> Pacific Wines Inc.

Uncork the magic
> (*Korbel Brut Champagne*) F. Korbel & Bros. Inc.

We will sell no wine before its time
> (*Paul Masson*) Browne Vintners Co.

When you mix with CinZano, you mix with the best
> (*CinZano*) Schiefflin and Co.

Wines of California. Since 1882.
> (*Christian Brothers*) Fromm and Sichel Inc.

Winning. Worldly. Well bred.
> (*Martini & Rossi vermouth*) Renfield Importers Ltd.

WRITING INSTRUMENTS
See also OFFICE EQUIPMENT AND SUPPLIES

All write with a Waterman Ideal Fountain Pen ... all wrong if you
    don't
        (*Waterman pens*)

Always sharp, never sharpened
        (*Eversharp pencil*) Wahl Co.

Always writes all ways
        Sheaffer Pen Co.

America's finest writing instruments since 1846
        A. T. Cross Co.

A pen is only as good as its point
        C. Howard Hunt Pen Co.

Behind every happy thumb, there's a Scripto
        Scripto Inc.

Crafted to express a lifetime
        A. T. Cross Co.

Creating new ways for America to write
        Pentel

Creator of advanced writing instruments
        Micropoint Inc.

Engineering with imagination
        Scripto Inc.

Fill with water, write with ink
        (*Camel fountain pen*)

Give Eversharp and you give the finest
        (*pencils*) Wahl Co.

Ink that absorbs moisture from the air
        S. S. Stafford

Insures a new kind of faultless effortless writing
        (*pens*) Eberhard Faber

It's a mark of distinction to own a Parker Pen
        Parker Pen Co.

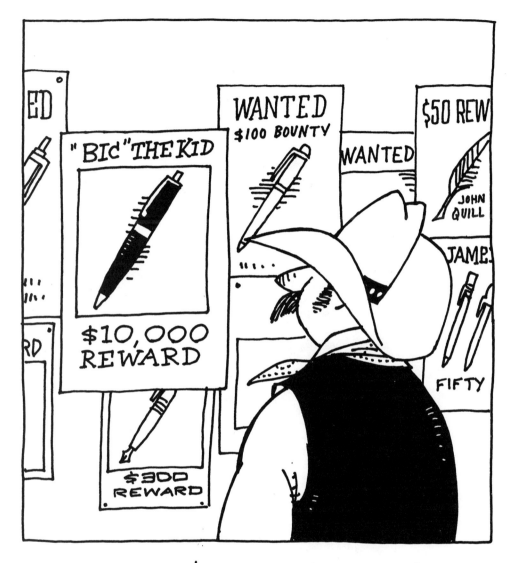

THE WORLD'S MOST WANTED PEN

It snuggles in your fingers
    Dixon Pencil Co.

Makes its mark around the world
    (*Waterman pens*)

Masters in the art of writing
    (*Montblanc CS-Line Pens*) Koh-I-Noor Rapidograph Inc.

Originators of the world-famous Utility ball pen
    Lindy Pen Co. Inc.

Paint with pencils
    Eberhard Faber

People take to a Pilot like it's their own
    Pilot

Permanent as the pyramids
    (*eternal ink*) C. M. Higgins & Co.

Right to the point
    Conklin Pen Mfg. Co.
    Wallace Pencil Co.

Smooth as silk, strong as steel
    Dixon Pencil Co.

Spot it by the dot
    Sheaffer Pen Co.

The art of writing
    Mont Blanc

The balanced pencil
    Swaberg Mfg. Co.

The ink that never fades
    Sanford Mfg. Co.

The pencil that uses its head
    Samuel Kanner

The pen that fills itself
    Conklin Pen Mfg. Co.

The pen with the tempered point
    Wahl Co.

The personal business gift
A.T. Cross Co.

We've got your number
Esterbrook Steel Pen Co.

World's most wanted pens
Parker Pen Co.

Write around the world
Alexander Mfg. Co.

Writes a strong, rich blue
Carter's Ink Co.

Index

All references are to page
numbers within the text

A human interest newspaper / 227
A journal for all who write / 227
A Kansas product from Kansas farms / 205
A King can have no more / 209
A lady to her gloved finger tips / 355
A liberal church journal / 227
A life preserver for foods / 168
A liquid finish that decorates as it preserves / 217
A little dab will do ya / 157
A little IBM can mean a lot of freedom / 84
A little varnish makes a lot of difference / 217
A live picture tabloid newspaper for all the family / 227
A living tradition in furniture / 151
A load for every purpose and a shell for every purse / 131
A lopsided diet may ruin your canary's song / 246
A love of a glove / 355
A lovelier skin with just one cake / 314
A magazine for all Americans / 227
A magazine for farm and home / 227
A magazine for farm women / 227
A magazine for southern merchants / 228
A magazine of better merchandising for home finishing merchants / 228
A magazine of good, clean humor / 228
A magazine only a homemaker could love / 228
A magazine with a mission / 228
A man of character / 256
A man who can't remember his last hailstorm is likely to get one he will never forget / 180
A man you can lean on, that's Klopman / 326
A massage for the gums / 103
A midget in size, a giant in power / 191
A mile of silk, inspected inch by inch / 174
A million Americans can't be wrong / 141
A million and one uses / 13
A million in service ten years or longer / 168
A million yards of good will / 214
A mind is a terrible thing to waste / 287
A minute to learn. A lifetime to master. / 343
A miracle in the rain / 75
A monthly business paper for chain store executives / 229
A monthly magazine devoted to more profitable painting / 229
A more enlightened approach / 27

A more intelligent approach to building shoes / 141
A most remarkable airline / 17
A mountain of flavor in every spoonful / 82
A musical instrument of quality / 292
A "must" for every wardrobe / 75
A national magazine for dry goods and department stores / 229
A national publication devoted to ship operation and shipbuilding / 229
A national publication for the wholesale grocer / 229
A national rider never changes his mount / 319
A new frame if the wind breaks it / 355
A new high in whiskey smoothness / 196
A new kind of excitement / 27
A new talc with a new odor / 224
A new time. A new GM. / 27
A newspaper for everybody; it goes into the home / 229
A newspaper for the makers of newspapers / 229
A noble Scotch / 196
A pen is only as good as its point / 362
A penny a night for the finest light / 193
A personal blend / 322
A personalized service that comes to your home / 96
A pillow for the body / 43
A pinch is all it takes / 330
A pip of a chip / 135
A pipe's best friend is fragrant Heine's blend / 330
A pippin of a drink / 51
A place to discover / 302
A policy to do more / 181
A powerful constructive force in the development of Georgia / 229
A precious bit more than a laxative / 107
A proud paper for a proud industry / 229
A public office is a public trust / 257
A radio that you can play / 292
A rainbow of distinctive flavors / 196
A *real* cigarette / 330
A real education for the real world / 304
A real magnetic horn / 34
A real safe, not a pretense / 214
A republic can have no colonies / 257
A roller rolls and there's ice / 168
A 'round the year coat / 75
A rug for every room / 133
A sack of satisfaction / 39
A sensible cigarette / 331
A shade better than the rest / 355

The Aetna-izer, a man worth knowing

369

Beauty bath for your teeth / 103
Beauty by the brushful / 217
Beauty in every box / 96
Beauty insurance / 157
Beauty *is* only skin deep; Luminiere controls the skin / 96
The beauty laxative / 113
Beauty that protects / 217
Beauty through science / 157
Beauty treatment for your feet / 142
Because ... / 339
Because ˆ is the way you want to go / 84
Because a better fit means better protection / 339
Because at ACL, we deliver / 349
Because I'm worth it / 96
Because it might rain / 75
... because it's nice to look younger than you are / 157
Because lips that feel lifeless aren't worth a look / 96
Because so much is riding on your tires / 34, 328
Because the music matters / 22
Because there *is* a difference / 181
Because you don't stop being a junior when you become a woman / 75
Because you love nice things / 174
Because you only want the best for your baby / 38
Because you're not just treating a fever. You're treating a child. / 107
Because you're only young once / 38
The bedspring luxurious / 44
Beer is as old as history / 46
The beer of friendship / 49
Beer that grows its own flavor / 46
The beer that made Milwaukee famous / 49
The beer that made the nineties gay / 49
The beer that made the old days good / 50
The beer that makes friends / 50
The beer with the 4th ingredient / 50
Before it's a memory, it's a Polaroid / 252
Before you dress, Caress / 315
The beginning of taste / 69
Behind every happy thumb, there's a Scripto / 362
Behind every Olga there really is an Olga / 352
Behind the enduring institution, successful customers / 127
Behind the panels of better built sets / 292
Bejeweled by Gaylin / 188
Belcraft Shirts, your bosom friend / 75

Believe your own ears / 292
Bell and Howell brings out the expert in you (automatically!) / 252
Beloved by brides for almost a century / 188
Below skin level shave / 309
Bends with your foot / 142
Bent like a dentist's mirror to reach more places / 103
Berkley Ties the world / 75
The best and nothing but the best is labeled Armour / 206
Best anti-freeze since mink / 34
Best because it's pan-dried / 65
Best beer by far at home, club, or bar / 46
Best bet in Baltimore / 230
Best bet's Buick / 27
Best built, best backed American cars / 27
The best-built, best-selling American trucks are built Ford tough / 30
Best buy in rye / 197
Best by taste test / 317
Best by test / 39
The best comedy in America / 237
The best connections in West Africa / 19
Best cooks know foods fried in Crisco don't taste greasy! / 135
The best cooks use aluminum / 190
The best films you never saw / 298
Best for baby, best for you / 38
Best for juice and every use / 149
Best for rest / 142
Best for you and baby, too / 315
The best friend your willpower ever had / 164
Best glue in the joint / 13
The best has a taste all its own / 50
The best in tapes has "Able" on the label / 113
The best in the Union, in pocket tins / 337
The best-lookin' cookin' in town / 206
The best monitors you never heard of / 87
Best nickel candy there iz-z-z / 61
Best of all ... it's a Cadillac / 27
The best of the world's press / 237
The best seat in the house / 162
Best-selling aerosols are powered with Freon propellents / 68
The best tires in the world have Goodyear written all over them / 329
The best to you each morning / 66
The best tonic / 50
Best way to close an opening / 55
The best way to reach Maturity / 237
The best with the *most* on the ball / 320
Best year yet to go Ford / 27

Better a part-time president than a full-time phony / 258
Better banking, better service, better join us / 128
Better because it's gas ... best because it's Caloric / 168
Better business is our aim / 14
Better buy Birds Eye / 136
Better care for better kids / 107
Better hearing longer / 164
Better light brings better living / 288
Better little shoes are not made / 142
Better meals by the minute / 190
Better products for a better world / 168
Better products for man's best friend / 245
The better sex video series / 298
The better spread for our daily bread / 139
Better taste makes the difference / 39
Better than a mustard plaster / 107
Better than money / 128
Better than whisky for a cold / 107
Better things for better living through chemistry / 68
Better vision for better looks / 122
Better yet, Connecticut / 116
A better yield in every field / 123
Better your home, better your living / 151, 230
Betty's husband for president in '76 / 258
Between wood and weather / 217
Beware of B. O. / 315
Beware *Of Smokers* Teeth / 103
Beware where you buy your bee-ware / 123
BICYCLE is the card player's choice / 343
The big brother to the railroads / 350
The big cheese of potato chips / 139
The big hotel that remembers the little things / 178
The big sky country / 347
The Big Stick / 277
Big thinking in little sizes / 75
Biggest, brightest, best magazine for boys in all the world / 230
Biggest in the country / 230
The biggest *should* do more. It's only right. / 25
The bike you'll like / 300
Birth control that you control / 107
Birth control you can trust / 107
Birth state of the nation / 345
Birthplace of the nation / 116
The biteless blend / 337
The blades men swear by, not at / 310
A blend of all straight whiskies / 196
Blended whiskey of character / 197
A blending of art and machine / 26

The blond beer with the body / 50
Blue brutes / 203
The Blue Chip company / 184
Blue Sunoco, the over-drive motor fuel / 248
The blue tube with the life-like tone / 293
Blueprint of a perfect cocktail / 360
The body-building no-lye relaxer / 159
Body by Fisher / 27
Body by Soloflex / 163
The body cosmetic / 98
Body made in America / 163
Bonded for life ... because they're built that way / 341
Bonds that grow in security / 186
The boot with the muscles / 146
Boots that never say die / 142
Bores a 300-foot hole in the night / 193
Born in America. Worn round the world. / 75
Born in Canada, now going great in the 48 states / 46
Born of the breath of man, Waterford is life's child / 69
Born where a king of France was born / 197
Boston's most convenient hotel / 177
Boston's most famous hotel / 177
The bottled beer with the draught beer flavor / 50
Bowl where you see the Magic Triangle / 319
The Boy Scouts' magazine / 237
The boys in blue will see it through / 278
Brain-built boxes / 220
Brains & Beauty / 84
The brand that always puts flavor first / 139
The brand that fits / 80
The brand with the grand aroma / 337
The brandy of Napoleon / 200
Brayco Light makes all things clear / 193
Bread is your best food, eat more of it / 39
Break away from the ordinary / 197
Breakfast of champions / 65
Breaks the static barrier / 70
Breathin' brushed pigskin / 142
A breathless sensation / 61
Bred, not just grown / 123
The brew that brings back memories / 50
Brew that holds its head high in any company / 46
Brew with a head of its own / 46
Brewed in the British manner / 46
Brewed *only* in Milwaukee / 46
Bright by day, light by night / 14

China by Iroquois for the hosts of America / 69

Chlorine ointment, better than iodine / 108

Chock Full O' Nuts is that heavenly coffee / 82

Chocolate bar flavor you can eat with a spoon / 136

The chocolates with the wonderful centres / 63

A choice for a change / 255

The choice for taste / 83

A choice—not an echo / 256

Choice of better mechanics / 341

The choice of champions / 250

The choice of noted music critics / 293

A choice of over a million women / 168

The choice of successful men / 337

The choice of the crew and the big boss, too / 58

Choice of the masters / 212

The choice you make once for a life-time / 189

Choose Crisco and put your money on good taste every time / 40

Choose your piano as the artists do / 212

Choosey mothers choose Jif / 136

Chronicle of current Masonic events / 230

Churned from sweet (not sour) cream / 100

Cie. For all the women you are. / 224

The cigar made with good judgment / 337

The cigar that breathes / 337

A citizen, wherever we serve / 288

The city that does things / 117

The city with a rhythm all its own / 347

The civilized way of shaving / 310

Clairol is going to make someone beautiful today / 157

Class magazine in a class by itself / 231

A classic in wood / 312

Classics in their own time / 152

Classics of optical precision / 252

Clean clear through / 197

The clean, convenient fuel / 167

Clean hair means a healthy scalp / 157

A Clean Home newspaper / 226

Clean house with Dewey / 258

Clean, smooth and unmistakably refreshing / 197

A clean that's cleaner than bath tissue alone / 220

A clean tooth never decays / 103

Clean up with S. O. S. It's easy. / 71

The clean way to kill dirty rats / 246

Cleaner, drier, better / 339

Cleans as it fizzes / 103

Cleans as it polishes / 70

Cleans easier, works faster, won't scratch / 70

Cleans in a jiff / 70

Cleans like a *white tornado* / 70

Cleans the impossible washload / 70

Cleans with a caress / 315

Cleans without beating and pounding / 169

Clear heads call for Calvert / 197

Clear to the ear / 292

Cleveland runs well in England / 258

Cleveland's better food markets / 302

The climate control fabric / 327

Close. But no lumps. / 136

The close electric shave / 311

The closer he gets ... the better you look! / 159

Clothes in the New York manner / 76

Clothes that enhance your public appearance / 76

Coast to coast overnight / 17

Coast to coast to coast / 17

Coast to coast, we give the most / 177

The coat with nine lives / 219

The coffee-er coffee / 83

Coffee rich enough to be served in America's finest restaurants / 82

The coffee that lets you sleep / 83

Coffee, the American drink / 82

The coffee without a regret / 83

Coke is it / 317

Cold and silent as a winter night / 169

Colgate helps stop cavities before they start / 103

College is America's best friend / 287

Colombian Coffee. The richest coffee in the world. / 82

The colorfast shampoo / 159

Colors hair inside, as nature does / 157

Come alive! / 317

Come alive ... Revive / 157

Come and say G'day / 346

Come home, America / 258

Come home to comfort / 165

Come home to quality. Come home to Andersen. / 56

Come on, breeze, let's blow / 169

Come on over to the right light / 149

Come on, you sunners / 322

Come rain or fog there's no shaker-clog / 90

Come ride with us / 209

Come to Israel. Come stay with friends / 346

Come to Jamaica and feel alright / 346

Come to Kentucky! It's a profitable move! / 116

Come to life in Hawaii / 346

Driving in its purest form

For heating and cooling ... gas is good business / 167

For her. For him. Forever. / 225

For her greater stimulation and pleasure / 109

For home lovers in cities, towns, and suburbs / 232

For imagination in communication, look to 3M business product centers / 93

For important clothes, it's Kerman Stores / 302

For industry, shop, farm and home / 341

For lazy people / 103

For matching lips and fingertips / 97

For men of distinction / 198

For men who care what they wear / 355

For men who dress for women / 78

For men who know fine whiskies / 198

For men whose emotions run deep / 225

For more good years in your car / 36

For natural feeling and sensitivity / 109

For oil marketing / 232

For penetrating relief get Hall's Vapor Action / 109

For people who have other things to spend their money on / 143

For people who love coffee, but not caffeine / 82

For people who travel ... and expect to again and again / 202

For people who'd rather invest money than time / 128

For real enjoyment / 332

For real smoking pleasure / 332

For relief you can trust / 109

For serving ... it's Erving / 222

For shaving without brush or lather / 309

For sheer loveliness wear Chatelaine Silk Hosiery / 175

For smooth shaves / 309

For smooth white hands tomorrow use Thine Hand Creme tonight / 97

For strength where the stress comes / 207

For superb personal movies / 253

For that breath-taking moment / 188

For that certain kind of woman / 302

For that "come hither" look / 97

For that deep down body thirst / 52

For that good-looking feeling / 78

For that smart sun-tan look / 97

For the active woman of today / 143

For the anemia of RETROVIR-treated HIV infected patients / 109

For the beautiful point of view / 56

For the best in paperbacks, look for the Penguin / 289

For the best in rest / 43

For the climate of excellence / 289

For the committed quitter, membrane controlled / 109

For the decorator touch / 186

For the difference it makes / 97

For the fullest, thickest, fluffiest hair you can have / 158

For the home that enjoys home life / 212

For the king of old-fashioneds / 198

For the lift of your lifetime / 352

For the lightest, fluffiest popcorn there's only one, Orville Redenbacher / 137

For the love of Ike vote Republican / 261

For the man on the move / 78

For the man who believes his own ears / 292

For the man who cares / 198

For the men in charge / 232

For the nicest youngsters you know / 78

For the one man in 7 who shaves every day / 309

... for the period before your period / 109

For the rest of the night / 78

For the REST of your life / 152

For the smart young woman / 233

For the smile of beauty / 104

For the tummy / 109

For the well-dressed salad / 91

For the winning edge / 143

For the woman who dares to be different / 225

For these symptoms of stress that can come from success / 109

For those confident few who have acquired a taste for simplicity / 78

For those friskie years / 78

For those letters you owe / 222

For those who can hear the difference / 22

For those who dress from the ground up / 143

For those who go first class / 202

For those who must make best impressions / 214

For those who really like to eat / 206

For those who think young / 317

For those who want *every* puff to taste as fresh as the *first* puff! / 332

For those with time for quality / 332

For Wilmington, the Carolinas, and the South / 128

For women whose eyes are older than they are / 97

For you and your town / 233

For young men and men with young ideas / 333

For younger young men / 78

HUSH takes the odor out of perspiration

Imagination in steel for the needs of today's architecture / 208
Imagine what we can do together / 94
Important to important people / 233
Imported from Spain, of course. True sherry is. / 360
The imported one / 201
In a class by itself / 22
In a word, confidence / 208
In a word ... it's Selig / 152
In electricity, it's Edison from start to finish / 118
In garden or in fields, Schell's seeds produce best yields / 124
In harmony with home and air / 293
In home, health, farm and industry, science in action for you / 68
In Hoover we trusted, now we are busted / 266
In keeping with a fine old tradition / 178
In metals, plastics and paper Budd works to make tomorrow ... today / 94
In partnership with all America / 295
In Philadelphia nearly everybody reads the Bulletin / 233
In rhyme with time / 358
In San Francisco it's the Palace / 178
In step with fashion / 144
In the air or outer space Douglas gets things done / 15
In the twinkling of an eye / 324
In touch with tomorrow / 120
In your guts you know he's nuts / 266
In your heart you know he's right / 266
"An inch of Pinch, please." / 196
An independent newspaper / 229
The industrial bar code experts / 88
Industrious Maine, New England's big stake in the future / 116
Industry is on the move to Iowa / 116
Industry-owned to conserve property and profits / 182
Industry Spokesman to CPI management / 233
Industry's friendliest climate / 116
Inexpensive. And built to stay that way. / 28
Information. Not automation. / 85
The information service you won't outgrow / 88
The ingenuity of people, the power of computers / 88
Ink that absorbs moisture from the air / 362
The ink that never fades / 364
The inner secret of outer beauty / 353
Innovation. Precision. Integrity. / 22

Innovation working for you / 94
Inside the rim of adventure / 346
Inspection is our middle name / 182
Install it, forget it / 293
Instant news service / 187
Instant relief of feminine itching / 110
Instantly known when blown / 118
The instrument of the immortals / 213
Insulate as you decorate / 56
Insure today to save tomorrow / 182
The insured pipe / 314
Insures a new kind of faultless effortless writing / 362
The intelligent choice / 121
An international daily newspaper / 229
The international one / 326
The interrupting idea / 14
Invented by a doctor—now used by millions of women / 339
Inventor and scientist make dreams come true; the insurance man keeps nightmares from happening / 182
Invest in memory insurance / 222
Invest in rest / 43
Invest with confidence / 129
Investing with a sense of direction / 129
Iowa's greatest evening paper / 234
The iron with the cool blue handle / 173
Irons while it steams / 170
Is it live? Or is it Memorex? / 23
Is it true ... blondes have more fun? / 158
Is the Telegram on your list? / 234
Is your refrigerator a Success? / 170
I'se in town, honey / 40
Isle of June / 116
Isn't it worth it? / 72
Isn't that you behind those Foster Grants? / 122
It beats, as it sweeps, as it cleans / 170
It beats talking! / 215
It beats the Dutch / 52
It brings out the best in all of us / 288
It can help you look younger too / 97
It cleans your breath while it cleans your teeth / 104
It costs no more to reach the first million first / 234
It could be what's missing in your cooking / 40
It could change the way you think about American automobiles / 28
It deserves to be preserved / 253
It filters the smoke / 312
It floats / 315
It happens in two seconds / 110
It is better to have it and not need it than to need it and not have it / 182

393

It is our business to help your business / 234

It is profitable to produce in Massachusetts / 116

It is what it eats / 343

It just feels right / 28

It keeps your engine running like new / 249

It leaves you breathless / 199

It lox the sox / 175

It lulls the skin / 310

It makes a difference / 249

It makes a dust magnet of your dust mop or cloth / 72

It may be your car, but it's still our baby / 36

It might have been worse / 266

It more than satisfies, it agrees / 82

It must be good to be a Gund / 343

It pays to be particular about your oil / 249

It pays to Discover / 128

It pays to know when to relax / 182

It pays to think about it / 182

It pays to use good tools / 341

It puts the sunshine in your hair / 158

It raises the dough / 40

It remembers so YOU can forget / 358

It snuggles in your fingers / 364

It speaks for itself / 23

It splits in two / 40

It started me smoking cigars / 334

It stays on the salad / 91

It S-T-R-E-T-C-H-E-S and springs back / 358

It takes a big airline / 18

It takes a man to help a boy / 288

It takes leather to stand weather / 144

It takes needles to make shirts / 308

It tastes as good as it tests / 104

It tastes good to the last crumb / 40

It will tell your eyes before your eyes tell you / 180

It won't dry your face like soap / 315

It wouldn't be America without Wonder / 40

Italian wines. The quality of life—Vino. / 360

It's a big country. Someone's got to furnish it. / 152

It's a dynamite taste / 48

It's a good time for the great taste of McDonald's / 300

It's a lucky day for your car when you change to Quaker State Motor Oil / 249

It's a mark of distinction to own a Parker Pen / 362

It's a matter of life and breath / 288

It's a pippin / 333

It's a winner / 54

It's all in fun / 225

It's all in the finish / 218

It's all in the wheel / 341

It's all in this little yellow box / 137

It's always a pleasure / 302

It's always a shade better / 72

It's always coal weather / 167

It's always Fehr weather / 48

It's as easy as FTD / 154

It's beer as beer should taste / 48

It's better because it's made of Koroseal / 327

It's better in the Bahamas / 346

It's better, not bitter / 48

It's better than it used to be, and it used to be the best / 48

Its blend is our secret, its fragrance your delight / 333

It's blended, it's splendid / 48

It's bug tested / 245

It's good because it's fresh / 333

It's good for you, America / 52

... It's good to have a great bank behind you / 129

It's in the bag / 91

It's in the fit / 78

It's it and that's that / 48

It's like homemade / 137

It's love at first bite / 137

It's McKinley we trust to keep our machines free of rust / 267

It's mild and mellow / 333

It's moisturized / 333

It's more than a cruise, it's the Love Boat / 306

It's More you / 334

It's not a home until it's planted / 191

It's not Jockey brand if it doesn't have the Jockey boy / 78

It's not just a truck anymore / 29

It's not just any snack / 137

It's one of the three great beers / 48

It's pure chewing satisfaction / 62

It's quick-wetting / 310

It's smart to choose the finest sterling / 188

It's smart to conform with Reo-Form / 352

It's sudsy / 72

It's the easiest / 110

It's the flavor / 199

It's the life they lead, it's the book they read / 234

It's the little daily dose that does it / 110

It's the next thing / 85

It's the only way to handle a perm / 158
It's the real thing / 318
It's the right thing to do / 288
It's the tops for kitchen tops / 72
It's the water / 48
It's the woman-wise range / 170
It's the yarn that counts / 308
It's time for a change to Gallo / 360
It's toasted / 334
It's ugly, but it gets you there / 29
It's uncanny / 137
It's "velveted" / 199
It's what's inside that counts / 40
It's wise to conveyorize / 204
It's worth it / 354
It's worth the trip / 300
Ives Toys make happy boys / 343
Ivory is kind to everything it touches / 315
Ivory tips protect your lips / 334
Jack of all trades and master of plenty / 341
The jack that saves your back / 342
Jamaica's legendary liqueur / 199
James Buchanan—no sectionalism / 267
Jeans for the way you live and love / 78
Jersey City has everything for industry / 116
Jet action washers / 170
The jet that justifies itself / 16
The jet with the extra engine / 20
The jewel of patent leather / 146
Jewelers to the sweethearts of America for three generations / 188
Jewelry for the home / 193
Jewelry of tradition for the contemporary man / 188
The Jewish market at its best / 239
John and Jessie forever! Hurrah! / 267
Join the first team. Reach for Winston. / 334
Join the knit parade / 308
Join the Pepsi generation / 318
Join the regulars / 110
Join the "regulars" with Kellogg's All-Bran / 65
Join with Bostik for better bonding / 13
The Journal covers Dixie like the dew / 239
A journal for all who write / 227
The journal of diagnosis and treatment / 239
Judged best by the just / 334
Just a darn good shaving cream / 310
Just a "shade" better / 56
Just as if you were there / 293
Just do it. / 144
Just enough Turkish / 334

Just everyday things for the home made beautiful by Stevens / 43
... Just for the sun of it / 306
Just for the taste of it / 318
Just form and fry / 137
Just plane smart / 18
Just plug in, then tune in / 293
Just rub it on the gums / 104
Just slightly ahead of our time / 120
Just smooth, very smooth / 199
Just the kiss of the hops / 48
Just to show a proper glow / 97
Just wear a smile and a Jantzen / 79
Just what works / 79
K-Y Jelly. The safer choice. / 110
Kalamazoo, direct to you / 166
A Kansas product from Kansas farms / 205
Kawasaki lets the good times roll / 209
Keep a roof over your head / 182
Keep children's feet as nature made them / 144
Keep cool with Coolidge / 267
Keep faith with our sons—bring America into the League of Nations—Vote for Cox and Roosevelt / 267
Keep fighting, keep working, keep singing, America / 110
Keep going with Pep / 65
Keep hair-conditioned / 158
Keep heat where it belongs / 56
Keep in step with Paris / 144
Keep in step with youth / 144
Keep it under your hat / 158
Keep kissable with Flame-Glo Lipstick / 97
Keep mechanics good tempered / 342
Keep Missouri in the center of your thinking / 117
Keep regular the healthful way / 150
Keep that great GM feeling / 36
Keep that schoolgirl complexion / 315
Keep the home fire burning / 167
Keep the stars in your eyes / 97
Keep the weather out / 56
Keep your bob at its best / 158
Keep your eye on Maidenform / 352
Keep your floors beautiful always / 72
Keep your health in tune / 163
Keep your income coming in / 129
... Keeping tradition alive / 152
Keeps a head / 48
Keeps America on time / 358
Keeps breath pure and sweet 1 to 2 hours longer / 104
Keeps cows contented from sunrise to sunset / 124
Keeps step with the weather / 166
Keeps the shape / 327

395

*A liquid finish
that decorates
as it preserves*

Makes night time plain as day

Makes old things new, keeps new things bright / 72
Makes pancakes mother's way / 40
Makes products better, safer, stronger, lighter / 57
Makes that long haul to the curb seem shorter / 190
Makes the skin like velvet / 97
Makes water wetter / 72
Makes your husband feel younger, too ... just to look at you! / 158
Makes your teeth feel smooth as silk / 104
Makin' it great / 300
Making good connections / 86
Making houses into homes / 166
Making petroleum do more things for more people / 249
Making smoking "safe" for smokers / 334
Making the world more productive / 86
Making the world safe for baby / 152
Making the world sweeter / 62
Making your world a little easier / 170
The makings of a nation / 337
Man alive! Two for five / 334
A man of character / 256
The man of the hour / 279
The man of the hour is Eisenhower / 279
The man of the hour—Woodrow Wilson / 279
The man that can split rails can guide the ship of state / 279
Man, that's corn / 124
Man to man, Roi-Tan, a cigar you'll like / 334
A man who can't remember his last hailstorm is likely to get one he will never forget / 180
The man who cares says: "Carstairs White Seal" / 201
The man with the plan / 184
A man you can lean on, that's Klopman / 326
Manning the frontiers of electronic progress / 120
Man's greatest food / 138
The man's magazine / 240
The man's styleful shoe on a real chassis / 147
Mar-VEL-ous for dishes, stockings, lingerie, woolens / 72
The mark of a good roof / 58
Mark of excellence / 29
The mark of modern pajamas / 80
Mark of quality throughout the world / 326
The mark of the well-built house / 58

The mark of the world's most famous hat / 356
The mark that is a message in itself / 223
The market with the "rainbow round its shoulder" / 240
A massage for the gums / 103
The massive men's market in print / 240
Master of mathematics / 215
Master the moment / 129
The master wood of the ages / 58
The master's fingers on your piano / 213
Masters in the art of writing / 364
Match him / 269
Matched tools for *unmatched* performance / 342
Matchless cooking / 170
Matchless in outdoor excellence / 54
The material difference in building / 58
The mattress that feels so good / 44
Maxell. It's worth it. / 86
The maxx for the minimum / 303
Maybe she's born with it. Maybe it's Maybelline. / 98
Maybe we're better / 25
Mazola makes good eating sense / 138
McCarthy and peace in '68 / 269
McDonald's and you / 300
McKinley and the full dinner pail / 269
Meals without meat are meals incomplete / 206
The meanest chore is a chore no more / 73
Means more mileage / 329
Means safety made certain / 35
Measure yourself for a Kelly / 334
The medal Scotch of the world / 201
Medically proven to help you lose weight / 110
Meet me at the fountain / 303
Meet me at the Music Box / 303
The meeting place of the thrifty / 303
Mellow as the greeting of old friends / 318
Mellowed in wood to full strength / 91
Membership has its privileges / 129
Men wear them everywhere / 145
Men who build America trust this trade mark / 57
The men will need their horses to plow with / 279
Mends everything but a broken heart / 13
Menthol-cooled / 335
Merchandise well displayed is half sold / 14
Mercury. Where comfort and control come together. / 29
Meredith moves merchandise / 14
Merrill Lynch is bullish on America / 187

More stars than
there are in
heaven

More than a
cedar chest, a
piece of fine

*The New York
Agent in your
community is a*

Quaker Oats.
It's the right
thing to do.